D0207821

Usability

USABILITY:
Turning Technologies into Tools

Edited by

Paul S. Adler
Department of Management and Organization
School of Business Administration
University of Southern California

Terry A. Winograd
Computer Science Department
Stanford University

New York   Oxford
Oxford University Press
1992

Oxford University Press

Oxford   New York   Toronto
Delhi   Bombay   Calcutta   Madras   Karachi
Kuala Lumpur   Singapore   Hong Kong   Tokyo
Nairobi   Dar es Salaam   Cape Town
Melbourne   Auckland

and associated companies in
Berlin   Ibadan

Copyright © 1992 by Oxford University Press, Inc.

Published by Oxford University Press, Inc.,
200 Madison Avenue, New York, New York 10016

Oxford is a registered trademark of Oxford University Press

Library of Congress Cataloging-in-Publication Data
Usability: turning technologies into tools/edited by Paul S. Adler and Terry
A. Winograd.
p.   cm.
Includes bibliographical references and index.
ISBN 0-19-507510-2
1. System design.   2. Automation.   3. User interfaces (Computer
systems)   I. Adler, Paul S.   II. Winograd, Terry.
QA76.9.S88U73   1992
670.42′7—dc20   91-39416

9 8 7 6 5 4 3 2 1

Printed in the United States of America
on acid-free paper

Preface

In the past few decades, we have witnessed a tremendous increase in the complexity and power of the tools we use in the office and industry. The book you are holding, for example, is the product of a personal computer used to type the text, a telecommunications network used to coordinate the revisions, photocopiers and printers used to produce copies, and manufacturing equipment used to fabricate the paper and apply the binding, and much more. Gone are the mechanical typewriters and the manual production processes that would have been used not so long ago.

This technological mutation has led to great improvements in productivity and quality in many types of work; but if our tools have become more powerful and flexible, it is because the technologies embedded in them have grown more complex, and as a result the challenge of designing effective tools has become more difficult. For users to exploit the full range of the new tools' potential function—indeed, to use them successfully at all—"usability" must be a high priority in the process of designing these tools. This book proposes new approaches to the "design for usability" challenge.

The chapters of this book began as contributions commissioned for a seminar on "Technology and the Future of Work" conducted at Stanford University in March 1990. The seminar brought together 200 senior managers and union leaders from U.S. industry, and 50 leading researchers from the U.S., Europe, and Asia. A companion volume, *Technology and the Future of Work*, edited by Paul Adler (Oxford University Press, 1991), presents the seminar contributions focused on the conditions required for effective technology *implementation;* it addresses the need in industry for new skills, new training approaches, new labor/management relations, and new strategic management practices. The present volume focuses on the technology *design* issues and brings to a wider audience revised and edited versions of the contributions focused on design for usability.

The seminar was conducted under the auspices of the Stanford Integrated Manufacturing Association. Funding was provided by several Association sponsors: Apple Computer, Inc., Digital Equipment Corp., Ford Motor Co., General Motors Corp., Hewlett-Packard Co., and IBM Corp. Representatives from these companies helped shape the agenda, and we owe special gratitude to Reesa Abrams, Chris Duncan, Al Jones, Frank West, and Stuart Winby for their contributions to the planning effort. Stanford faculty colleagues Elliott Levinthal, Warren Hausman, and Dick Scott provided valuable guidance and support. Susan Sweeney's help with the logistics and Cecilia Wanjiku's secretarial support were indispensable. Greg Tong provided invaluable editorial help in refining successive drafts of the chapters. Thanks too to Don Jackson and Herb Addison at Oxford, for their consistent encouragement and support. Above all, we must thank the contributing authors. Their patience and responsiveness made the editors' role a pleasure.

Tarzana, Calif.   P.S.A.
Stanford, Calif.   T. A.W.
November, 1991

Contents

Contributors

Paul S. Adler is associate professor at University of Southern California's School of Business Administration. He began his education in Australia and moved to France in 1974, where he received his doctorate in Economics and Management while working as a research economist for the French government. Before joining U.S.C. in 1991, he was a visiting scholar at the Brookings Institution, a visiting assistant professor at Columbia University, a post-doctoral research fellow at the Harvard Business School, and an assistant professor at Stanford University.

John Seely Brown is vice president, Advanced Research at the Xerox Palo Alto Research Center and co-founder and associate director of the nonprofit Institute for Research on Learning in Palo Alto, California. Brown received his bachelor's degree in math and physics from Brown University, his master's of mathematics from the University of Michigan, and his Ph.D. in computer and communication sciences from the University of Michigan.

Debra Cash is currently a principal writer in Digital's Media Communication Group. She has a longstanding interest in modern cultural and intellectual history and is a regular contributor to M.I.T.'s *Technology Review* and to the *Boston Globe.*

Elizabeth Anne Clemens is a principal of Da Vinci Group, a human factors consulting firm. Previously, she worked in the Human Factors Department at Digital Equipment Corporation, where she was involved in the application of human factors to the design of computer systems.

J. Martin Corbett has a background in organizational psychology and studied at the Universities of Leeds, Lancaster, and Bath before joining the "Human Centered Technology" research team at the University of Manchester Institute of Science and Technology. He then became a research fellow with the Medical Research Council at the University of Sheffield and is currently lecturer in organizational behavior at the University of Warwick Business School. His recent publications include *Crossing the Border: The Social and Engineering Design of Computer Integrated Manufacturing Systems* (co-authored with Lauge Rasmussen and Felix Rauner). He is vice-chairman of the International Federation of Automatic Council's Technical Committee on the Social Effects of Automation, head of the U.K. Group within CAPIRN (International Research Network on Culture and Production), and associate editor of the *Journal of Occupational Psychology.*

Paul Duguid is a member of the research staff of the Institute for Research on Learning in Palo Alto, California. He is a graduate of Bristol University in England and Washington University in St. Louis.

Pelle Ehn is associate professor at the Department of Information and Media Science, University of Aarhus, Denmark, and was previously a researcher at the Swedish Center for Working Life. He has a Ph.D. in computer and information science from the University of Umeå, Sweden. Since the mid-1970s, he has been active in the field of skill-based participatory design through a variety of projects including the DEMOS project, the UTOPIA project with newspaper workers, a repair shop, a warehouse, and a steel mill. He has published *Work-Oriented Design of Computer Artifacts* (Hillsdale, N.J.: Erlbaum, 1989), co-edited with G. Bjerknes and M. Kyng, M.; *Computers and Democracy—A Scandinavian Challenge,* (Brookfield, Vt.: Gower, 1987); contributed to J. Greenbaum and M. Kyng (eds.) *Design at Work* (Hillsdale, N.J.: Erlbaum, 1991).

Bill Hartman holds an M.S. in mechanical engineering from The University of Wisconsin. He is director of Industrial Design and Human Interface Design at Xerox Corporation, where he has worked for 26 years. Most of his experience is in the areas of product engineering and product and technology design and development.

Charles D. Kukla is a system designer responsible for defining and applying user interface technologies in manufacturing for Digital's Computer Integrated Manufacturing and Product Development Group. He has spent over 15 years in various roles as an operator, project manager, and designer in manufacturing organizations. He holds a B.A. in chemical engineering and an M.S. in engineering with a concentration on mechanical engineering.

Robert S. Morse is a principal of Da Vinci Group, a human factors consulting firm. He worked previously as a senior human factors engineer at Digital Equipment Corporation, where he was involved in human factors research and design of computer systems.

John Rheinfrank holds a Ph.D. in systems engineering from The Ohio State University. He is an executive vice president at Fitch RichardsonSmith and an affiliate research scientist with the Institute for Research on Learning.

Harold Salzman received his Ph.D. in sociology from Brandeis University. He was a research associate at the Center for Technology and Policy and an adjunct assistant professor in the Department of Sociology at Boston University. He is currently director of the Technology, Work and Organization program, a joint program of the Labor-Management Center and Urban Research Institute at the University of Louisville.

Arnold Wasserman holds an M.A. in history and theory of design from the University of Chicago. He is currently dean of the College of Art and Design at the Pratt Institute. He was an industrial designer for more than 30 years and held the positions of vice president of Corporate Industrial Design and Human Factors at Unisys, manager of Industrial Design/Human Factors at Xerox Corporation, and director of Corporate Industrial Design at NCR.

Terry Winograd is professor of computer science at Stanford University. He has published widely on natural language understanding by computers. His most recent book is *Understanding Computers and Cognition: A New Foundation for Design* (Addison-Wesley, 1987) co-authored with Fernando Flores. He is a board member and consultant to Action Technologies, a firm developing workgroup productivity software, and has served as the national president of Computer Professionals for Social Responsibility, of which he was a founding member.

Usability

CHAPTER 1

The Usability Challenge

PAUL S. ADLER AND TERRY WINOGRAD

All too often, new technologies are introduced into the workplace without sufficient planning for their implications for the workforce. To the extent that businesses do plan for these implications, their approach is often governed by two related myths—the idiot-proofing myth and the deskilling myth. In each, technology plays a heroic role, rescuing efficiency from a workforce presumed to be unreliable.

In the idiot-proofing myth, the hero is a machine so perfect that it is immune from the limitations of its users. System design based on this perspective is more concerned with how to keep operators from creating errors than with enabling operators to deal with the inevitable contingencies of the work process. The deskilling myth extends the idiot-proofing myth, offering a system so idiot-proof that the business can presumably get along not only with proportionately fewer workers, but also with workers who are on average less skilled and less expensive.

Contradicting these myths, an emerging body of research suggests that in the vast majority of cases, new technologies will be more effective when designed to augment rather than replace the skills of users. The key challenge in designing new technologies is how best to take advantage of users' skills in creating the most effective and productive working environment. We call this the *usability challenge.*

To meet the usability challenge, industry needs to develop more appropriate usability criteria and to implement more effective processes to assure usability. This book provides a background of concepts and experiences that can offer insight into defining these criteria and processes.

This introductory chapter situates the usability challenge in its organizational context, develops some core concepts of usability, and outlines the subsequent chapters' contributions. Our first task is to articulate more clearly what we mean by usability.

BEYOND TRADITIONAL HUMAN FACTORS ENGINEERING

The design of systems for human use has long been associated with the discipline of "human factors," in which the operator is seen as a component of a larger system, and the job of the designer is to produce an "interface" that ensures the most efficient fit of this component into the system. The premise of this volume is that we need a concept of usability that goes beyond the traditional model because this model suffers from at least four interrelated limitations.

First, the traditional model treats the user primarily from a physical/mechanical point of view. While physiological issues will always be relevant, the development of new technologies has forced us to focus on the cognitive and social aspects of users when designing equipment. As work has become less physical and more mental, the key criteria of effective worker performance have shifted from the speed or range of motion of their limbs to the quality and flexibility of their thinking. Unfortunately, the cognitive theories used in most human factors work focus on the lower levels of cognitive functioning—such as character recognition and mnemonic abbreviations—and are ill suited to understanding the higher cognitive functions of complex reasoning processes and social interaction.

Second, the perspective usually adopted in human factors practice is one in which the human is viewed as a system component with a particular repertoire of actions and potential for breakdown. This view conceals the active role that people take in interpreting situations, in learning and adapting in their work, and generally in performing higher-level functions of monitoring and changing the system. Design techniques suited to maximizing the throughput of a speed-limited processor are simply irrelevant to the task of augmenting the capacities of the worker to act as an observer and designer of actions.

While the first two limitations constrain our understanding of the usability objective, the third and fourth limitations of traditional human factors pertain to processes for ensuring usability. The traditional human factors approach takes as given the basic form of the technology and asks how the details of a device can be modified to fit better the limits of human function. As a result, the typical human factors effort is given low priority among a design team's objectives. Usability issues are often left to the latest possible date, by which time modifications are more expensive to make. This traditional industrial practice has shaped the human factors field: human factors engineers are more at ease in responding to a proposed design than in articulating usability criteria for, and contributing directly to, the initial design concepts.

Finally, the human factors process has typically accorded the central role to engineering experts. The expertise of human factors engineers is seen as necessary to predict operating difficulties of which users may not even be aware, such as the long-term effects of poor posture. Users appear in such a usability process only as parameters of human performance identified in laboratory studies and summarized in handbook tables. The traditional approach allows that, in extreme cases, the technical novelty of the system being designed might take the engineer beyond the envelope of prior research. In such cases, some user testing might be required to ensure usability.

These expert-centered approaches may have made sense when the key usability issues were primarily physiological and lower-order cognitive ones. But when the effectiveness of a system depends on how well it supports higher-order cognitive activities and social interaction, there is often no substitute for direct user participation in the design process.

The traditional criteria and processes may have sufficed at lower levels of automation, when there were often only a few ways to implement a given capability. With computer-based systems, however, usability is often the primary consideration in whether the design will be effective in use. For companies whose business is designing and selling new equipment, usability often determines market success or failure; for departments designing equipment for in-house use, efficiency and quality of use can have important competitive repercussions.

By relegating usability to its traditional place, the conceptual design effort fails to come to grips with key issues that will govern the ultimate success of the equipment being designed. It is thus hardly surprising that seventy-five percent of companies that implement advanced manufacturing technologies do not achieve the performance they anticipated because of unforeseen problems with the interaction of human and machine (Corbett, Chapter 6 of this volume, citing Majchzrak, 1988).

The pace of technological change today makes usability assurance both more important and more difficult. The expanding functionality of new generations of systems—especially computer-based systems—widens the gap between the performance of well-designed systems and that of poorly designed systems. At the same time, the increasing complexity of the new systems reveals the limits of our current understanding of what constitutes usability and how to design for it.

USABILITY AND USE: THE LINK BETWEEN EQUIPMENT DESIGN AND WORK DESIGN

Industrial practice in the area of equipment design has been hobbled not only by the narrow views of usability discussed in the previous section, but also by some invisible assumptions about the ultimate goal of equipment design. Designers have long been encouraged to assume that the most effective designs will be those that minimize reliance on users' skills and users' involvement in the production process. This belief is encouraged first by its consistency with the widespread deskilling myth, and second by the sociopolitical pressures that shape design.

First, viewed as an engineering and economic problem, this idiot-proofing approach reflects a commitment to the deskilling myth. It heels to the belief that automation will typically reduce not only the number of employees per unit of output, but also the average level of skill required of the users, and thus reduce the average per-hour labor cost.

Although such a double gain can be obtained in a small minority of cases, a growing body of research shows that, in the majority of cases, the effective use of new technologies requires a workforce that is more skilled, not less (Adler, 1991). The most profitable way to use most new technologies appears to be two-pronged: invest in user training and broaden job responsibilities. The resulting improvements in productivity and quality greatly outweigh the added per-hour labor cost.

Second, viewed as an organizational problem, the design of work and equipment is strongly influenced by the sociopolitical realities of industrial life. In practice, involving users in the design process is difficult: It takes time, and users' input is often contradictory. Moreover, as argued by an important stream of research following from Braverman's seminal book (1974), asymmetric distribution of economic rewards, status, and power between managers and employees creates great tension in all aspects of job and equipment design.

For research on designing for usability to benefit industrial practice, we must be sensitive to the organizational context in which the research results might be implemented. In order to better understand the forces shaping this context, let us describe a prototypical situation—one that is depressingly common—in which employees resist and even sabotage the implementation of new technology, and managers insist that work design and equipment design minimize user skill requirements and job responsibilities.

In this hypothetical situation, managers see employees as recalcitrant and unreliable. Whatever the accuracy of this perception, it leads to a self-fulfilling prophecy. Managers adopt policies and behaviors that give employees every reason to act in recalcitrant and unreliable ways, thus confirming managers' beliefs (Walton, 1990). Managers' distrust of employees is mirrored in employees' distrust of managers. Employees contribute to tensions when they fear that their work will be deliberately regimented by new technologies and that they may be laid off as a result of investments in automation. Managers fear that any guarantees to protect workers against layoffs will weaken the effectiveness of the sanctions they use to buttress their managerial authority. Without such protection, employees become very reluctant to accept flexibility in job assignments. The union, on the defensive, therefore clings to existing job definitions and skills and opposes reorganization.

In organizations characterized by such an interlocking set of assumptions and self-fulfilling prophecies, designers find it difficult to operate with anything but a deskilling/idiot-proofing assumption. Usability in this context is reduced to a simplistic concept of "user friendliness" as measured by the time it takes for operators to learn the rote routines that they are expected to use. As a result, new technologies can realize only a fraction of their potential benefits.

By contrast, in organizations that have established a different set of assumptions to guide management–employee relations, work design and equipment design take on a quite different logic and the business payoff can be enormous. By building a context of mutual commitment, employees and managers can use technology to enhance user capabilities rather than to deskill—to "informate" rather than to "automate" tasks (Zuboff, 1988).

USABILITY CRITERIA: USABILITY AS A DIALOGUE OF CHANGE

To break free of the prevalent myths and go beyond current practice, we must articulate new criteria of usability that are appropriate to the tasks of modern computer-based system design and the interwoven tasks of work design. The papers brought together in this volume revolve around a common, powerful thesis: The key criterion of a system's usability is the extent to which it supports the potential for people who work with it to understand it, to learn, and to make changes. Design for usability must include design for coping with novelty, design for improvisation, and design for adaptation.

Usability thus construed assumes a communications dimension. The technology itself, even when it is not intended as a communications product, serves as a communication medium between user and user and between designer and user. A realistic characterization of work—even routine work—is that it is essentially entwined with communicative actions generated to deal with the novel situations that continually arise and with the need to interpret the intentions embodied in the machines. The user needs to learn the machine's potential and to deal effectively with the breakdowns and contingencies that inevitably occur.

Several of the chapters in this volume take a communications perspective explicitly, speaking of "design languages," "conversations," and "user-orienting design." One aspect of this communication is the dialogue between designers and operators that is implicit in the structure of equipment itself. As the case studies demonstrate, this kind of communication is embedded in every kind of artifact. Through their structure and appearance, designed objects express more or less effectively what they are, how they are used, and how they are integrated with the embedding context. Users read the artifact in much the same sense as they read a road sign or a book. They interpret symbols relying on cues from both the tool and the context, to understand the state of the system, the potential for acting on it, and the results of those actions. The user thus bridges "gulfs" of interpretation and action between the device and the field of perceptions and actions (Norman, 1986).

When our perspective shifts from viewing users as mechanistic "human components" to viewing them as dialogue partners, the key design criteria shift to those of communicativeness. We begin to consider how the design contributes to understanding, learning, and helping users go beyond narrow definitions of what needs to be done. Carrying this further, we start to look beyond the particular system being designed to the larger technical world in which it has emerged, with its background of design languages that are already prevalent.

New design evolves not in isolation but by adopting and extending these already understood languages. The innovative is understood in terms of the familiar. This applies to all areas of industrial design, and is nowhere more evident than in the world of computer interfaces, where a primary concern for any new application program is the way that its interpretation by users will fit *de facto* standards, such as Lotus 1-2-3 and the desktop metaphor of Apple's Macintosh computers.

Another aspect of the communications perspective on designing for usability is the dialogue among users. An important characteristic of newer computer-based systems is the way they tend to link work across traditional physical and organizational boundaries. Systems often link planning, production, finance, logistics, and other business processes. Many key work processes in industry today (especially those dealing with nonroutine issues) hinge on communication among previously discrete activities. In designing the work of an individual in a such a setting, we cannot take the traditional Tayloristic approach and minimize interdependence. When interdependence is a central feature of organizational effectiveness, we must design from the outset for collaborative rather than individual work. For new technologies to be effective in such organizations, they must support users' efforts to coordinate their work with others and support the work group's efforts to learn and adapt.

Current practice in system design tends to emphasize formalized information flows and preplanned communication patterns. The significance of informal and adaptable communication patterns is often neglected by computer professionals. In part, this is due to the difficulty of making such processes visible and predicting their evolution. Traditional design practice also reflects the prevalence of the older models of technology and organization, models we have argued are increasingly obsolete. The chapters in this volume argue for a new emphasis on the collective dimension of work.

THE USABILITY ASSURANCE PROCESS: THE ROLE OF THE DESIGNER

Just as we need new criteria for usability, we also need new processes for assuring that designs meet these criteria. Efforts to meet this need lead us to new interpretations of what it means to design, and of the role to be played by the designer. To treat usability as a dialogue among many parties, one must know how and when the dialogue begins, and how it is carried out through the course of the design process.

One point on which there is broad agreement is that usability assurance efforts will be most effective when they begin early in the design process, rather than take the form of a supplement at the tail end. In many cases, system usability is largely determined by early decisions because they reflect basic assumptions that then pervade the details of design. A naive observer might hypothesize that the flexibility of software would make early intervention less important in the design of computer-based systems than for purely mechanical technologies. However, even though the local details of software designs are often very plastic, usability depends less on such local details than on the fundamental structure of the design, and this structure is very difficult to modify once a design project is underway.

Not all design projects require extensive usability input in the early phases. When the system is a mere extension of an already proven design, usability considerations in the early phases of design can take the form of explicit or implicit standards or guidelines, and usability can be assured by downstream tests and minor modification. But when the new design is more novel, there is less past practice to act as guide, and the active and explicit consideration of usability in the earliest phases becomes essential.

If usability is to be integrated into the early phases of design, it will no longer suffice for usability experts to evaluate designs submitted to them. Design for usability must play an active role in determining design objectives and early conceptual designs. Usability experts must assume new roles and use new skills. As an analogy, consider how an architect works with a client in developing a plan for a house or building. The work involves bridging between what can be built, given the engineering and economic constraints, and what would be useful, given the client's needs. The architect stands with one foot in the technical engineering domain and one in the human social domain. Equipment design needs to involve a similar new "mediator": the automation architect who can bridge engineering and social demands in the design of computer-based technological systems (Hooper, 1986).

One aspect of this new design work is the ability to offer potential clients/ users a vision of what is possible: a vision that they can understand fully enough to anticipate the consequences of a project. The formal languages of system analysis are foreign and opaque to users. In their place, designers must develop a variety of other techniques, such as mockups, profession-oriented languages, partial prototypes, and scenarios that provide an extended "language" for communicating with people who are familiar with the work context and who can best anticipate how the new system might change it. This multimodal dialogue is the context in which designers and their clients together can go beyond the traditional usability approaches.

ABOUT THE BOOK

This volume brings together a set of papers from a body of research on design for usability that is emerging in the United States and Europe. It adds to a growing literature that approaches questions of design and usability from points of view such as cognitive psychology (Norman, 1988; Norman and Draper, 1986) and the sociology of work and technology (Adler, 1991, Suchman, 1987; Zuboff, 1988). The chapters also reflect, in varying degrees, the increasingly sophisticated work in practice-oriented subdisciplines such as work-oriented systems design (Ehn, 1989; Greenbaum and Kyng, 1991; Winograd and Flores, 1986), computer-supported cooperative work (Greif, 1988), and human–computer interaction (Laurel, 1990; Helander, 1988; Shneiderman, 1987).

The present volume is unusual in that it spans these diverse perspectives. Our objective is to highlight the ways they enrich each other.

Most of the papers collected here were commissioned as background briefing for a seminar titled "Technology and the Future of Work" conducted at Stanford University on March 28–30, 1990. Two hundred leaders from industry and fifty researchers, including the paper authors, attended the seminar. Their enthusiastic response encouraged us to believe that the set of issues was well defined and that the papers deserved wider circulation. A companion volume (Adler, 1991) presents papers on the *impact* of new technologies on work organization, training, employee relations, and business strategy; the present volume focuses on the *design* of new technologies.

Our approach has been multidisciplinary, since researchers from a variety of fields—both those concerned with tool design and those addressing the broader context within which new tools are designed, introduced, and used—have much to contribute to our understanding of usability. The following chapters will therefore be of interest to researchers in computer science, mechanical engineering, design studies, and human factors, as well as in sociology, organizational behavior and human resource management, industrial relations, education, and business strategy.

This volume also addresses the industrial practitioner community. A distinguishing feature of the assembled authors is their relatively "real-world" — as opposed to purely academic—orientation. Practitioners in R&D, design, manufacturing engineering, personnel/human resources, industrial relations, and general management should find valuable guide-posts to help them in their efforts.

We have organized the chapters into three sections. The first section focuses on case studies that illustrate the broad dimensions of usability and the major themes of the book.

John Rheinfrank (Fitch RichardsonSmith), Bill Hartman (Xerox Corp.), and Arnold Wasserman (Unisys Corp.) present a detailed case study of a redesign effort that yielded a particularly rich set of new usability concepts. "Design for usability: crafting a strategy for the design of a new generation of Xerox copiers" describes the development of a coherent design language that was the basis for a new concept of usability for copiers. The core of this broader concept of usability is to provide users of copiers with a "glass-box" view of the system, one that enables them to manage the various contingencies that inevitably arise in photocopying. Their design process exemplifies the use of artifacts such as models and mockups in communicating new design possibilities to people outside the design team, in this case, Xerox management as well as potential customers.

In their paper, "Designing effective systems: A tool approach," Charles Kukla (Digital Equipment Corp.), Elizabeth Anne Clemens (Da Vinci Group), Robert Morse (Da Vinci Group), and Debra Cash (Digital) present an expanded approach to system design that integrates human factors, organizational design, and systems engineering throughout the design process. The authors argue that as operational environments become more dynamic, traditional design approaches are increasingly inadequate because they are blind to how workers contribute to making operations smooth and safe. The approach proposed by the authors is distinctive in the importance it accords to integrating the modeling of the production process and the operational environment with a rigorous analysis of workers' conversational structures and the role they play in dealing with the nonroutine aspects of production. This approach is demonstrated in action by a case study of the design of a chemical processing plant.

The second section presents three chapters that draw on multiple case studies to draw some general conclusions about the relationship between technology design and the nature of work and skills.

Hal Salzman (Boston University), in his chapter on "Skill-based design: productivity, learning and organizational effectiveness," presents one of the first large-scale empirical studies of the penetration of what he calls "skill-based design" principles in equipment manufacturing. He argues that the design process that best capitalizes on automation's potential will embody a commitment to using the full range of worker skills to improve the overall production process. Salzman believes that the traditional approach, in which workers are considered only as unreliable system components, is in conflict with strategies that require greater worker involvement to improve quality and productivity. He shows how the traditional approach is articulated in design textbooks, and then, through a survey of design policies and practices in U.S. manufacturing firms, assesses how far the new approach has penetrated industrial practice.

Pelle Ehn (University of Aarhus, Denmark), in "Scandinavian design: on participation and skill," summarizes some of the recent Scandinavian experiences in participatory design, with specific reference to the DEMOS and

UTOPIA projects. Ehn discusses the key role played by unions in supporting a "work-oriented" design philosophy and argues that, without an institutionalized voice, workers' participation in design quickly loses significance and momentum. To conceptualize the role of the designer in the new process, he builds on Wittgenstein's ideas on language games. He presents design as a process in which designers and users must develop a new, shared language game.

The chapter by Martin Corbett (Warwick Business School), "Work at the interface: advanced manufacturing technology and job design," summarizes a series of University of Manchester and ESPRIT projects designed to identify general criteria of usability and to specify a collaborative design process capable of assuring that usability in advanced manufacturing systems. His paper focuses on five key problem areas: the allocation of functions between worker and machine, the design of the overall system architecture, the control characteristics of the interface, the informational characteristics of the interface, and the allocation of operating responsibilities.

The final paper, in a group by itself, is by John Seely Brown (Xerox Corp.) and Paul Duguid (Institute for Research on Learning). In "Enacting design for the workplace" they address several of the topics we have introduced in these opening pages. They reflect on the folly of idiot-proofing, the insights offered by thinking of using new technology as like reading a book, the analogy between product design and building architecture, and most of all, the importance of focusing on learning in product design. Like several of the earlier chapters, they argue that new tools should be designed to support learning through use; and they go on to argue that learning to use a new tool is a process of becoming a participant in a community of users. Good design should support this community-centered process. Moreover, since designs "enact" a certain view of the world, organizations need to understand that designers contribute to—or detract from—the organization's innovative capability.

CONCLUSION

This collection of essays makes a compelling case that new technologies will realize too little of their potential unless a new, broader concept of usability is made central to design. Usability must be elevated to the same priority as functionality.

However, in extending the view of design beyond the traditional idiot-proofing/deskilling assumptions, we create a dilemma. The old assumptions allowed designers to circumscribe their task very narrowly, and within the boundaries of these assumptions they could reasonably hope to reach their objectives. Once we abandon these assumptions, the design task becomes much less well defined, and the design objective may seem frustratingly remote since the designer must simultaneously design the equipment and the work organization in which the equipment will serve.

We believe that the potential power of new technology can only be tapped by squarely confronting this broader, more ambitious usability challenge. To do so we must revolutionize established design criteria and procedures. Indeed, the term *usability assurance* is inadequate to capture the nature of the task at hand. *Assurance* is too reassuring a term because it implies that we understand more than we really do about usability.

We believe that a more open-ended usability challenge confronts industry and researchers alike, and that this challenge requires a fundamental shift in our thinking and practice.

This shift puts a premium on designing for learning—learning at three levels. First, we need to design equipment that supports the kind of learning in which users come to understand how and why the system works as it does. Second, the equipment needs to be designed to support the kind of learning in which users discover how to adapt and extend the technology to satisfy the demands and contingencies of their work better. And finally, we need to create a design process that allows us to learn how better to tackle these daunting usability challenges.

In essence, the "usability challenge" is therefore one of contributing to the design of the "learning organization" —an organization that takes change as the primary constant, and is explicitly concerned with inventing and supporting equipment and processes by which it adapts to a continually changing world.

REFERENCES

Adler, P. S. (ed.) (1991) *Technology and the Future of Work,* New York: Oxford University Press.

Braverman, H. (1974). *Labor and Monopoly Capital—The Degradation of Work in the Twentieth Century.* New York: Monthly Review Press.

Ehn, P. (1989). *Work-Oriented Design of Computer Artifacts.* Falköping, Sweden: Arbetslivscentrum and Hillsdale, N.J.: Lawrence Erlbaum Associates.

Greenbaum, Joan, and Morten Kyng (eds.) (1991). *Design at Work: Cooperative Design of Computer Systems,* Hillsdale, N.J.: Erlbaum.

Greif, I. (ed.) (1988). *Computer-Supported Cooperative Work: A Book of Readings.* San Mateo, Calif.: Morgan Kaufmann.

Helander, Martin (ed.) (1988). *Handbook of Human–Computer Interaction.* North-Holland: Elsevier Science Publishers.

Hooper, K. (1986). Architectural design: An analogy, in D. Norman and S. Draper (eds.). *User Centered System Design—New Perspectives on Human Computer Interaction.* Hillsdale, N.J.: Lawrence Erlbaum, pp. 9–24.

Laurel, Brenda (ed.) (1990). *The Art of Human–Computer Interface Design,* Reading, Mass.: Addison–Wesley.

Majchzrak, A. (1988). *The Human Side of Factory Automation.* San Francisco: Jossey–Bass.

Norman, D. A. (1988). *The Psychology of Everyday Things.* N.Y.: Basic Books, Inc. Reprinted as *The Design of Everyday Things* (paperback).

Norman, D. A. (1986). Cognitive engineering, in D. Norman and S. Draper (eds.). *User Centered System Design—New Perspectives on Human Computer Interaction*. Hillsdale, N.J.: Lawrence Erlbaum, pp. 31–62.

Norman, D. A., and S. Draper (eds.) (1986). *User centered system design—New Perspectives on Human Computer Interaction*. Hillsdale, N.J.: Lawrence Erlbaum.

Shneiderman, B. (1987). *Designing the User Interface: Strategies for Effective Human–Computer Interaction*. Reading, Mass.: Addison–Wesley.

Suchman, L. A. (1987). *Plans and Situated Actions—The Problem of Human–Machine Communication*. New York: Cambridge University Press.

Walton, R. E. (1990). *Up and Running: Integrating Information Technology and the Organization*. Boston: Harvard Business School Press.

Winograd, T., and F. Flores (1986). *Understanding Computers and Cognition—A New Foundation for Design*. Norwood, N.J.: Ablex.

Zuboff, S. (1988). *In the Age of the Smart Machine*, New York: Basic Books.

CHAPTER 2

Design for Usability: Crafting a Strategy for the Design of a New Generation of Xerox Copiers

JOHN J. RHEINFRANK, WILLIAM R. HARTMAN, AND ARNOLD WASSERMAN

As designers, we view our work not merely as the production of products, but also as the creation of evocative and evolutionary artifacts that play important roles in shaping people's lives. Well-designed artifacts tell people what functions they perform and how they perform them—this is why they have been designed, not merely produced or created. More important, through their design, well-designed artifacts also participate in the construction of human experience. In particular, carefully crafted artifacts can participate in the construction of human experiences surrounding how they (the artifacts themselves) can be used. Thus, we arrive at "Design for Usability," a phrase we use to refer to the design of an artifact's use through the design of its physical presence in the world.

This chapter, then, is about a shift in perspective from "design as the post hoc application of form and appearance elements to functionality, with the intent of communicating that functionality" to "design as the conscious crafting of usability, through the skillful development of form and appearance elements, with the intent of providing people with the resources to perceive and construct usability themselves." Expressed another way, we are talking about turning innovative concepts into everyday and universal operations through the design of things. As we said to ourselves while working on the "Design for Usability" project we are about to describe: "If we could make the experience of using a Xerox photocopier as simple and straightforward as the experience of walking through a door, then we will have made a truly usable copier."

We will demonstrate the process of designing according to this shift in perspective through a case study of a successful photocopier-design collaboration between Xerox Corporation (Xerox) and Fitch RichardsonSmith

(FRS). Historically, Xerox has always pursued the goal of creating products and services intended to improve how people work and the overall quality of people's work lives. More recently, Xerox copiers have not been designed as objects, but as artifacts that galvanize the work culture at Xerox to produce them and the widely distributed work culture of Xerox's customers to make them part of their everyday activities. How did this shift occur? The answer to that question is the subject of the rest of this chapter—a description of the formative stages of one of Xerox's largest strategic design initiatives: the design and development of the 10- and 50-series of copiers between 1980 and 1990.

The first section of this chapter presents the experiental design semantics foundation for our "Design for Usability" approach. Here, we also define the concept of "Design Language" and describe how it is used by designers, users, and corporations to convey both functionality and experience. The second section presents a short history of the development of the Xerox copier technology and early products, followed by a description of the business context that called for a different design perspective in the 1980s. The collaborative structure and the work process of the project are described in the third section. The formulation of the Xerox Design Language is outlined in the fourth section. The fifth section contains a discussion of the impact of the work on the product, on corporate learning and acceptance, and on future design projects. The conclusion summarizes a few of the larger conceptual shifts that came out of the work.

DESIGN SEMANTICS: PRODUCT AND EXPERIMENTAL SEMANTICS

Our work has taught us the value of a language- and communication-based approach to the design of products and the use of those products. From traditional linguistic and communication arenas we are able to draw on the insights of semiotics (the study of meaning), product semantics (the expression of meaning through form), and situation semantics (the expression of meaning through action) to help us frame our approach. From this foundation, we have arrived at the idea of "experiential semantics," which we define as the design of meaningful experiences through the production of an emergent and evocative integration of both form and action. Although still largely unexplored, we believe that experiential semantics can provide a powerful new framework for design.

Within this framework, we see meaning in design not just as the built-in sense of an object, but also as the *quality of sense-making that objects have and can produce*, especially with respect to their surroundings. In other words, design is more than making meaningful objects; it is crafting "whatever it is" about objects that lets them participate in the creation of meaningful experiences. According to this view of meaning, the sense of an object cannot be separated from the experience in which that object simultaneously sits and helps to create.

We can contrast this notion of experiential semantics with the traditional concept of "product semantics." In the traditional concept, the focus has been on objects' forms (such as whether doors are rectangular or arched), on objects' surface treatments (whether door surfaces are plain, painted wood, or glass), and on the deeply embedded meanings (expressions of doorness) that those forms, surface treatments, and objects carry and convey for both designers and users. One common assumption has been that objects (revolving doors) and the elements of objects (thin horizontal metal handles) evoke meaningful actions (push here and walk around in circles) for people interacting with objects (going through doors).

Product semantics helps make clear *how* objects participate in the production of meaning and how they are interpreted—not what they mean. For the most part the product semantics approach has failed to clarify (1) the overall experiences that result from the combination of object, interpretation by people, and interaction between people and objects; (2) the feelings or attitudes that people produce about those experiences; and (3) how designers can use an understanding of these experiences and feelings in their work. Since designers have often been unclear about how objects themselves contribute to the experiences people have with them, and about how those expressions become meaningful through interaction, they have often only been able to design experiences through objects in an intuitive and haphazard (although frequently surprisingly successful) way.

From a product semantics point of view, a good door has a handle that, whether ceramic or metal, is obvious and clearly communicates "grasp here to open or close." From an experiential semantics point of view, a good door makes all of the experiences associated with doors (such as invitation, privacy, and passage) available to people without making people think explicitly about them—without making people think, "I must now pass through this door by manipulating a handle." More importantly, a person can literally and figuratively go "through" a door to the rich set of feelings which the door is about. Experiential semantics is therefore concerned more with making doors (or copiers or cars) that have (1) radically more appropriate substance and (2) a collaborative quality that allows them to integrate with the experiences of those who use them.

Experiential semantics helps to make clear how both people and objects participate in the creation of experiences. Designers can take advantage of this knowledge in their work by consciously considering—and designing—not only *the properties of objects* that contribute to the creation of experiences, but also *the emergent properties of objects in the context of the abilities that people have to interact with objects and each other.*

Designing from an Experiential Semantics Perspective

Designing from an experiential point of view means designing the resources that people use to frame those events that constitute their experiences when they interact with objects. To accomplish this, one designs objects that will produce or evoke specific events that lead to specific experiences in specific situations. The events to which we are referring are dynamic actions, not static situations. Thus, the shift from product semantics to experiential semantics entails shifting from thinking about objects as nouns (doors) to thinking about objects as verbs (open, close). To carry this analogy one step further, experiences can be seen—and designed as—sequences of verbs (open: perceive door, approach door, grasp handle, and so on).

We call the decomposition of an experience into events the "unfolding of meaning," and we can design experiences (as enfolded meaning) according to the patterns created by the unfolding of events. In design terms, the situated, almost archetypical, presence of a good door can be made clear through a sequence of revelations (articulated through form) about what doors have been, what doors are, what this particular door is, and how this particular door functions in its current context. A good door invites us to approach it when we first see it, makes obvious to us where we are to open it, makes clear to us that it is a means of transition from one place to another, and helps create experiences of invitation, privacy, and passage.

A good door allows us to use an enormous range of physical resources without even thinking about them—or about ourselves as users of doors. We simply move through doors to the other side. This is the spirit with which we approached the development and design of a line of copiers for Xerox.

Design Languages

Just as spoken languages are the basis for our conversations with people, so design languages are the basis for our interactions with products and services. Spoken languages consist of words and rules of grammar. By analogy, design languages consist of design elements and guidelines for their combination. People use spoken language to express themselves. Product designers use design languages to design expressive objects. When a designer uses a design language to design a product, the resulting product expresses what it is, what it does, how it is to be used, and the experiences to which it has the potential to contribute. When people use a design language to use a product, the resulting experience of use is simple and straightforward. The best design languages take the design of experience one step further by making interactions between people and objects pleasant and continuously meaningful. Design languages play a very important role in the expression of the "unfolding of meaning" of objects. Essentially, design languages are (1) the means by which designers build meaning into objects, (2) the means by which objects express themselves and their meanings to people, and (3) the means by which people learn to understand and use objects, and engage in experiences associated with objects.

Design languages are present everywhere in our manmade environment. For example, in urban design and architecture, a definite language of form, materials, and structure has been used to help produce the buildings, neighborhoods, and social patterns of suburban Amsterdam. This design language is different from the one used to help produce the buildings, neighborhoods, and social patterns of suburban Columbus, Ohio. The suburbs of Amsterdam have almost no grass. The typical Columbus suburb has spacious lawns and gardens. In Amsterdam, residential buildings are attached to each other and built of masonry or stone. In Columbus, buildings are widely separated and mostly of frame construction. These are not "stylistic" differences; these are content-based differences—differences that have developed over time in response to local interpretation of the underlying concept of "house." In Amsterdam, there are few lawns because there is very little space, not because the Dutch do not like grass. In Columbus, most houses are built of wood, not stone, because trees are plentiful. There are clearly two different design languages at work here. Each has its own set of design elements and its own guidelines for use. Each results in the construction and realization of a different "housing experience." When new houses are constructed in either Amsterdam or Columbus, the appropriate design languages are used.

Doors too have a design language. A wooden door with obvious hinges and a round doorknob expresses to the user that the object is a door and that, as a door, it should be opened and closed in a certain way. If the same door is surrounded by a wonderful, hand-painted wooden frame at the entrance to a bedroom in a family home, then its meaning in the context of the house is obvious, as are its contributions to the experiences that occur in the house. By contrast, a harsh glass door at the entrance to a glass-fronted public building with no obvious hinges and with a small steel plate as a handle does not communicate "doorness" so clearly. Nor is its meaning clear within the context of the surrounding glass wall that is the outside of the building. Furthermore, such a door does not contribute to the experiences that occur during the entering and leaving of public buildings. In fact, people often make mistakes when using such doors—they walk into the walls next to the doors (behaving much like unsuspecting birds who do the same thing), or, if they find the doors, they falter when opening them. In this example, the design language of doors has been appropriately applied to the design of house doors and inappropriately applied to the design of building doors. The designer of the wooden bedroom door was designing experiences having to do with privacy and togetherness in families. The designer of the glass building door should have been—but was not—designing experiences having to do with the significance of entering and leaving public spaces.

Design Languages and Learning

We have given two examples of how the use of design languages allows artifacts to express what they are and how they are used (product semantics) as well as their integration with the richness of the embedding context (experiential semantics). Designers can also use design languages to give people strong cues and powerful resources for learning by using. They can do so by shaping their designs to take advantage of what people already know and have the potential to do. For example, a designer who understands "the design language of door handles" and applies this understanding to the design of "opening things" can provide people with physical cues for "how to open things" by using handles that (1) correspond to the contexts of the artifacts being designed and that (2) clearly communicate "open here" in those contexts.

A designer who pays attention to the design language of "handles and doors and opening" would not put a steel plate handle on a plate glass bedroom door. Instead, the designer might draw on the qualities of handles that people already understand—and know how to use—to design door handles (openings) appropriate to the privacy and intimacy that bedrooms afford. By attending to what people already know, designers can provide people with powerful cues for accepting and effortlessly learning how to use newly designed artifacts.

One thing designers can do to help people learn is to reveal functionality—through "glass-box" design—rather than to conceal it—through "black-box" design. In a "black box" all functionality is opaque or hidden from view, and people accomplish their goals by pushing buttons that signify nothing whatsoever about the inner workings of the box. To accomplish this, the technology is made "foolproof." (Note the degrading reference to the assumed "competence" of the user). In a "glass box," functionality is revealed, and people are provided with the opportunity to comprehend the inner workings of the artifact they are using. A well-designed glass box selectively reveals to people just enough information about "how to use the artifact" and "how the artifact works" for people to accomplish their goals or to do tasks. This selective revelation can be done by allowing the "meaning" of the full experience of using the artifact to unfold gradually according to need, over time, as the artifact is used.

Design languages also make it easier for people to learn by allowing patterns of use to be transferred from one artifact to another. Designers can help users transfer patterns of use by consciously and consistently understanding and applying one design language across a product offering. People can then take advantage of the resulting similarities in how products are used, often without any conscious relearning. For example, design languages can be applied across product lines to create families of products. The members of these families resemble one other with respect to their forms and interaction styles. Thus, when people learn about one family member's form and inter-action style, they can transfer this learning to other members of the same product family, adding to the overall usability of the entire product offering. The standard Apple Macintosh interface is a good example of this: Users can easily learn new applications because they rely on similar and familiar icons and conventions of interaction.

Design Languages and Business

In the past ten years, it has become obvious that design languages can contribute to meaningful and successful design and market development strategies for businesses. Design languages can also unify a corporation's offerings with respect to appearance, functionality, and, most important, usability. Because of this, businesses can explicitly use design languages to create coherent product lines. When a corporation's products are presented to its markets in coherent ways, customers form a consistent—and increasingly more positive—impression of the corporation. This impression becomes stronger as customers are repeatedly exposed to a corporation's products. In the end, this impression plays a large role in determining future customer purchases—thereby also determining the success of the corporation.

The best design languages, however, do more than create coherence; they also create relevance—they ensure that the product line is relevant to customer needs and plays a crucial role in customers' everyday activities. Thus, the best design languages set an industry standard for coherence, relevance, and quality, and, once adopted by customers, force competitors to either adopt the same standards or produce equally strong alternatives. If a design language that is appreciated by customers becomes dominant in a market, it may take rival corporations years to make the changes necessary for effective competition.

The most relevant design languages can even profoundly recast an industry. For example, the move made by the Japanese to downsize cars and reorient them to respond to a broader range of customer lifestyles dramatically changed the competitive rules of the automotive industry. When a new or recast product line appears and convinces customers that it will meet their needs in a powerful way, then customers move toward it steadily and irreversibly. This is especially true when design languages are used to influence the whole spectrum of ways that a company communicates with its customers (advertising, customer service, literature, merchandising, and so on).

There is one quality of design languages that makes them potentially dangerous in an environment of accelerating change: They are most effective when they acquire power over time. Design languages typically are most powerful when they have become deeply held traditions, when people can unconsciously assume that they are valid and can continue to work through them rather than think about them and their appropriateness. In a changing world, a business might therefore find itself adhering to an outdated tradition that no longer "makes sense" to customers. In such a case, the business might become particularly vulnerable to a competitor whose product line addresses a set of needs that have suddenly become more salient. On the other hand, corporations that know how to use design languages and recognize their lifecycle limitations can use design languages to respond skillfully to the pace of change. A reflective corporation can identify, develop and implement a new design language quickly and effectively as part of the movement toward a dramatically better market potential.

XEROX, PHOTOCOPYING, AND PHOTOCOPYING MACHINES

Design languages have much to do with the concept of "crafting usability" that we wanted to implement in the Xerox photocopier project. Specifically, our approach to usability was to create a design language that would help designers create artifacts expressing (1) what copiers are, (2) how copiers are used, (3) what the experience of copying is, and (4) how copiers and copying are integrated into the embedding, constantly changing, work context.

Before we describe and illustrate some of the design language principles we developed to define and implement the new concept of copier usability, we will set the stage by describing the history of photocopying and photocopiers at Xerox.

The Invention

In the 1930s, Chester Carlson invented a technology that transferred images from one sheet of plain paper to another. We say he invented a technology, not a product, because his invention was essentially unusable outside the laboratory.

From the early 1940s through about 1960, Xerox worked with Battelle Memorial Institute to commercialize Carlson's original technology for making plain paper photocopies. When Battelle researchers talk about the early photocopy process, they call it "a usability nightmare." The process involved four or five discrete steps and was complicated and messy (using a camera, preparing plates and films, using chemical developers, turning papers in trays filled with black powder, etc.). As it was originally conceived, the process was barely workable in the laboratory. It would have been impossible in the workplace. Despite this, the focus of early research and development was to make *usable copies*—to produce higher-quality images more quickly and at higher volumes. There was some interest in making the copying process more convenient and reliable for users, but the overall concept of usability in the early days was "higher-quality, faster copying."

As the researchers worked on refining the technology, they also pursued creative applications of it. Once they began using the copying technology in their own work to share printed information with one another, the shift from using carbon paper to using photocopies was inevitable. As this shift gained momentum, the researchers finally began to develop notions of what usable copies would mean in a workplace setting. The experience enhanced their interpretation of usability. Suddenly, usability also meant *usable copying*.

The process of refining usability was transferred from the Xerox–Battelle team to the Xerox corporate culture along with the refined technology. The new Xerox goal became the production of usable copies *and* convenient copying.

The success story, of course, is that by the middle of the 1960s people around the world were using Xerox copiers and Xerox copies in offices to disseminate information. The technology moved into the workplace as a series of products, and the products became indispensable adjuncts to everyday work. Copiers were becoming the printing presses of the twentieth century.

Business Urgency

From the early 1960s to the late 1970s, Xerox dominated the photocopying market, largely as a result of its ability to capitalize on the inventions it discovered and patented during the earlier days of research and development with Battelle. But by the late 1970s and early 1980s, Xerox's share of the reprographics market had declined. Japanese manufacturers began to pose an external threat. This was compounded by legal challenges to the so-called "Xerox photocopier monopoly." Other blows were self-inflicted. Xerox was late in recognizing a business opportunity at the low end of the market. A few critical weak product introductions and product failures, and poor product reliability hurt the company's reputation. Management also had to contend with cost-containment problems, long product development and introduction times, and problems with product usability. What follows is a quick summary of some of these design/usability problems from a number of perspectives.

1. Difficult to use. From the perspective of the customer/user, Xerox photocopiers were often perceived as difficult to use. On some machines, walkup use (job programming, loading paper) was considered unnecessarily complex, and recovery from routine problems (fixing paper jams) was sometimes seen as unnecessarily difficult. In many cases, users simply abandoned machines they could not comprehend, operate, or fix, resulting in unnecessary service calls. The abandoned (but certainly fixable) machines were, of course,

unavailable for copying, adding to the user's perception that Xerox's machines could not be relied upon.

The job of operating the copier was primarily assumed by either secretaries, who had no extra time to spend "babying" difficult equipment, or by the growing ranks of walkup users, who had little or no copying experience. To compound this problem, the machines were not as communicative as they could have been. Flip-card decks were the main carriers of instructional and diagnostic information, and they were located "out of the way," far from the most common sources of user error. In addition, the products were difficult to explain, demonstrate, and sell, and formal training was almost always required for efficient use. All of this made the natural exchange of information about how to use the copier among office workers virtually impossible.

Then, Japanese reprographic products began appearing in offices and introduced customers/users to different styles of interaction with copiers. This is not to say that the interaction styles of the Japanese products were necessarily better, just that they did present an alternative to an existing interaction style that was negatively perceived by current customers and users.

2. Accelerating changes in use. As the volume of information in offices increased and the copier became more integrated into office life, making copies became a ubiquitous part of work. This changed the way copiers were used. Instead of relying on "key operators" (usually secretaries) to operate copiers and handle immense volumes of copying, office workers began to try to make their own copies. The conceptual switch from "an operator making copies" to "anyone making copies" was a move in the right direction in terms of usability, but unfortunately the Xerox reprographic products did not provide users with the corresponding resources to make this move.

3. Increasing functionality. Over time, copier functionality increased in two ways. The range of functionalities expanded, as did the sophistication of the functions themselves. As the capabilities of the products increased, the users' levels of frustration increased as well. People less skilled at copying were trying to accomplish more complex copying tasks that required more skilled execution. And, they were given little additional help from the copiers or the documentation.

4. Narrow design perspective. The pre-1980 Xerox copiers had been developed as though they were office furnishings meant to blend decoratively and functionally with other office objects and surrounding office environments. The design idiom was "a copier that complements its environment." Most of the Xerox design staff saw the design of reprographics products as "furniture making" or "cabinet making," where the goal was to conceal functionality wherever possible. Functional areas were revealed only when absolutely necessary.

As a result of this narrow design perspective, the human factors group was relegated to testing and solving "usability problems" within the framework of the established design. The overall impact of this flaw-fixing orientation was that, although the products were functionally usable, their forms did not offer users much organizational or conceptual support for the activity of making copies.

5. Reversion in strategic priorities. The prevailing attitude among the community of product developers called for reprographic products to be conceived, planned, and produced according to their speed, copy quality, cost, and technical reliability. This prioritization was based on the recognition that future competitiveness would require innovation along several of these fronts simultaneously. But, there was no agreed-upon concept for ease and convenience of use. Good usability was not defined as an overall design criterion or as a component of competitive strategy. Somehow, the organization had reverted to the 1940s goal of "making usable copies." The idea of "making usable copiers" seemed to have disappeared from the Xerox culture.

THE XEROX–FRS DESIGN COLLABORATIVE

The Players

In the early 1980s, in response to their perception of increased business urgency, Xerox began to work with FRS to co-develop and implement a comprehensive usability design strategy for copiers. The goal of the strategy was to produce more usable copies through more usable copiers.

From the Xerox side, the design directors were Arnold Wasserman (1980–1986) and Bill Hartman (1986–present). Participants from the Xerox internal design staff included product designers, human factors personnel (evaluation and testing), user interface designers, graphic designers, and system developers. Other participants from Xerox—content and process champions—included principal engineers, service strategists, trainers, salespeople, members of advanced development teams, marketing strategists, researchers, and planners.

From the FRS side, the project directors were Deane Richardson and John Rheinfrank. Richardson and Rheinfrank co-directed the project from 1980 to 1982; Rheinfrank directed the project from 1982 to 1986, and continues to work with Xerox. From 1986 through 1991, continued collaboration between Xerox and FRS has led to further application and extension of the work done in the 1980s, as well as new industrial design and human–computer interaction design initiatives. The FRS team assembled to work on the project included people with expertise in product design, user interface design, cognitive psychology, information design, graphic design, systems engineering, communications theory, and model making.

Developing a Usability Design Strategy

The Xerox–FRS team began with the challenge of designing photocopying products that would be easy and convenient to use. In an effort to provide people with more task-oriented support for copying, the Xerox–FRS team began to rethink the traditional human factors definition of usability. Driven in part by the increased functionality of new copiers, and in part by copier users' frustration at their own inability to understand and use the new functionality, the team began to develop a much broader definition of usability. Instead of responding to human factors flaws after they were discovered, the team tried to anticipate and provide the resources people would need for effective operation. Given the association that had grown at Xerox between the term *usability* and the old, narrow design perspective, the team realized that they needed another term to describe their work. They chose the term *operability* to refer to the new objective of "making copiers immediately useful." By changing terminology, the team effected a conceptual shift within Xerox. The shift was from reactive flaw fixing to proactive design for use, and from a narrow concept of usability to a broader one.

The conceptual transition was followed by a change in the way Xerox design work was done. By designing for the broader definition of usability, the Xerox–FRS team began designing copiers that communicated. For example, copier exteriors no longer resembled cabinetry, but began to communicate how the machines were organized in terms of operational regions (paper in, paper out, interior access) and in terms of functionality (multiple copies, collated copies).

Within the broader definition of usability, the Xerox–FRS team identified several strategic opportunities for immediate investment. Most of these were motivated by the growing feature richness and complexity of copiers. Key opportunities included: (1) learning while using and thus minimizing reliance on manuals, (2) transferring learning and skills from one machine to another, (3) embracing changing work practices, (4) differentiating Xerox products from competitive products, (5) taking advantage of available computation technologies to display information that would be relevant to trouble management, and (6) incorporating Xerox research staffs' considerable expertise into achieving all of the above.

Qualitative Field Research

To begin the design process, the Xerox–FRS team observed authentic situations of copier use. Members of the design team interviewed customers and users of copiers about patterns of use, likes, and dislikes. They participated in service calls where they were able to see copier breakdowns and repairs for themselves. They joined sales teams as they called on customers. Through sales and service training, team members became "experts" in the copier business. They also attended trade shows and went to local sales offices for hands-on experience with the full range of products available in the market.

Rapid Iterative Prototyping

The design process was iterative, as most design processes are. The team's strategy was to begin conceptual development of a 1990 product line in 1983. The first iteration of the design process consisted of foamware modeling of a projected product line. By foamware, we mean constructing progressively better understood physical representations of products out of foamcore, wood, paper, and other soft modeling materials. The second iteration involved the divergent generation of ideas and rough embodiments of product form and interaction style. The third iteration led to the convergent selection and representation of a final direction. The fourth, and final, iteration was essentially validation and refinement of the selected direction, and led to finished models of what became the 10- and 50-series copiers.

Because the prototypes had physical presence, each became the center of an almost theatrical experience that evoked conversation and interaction among developers, designers, and business decision makers. These scenario-based experiences included the simulated use of the prototypes by developers as though they were potential customers of the future product line. The prototypes were then refined according to the insights uncovered. This activity allowed the design teams to pursue their own and others' intuitions and creative interpretations freely and cost effectively.

Communicating the Results

To share the results of the rapid iterative prototyping, the design team chose to create communicative experiences rather than simply deliver results in the form of models and reports. Demonstration rooms were constructed at Xerox to display models of the entire projected product line. The models themselves, however, were not the stars of the show. Instead, they were used as the focal points for creating (staging) and enacting (acting out) events reflecting scenario-based hypotheses about how people would go about "making copies" in the future. Development teams, designers, senior managers, and executives "stepped into" the results.

In effect, the reviewers used models of copiers to act out events surrounding "making copies." The conversations they had, and the subsequent modifications (actual or suggested) they made to the models, helped shape the final product and interaction style design directions. An interesting side effect was that, through conversation, the participants in the project gradually developed an understanding of one another's capabilities and motivations. This contributed to increased internal understanding throughout the company.

The Xerox–FRS collaboration resulted in both a redefinition of usability and a transfer of the new interpretation of usability into the Xerox culture. The transfer phase of the effort was considerable—the team spent about a quarter of its time on design and development, and three-quarters of its time on planning and communication.

In pursuing the challenge of designing easy and convenient photocopying products, the Xerox–FRS team moved from designing copiers as single products to designing families of copiers that supported the transfer of learned skills. The team also developed a "new way of designing" that resulted in the integration of "design for usability" with "design for appearance and functionality." It was hoped that by designing and launching entire families of copiers unified through appearance, functionality, *and* usability, Xerox would be able to regain and maintain a key competitive edge in the marketplace.

THE XEROX DESIGN LANGUAGE

The iterative prototyping, simulation, and refinement of the products' forms, interaction styles, and uses led to the identification of a central set of insights about the everyday experience of using photocopiers to make photocopies. This set of insights was captured and communicated through a product and interaction style design language—the Xerox Design Language. In short, the Xerox Design Language consisted of a series of specific product and interaction style design recommendations (principles, sketches, photos of models, scenarios), plus guidelines for their application. The design elements and the guidelines were intended to be applied in a variety of situations to create near-optimum copiers and copying experiences. At the foundation of the Xerox Design Language was the notion of adding the "crafting of usability" to the "crafting of functionality and appearance" by considering the design of events-of-use as a part of the design of the product line.

Over the course of the project, the photocopier product prototypes, the elements that composed them, and their associated interaction styles became a generally accepted vocabulary of form and function. For example, members of the design team made frequent references to "that value of grey on the doors" or "the way this paper tray is inserted." "That value of grey on the doors" became a vocabulary element in the Xerox product design language in the sense that it retained its meaning when taken from one context and used in another: "Let's use that value of grey on this product's doors, too." Similarly, "the way this paper tray is inserted" became a vocabulary element in the interaction style design language: "Let's transfer that way of insertion to this paper tray too." Elements like these, plus guidelines for their use (for example, "Use that darker value of grey to indicate interior access by applying it to doors on machines") became a true designer's language. The elements and the guidelines for their use could be used in an almost infinite number of ways to make up various product configurations and create various user experiences, much as words and rules of grammar are used to make sentences and meaning.

The Xerox Design Language Applied

The Xerox Design Language took the form of a succession of informative views of the copier at various stages of the copying experience. As the views unfolded, they supported the formation of useful mental models of the machines' parts and the experiences of interacting with those parts. The views included step-by-step presentations of machine parts and their functions, and the corresponding task sequences. The views supported copying tasks by "talking the user through them" instead of concealing information or overloading users with incomprehensible or unrelated information. A list of some of the main views and categories of the Xerox Design Language follows, along with brief discussions of the design teams' intentions and accomplishments for each entry.

1. Gestalt view. The overall impressions or silhouettes of the products were designed not to conceal but to inform. The main categories of use were made clear; color and value coding were used to distinguish various areas of the product; and the machines were given an overall frontal orientation. (See Figure 2.1.)

Figure 2.1.

2. Work surface view. The work surfaces of the machines were designed according to a workbench metaphor. The flow of work was made clear through stations of work, manageable amounts of information were placed where they were needed, and the products were all designed to have identifiable central control/display surfaces. The goal was total support of the copying task—within arm's reach for the user. (See Figure 2.2.)

3. Access view. The points where the users could move to take actions beneath the outside surfaces of the machines were made obvious and nonthreatening. The surfaces were designed to be plain and straightforward, and the access points were made clear. The access view invited users to explore the interiors in a relaxed way rather than intimidating them. (See Figure 2.3.).

4. Interior view. One of the most significant innovations that came out of the project was the treatment of the interiors of the machines themselves. The interiors were designed to express various layers and degrees of interaction to users and service people. The user-accessible components of the interiors (such as paper loading, jam clearing, and simple maintenance) were placed in the visual foreground, and the technician-accessible components of the interior (more complex maintenance and repairs that needed to be done by customer or technical service staff) were placed in receding layers in the background. Color and value coding were used to indicate the various layers of interaction. Light colors and values were used for items in the foreground, and darker values were used for the items in the background. (See Figure 2.4.)

Figure 2.2.

Figure 2.3.

5. Control/display surfaces. The central control/display surfaces of the machines were designed to be active windows into the machines and their functionality. A careful blending of visual and verbal carriers of information was used. Both alphanumeric and mimic displays were used, and direct manipulation interfaces were emphasized. In all cases, the control/display surfaces were designed to be as clear and usable as possible. The individual controls went through many iterations of prototyping and user testing before guidelines were established. (See Figure 2.5.)

6. Communication graphics. The principle behind the design of the communication graphics was to offer sufficient instruction at the point of need, with links to more detailed information elsewhere. Instructional graphics, graphic signs and symbols, and the use of the Xerox identity were all considered in conjunction with the product form and the interaction style of the products. (See Figure 2.6.)

7. Total design: User/customer orienting. Finally, the broader concept of usability we came to call *operability* (incorporating functionality, appearance, and usability) were extended beyond the boundaries of the products themselves. A total (vertically integrated) design of the Xerox copier/copying experience was the team's goal. This included the presence of the copiers in advertising, the presentation of the products by salespeople, the configuration of a particular copying solution for a particular customer's needs, the merchandising of the products at point of sale, the packaging, the installing pro-

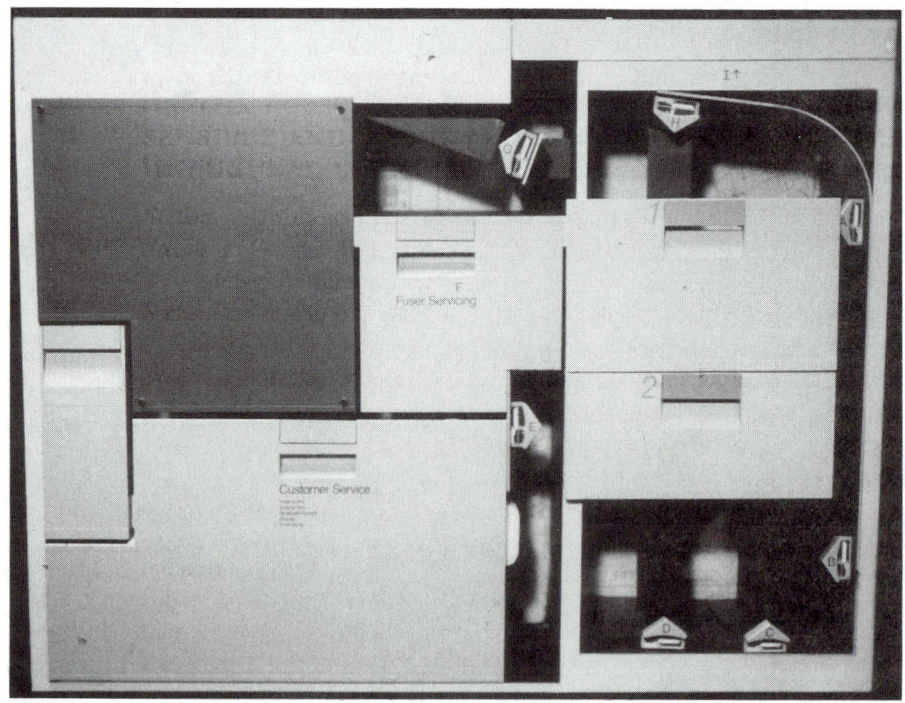

Figure 2.4.

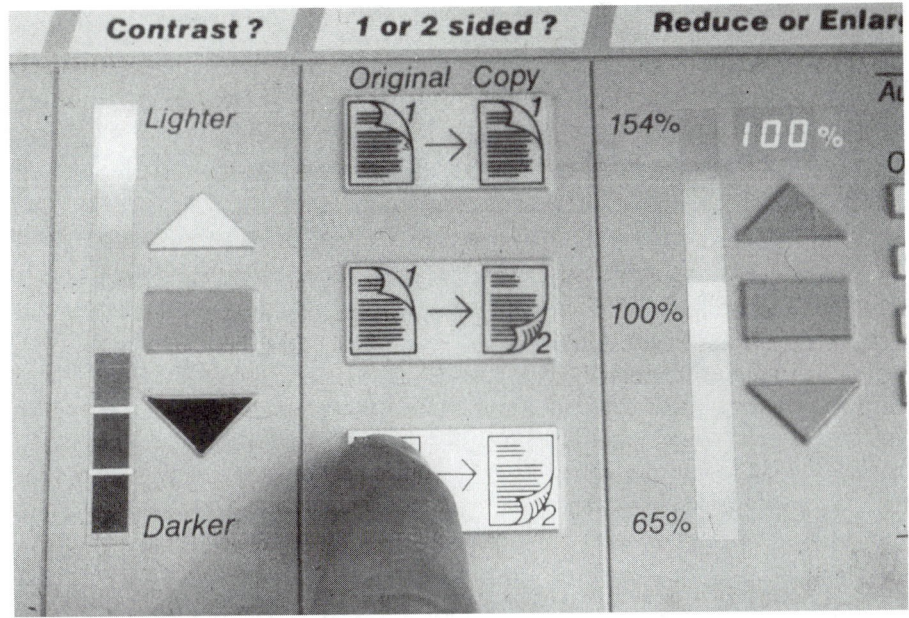

Figure 2.5.

Figure 2.6.

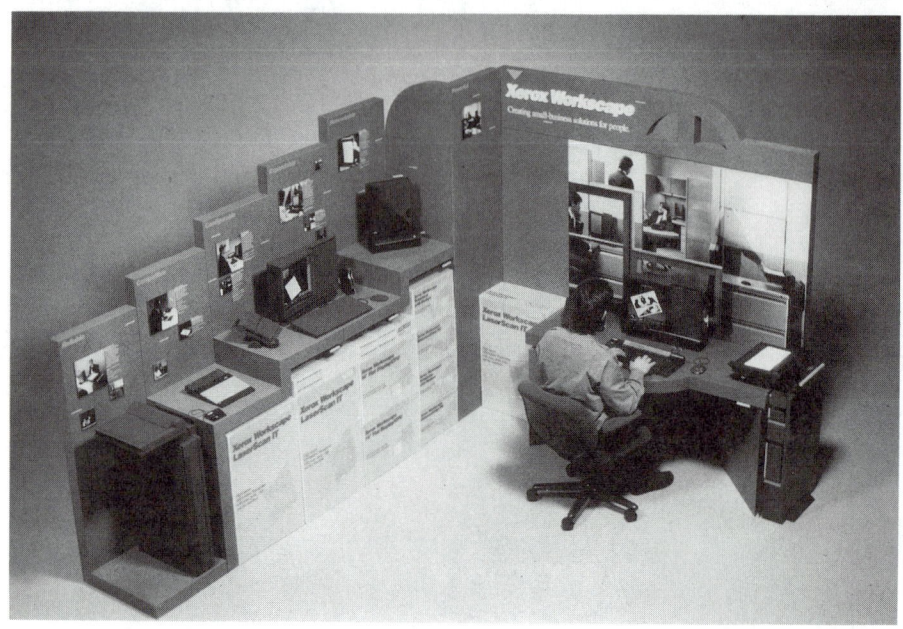

Figure 2.7.

cess, the learning-to-use process, and everyday use and maintenance. (See Figure 2.7.)

RESULTS

A Retrospective Account

Throughout the project, from 1980 to 1990, the Xerox–FRS team studied, learned, refined its understanding of usability, analyzed opportunities for applying discoveries, and took advantage of the resulting opportunities. During 1980 and 1981, the team went through several design language development iterations. From 1981 to 1982, the team stabilized almost all of the details of the design language. During this time, the team also incorporated early results into ongoing Xerox product development programs, namely, the 10-series copiers. In 1982 and 1983, the critical components of the next generation of products were tested, and piecemeal implementation took place. Draft guidelines were produced during this period. At the same time, internal Xerox validation and communication served to increase corporate understanding of the new usability initiative. In 1984 and 1985, the final guidelines were produced, constituting a comprehensive visual and verbal guide for the extensible design of families of Xerox copiers. (See Figure 2.8.)

Experiential Semantics

We demonstrated that a new conceptual framework—design semantics that includes both product and experiential semantics—could transform the design of products from machine-centered design through user-oriented design to user-orienting design. In the early days of Xerox, the key challenge was getting the machines to work. Subsequently, human factors engineering was applied to adapt the machine to people's limitations. Now we have shown that design can draw on people's capabilities by creating resources for people to orient themselves towards the use of products. The new approach allowed Xerox to move from the machine side to the user's side of the user–machine interface. Instead of design based on the engineers' knowledge of how machines worked, our approach was based on people's understandings of how they get their work done.

Marketability

We discovered that experiential semantics could add dramatically to the perceived value of products. By designing according to a meaningful set of guide-

Figure 2.8. *Design Guidelines* The approach was documented to provide the staff with a working tool for building any product that came into development. As the Xerox staff gained experience using the tool, it was modified several times to include evolving practices.

lines based on use and experiences rather than on simple functionality or appearance, we produced products that were much more useful to people at work and therefore much more marketable. The products were immediately more useful because people could understand and use them right away. They were also more useful in the long term because their increased functionality allowed them to contribute to the evolution of information-based office work in understandable ways. All of this played a role in contributing to an increase in market presence for Xerox.

Organizational Learning

The Xerox–FRS team learned how to "sell" into the larger Xerox organization. We used design teams, prototype products, and staged experiences to help others in the company buy into the product designs through participation in design activities. As Xerox and FRS worked together to put ideas into operation, FRS began to play more of a catalyzing role, while the internal Xerox team members became working champions of the ideas and builders of relationships and understandings within Xerox. This process continues today.

The design process also led Xerox to identify and overcome several internal organizational barriers. By the end of the project, design at Xerox was no longer a styling activity limited to the selection of colors and button shapes, but a central business activity that could contribute directly and substantially to market success. Traditionally, senior managers had limited time to devote to design projects, and, in the beginning, this was true in the case of the Xerox usability project. However, by the end of the project, senior management had become significantly more involved. Going into the project, Xerox had a rather rigid belief system that encouraged its designers to focus on speed, copy quality, and cost as the dominant design objectives. By the end of the project, the focus had expanded to include ideas about usable copiers and user-friendly copying. Finally, Xerox as a corporation took some important steps towards moving from a product development process based on technology to a product development process based on technology, users, and markets. This movement continues to influence the development strategy of Xerox.

Xerox team members came out of the project with feelings of increased design freedom and inventiveness. Their new skills and points of view diffused progressively throughout the company. The project led to better time commitments from developers and increased communication within and between development teams. Collaboration among the Xerox research groups and other parts of the company increased. The internal Xerox industrial design and human factors group became more visible throughout the company and began to play more of a role in linking product development with research and marketing. Finally, several members of the Xerox staff became strong champions of the expanded definition of usability. The work practices they developed helped make their groups at Xerox more effective.

Design Guidelines

The results and discoveries of the design project were communicated through two channels. One was fairly traditional: The team produced an extensive set of Xerox Design Guidelines for use by internal Xerox design staff. The second channel was less conventional: The team produced a series of staged experiences around the final models of the copiers after they had been delivered to Xerox. The product models, which were part of the experiences, helped to communicate the results in their own right.

The Xerox Design Guidelines were 300 pages long and included both visual and verbal information that clearly communicated the Xerox Design Language to designers. They documented both the design language and the design process that came out of the project. Communicating the process was crucial in helping other designers understand and implement the language.

The Guidelines themselves evolved over the course of the project. They were not simply created at the end of the project like most research reports. In their earliest form, they consisted of notes and sketches by participants in the project. These documents helped team members communicate with one another about their work. As the work progressed, the notes and sketches were developed and refined through an iterative process. The final guidelines captured much of the learning accumulated by the designers and developers while working on the project.

This accumulated learning was made more accessible to other designers through the organization of the written guidelines. Topics were presented in sections that corresponded to different categories of copiers and copying activity. There were sections such as "Access View," which provided information about how to design the parts of the machine that facilitated interior access, and there were sections such as "Control/Display Surfaces" that provided information about how to design the operating interfaces of the machines. The learning was also made accessible to other designers through a set of experiences. The use of demonstration rooms, for example, has already been described.

Ongoing Implementation

The usability guidelines produced as a result of the project are being implemented and continuously improved by Xerox internal design staff. Beginning in 1983, Xerox designers used the guidelines to help shape the total design, development, and delivery of the 10-series copiers. This continued well into the late 1980s. From 1987 through to the present, the usability guidelines were used in the design, development, and delivery of the 50s-series of copiers. They were also extended to ongoing Xerox products, systems, and human interface initiatives. Finally, in 1988 and 1989, the guidelines concept was used again by Xerox to help reorient their efforts toward 1995 markets and technologies, including integration with Fuji Xerox.

The design language itself was implemented within the Xerox community in a number of ways. Consider an analogy to written and spoken language. From a writing perspective, the Xerox Design Language is being used by the design community to produce products, systems, and services. From a reading perspective, the language is being used by the customer/user community to infer value for the products, to interpret the messages Xerox communicates about itself as a company, and to take action in specific contexts of use. From a conversational perspective, the Xerox staff is using the language collaboratively to craft a design strategy and tradition in concert with a market and technology environment. Xerox's clients are using the language collaboratively to craft a framework for incorporating Xerox products and services into ongoing work practices. Finally, from a literary perspective, the reprographic industry has perceived the Xerox Design Language as having established a benchmark for competitive excellence in the industry.

Next Steps: Computer–Human Interaction Design

The lessons of the photocopier usability project are also being applied to other aspects of Xerox's business. For example, the notion of design language that we developed and used has begun to play a role in Xerox human–computer interaction design initiatives. Just as product design languages give product designers a new way to think about designing products, human–computer interaction design languages can give software engineers a new way to think about interaction design.

One of the most exciting opportunities here is in the design of direct manipulation interfaces. Direct manipulation interfaces are essentially visual languages in their own right. They consist of elements (objects on the screen) and guidelines for combining the elements. One example is the system of files and folders on a Macintosh computer. With direct manipulation interfaces, users can create and use screen objects (or design language elements) themselves. This means that designers can use design languages when designing interfaces, and users can use variations or dialects of the same design languages when customizing the interfaces for their everyday work. In such situations, the designer would be providing the user with tools to create meaning and experience, rather than creating meaning and experience for the user.

Business Case

By designing and launching families of copiers that are unified through appearance, functionality, and usability, Xerox was able to regain and maintain a key competitive edge in the reprographics market. The success of the 10- and 50-series copiers in the market is a direct result of the shift from "designing for appearance" to "designing for usability."

CONCLUSIONS

Conceptual Shifts

The design project that caused a shift in design perspective from appearance and functionality to usability broadly construed also produced shifts in how Xerox conceived of its products. The major shifts are listed below.

1. From designing single product to designing product families. The Xerox Design Language helped Xerox unify its offerings. Instead of designing single products one at a time, the Design Language allowed Xerox designers to design entire families of products. The members of the product families shared common characteristics and interaction styles. This made the products easier for people to use and helped Xerox create a strong market statement.

2. From fool-proof products to user-orienting products. Because of its historical concentration on technology and functionality, Xerox had been trying to design technically superior products whose designs did not permit mistakes. Unfortunately, people always make mistakes. But those mistakes are also learning opportunities. When Xerox began designing successful interactions among people and copiers rather than pursuing the questionable goal of fool-proof copiers, users began to see Xerox copiers as more usable.

3. From technical reliability to perceived reliability. The traditional focus at Xerox was on product reliability and on avoiding breakdowns at all costs. The usability project helped Xerox make a shift in focus from technical reliability to perceived reliability. The goal became "to help the user operate the product efficiently" not "to protect the user from breakdowns." When users understood how to recover from paper jams effortlessly, paper jams became much less of a usability problem.

4. From design styling to design semantics. Design is often thought of as the application of styling details to functionality or technology. Xerox shifted to thinking about design as the creation of optimal experiences of use through the design of product form and interaction style. By moving from designing copiers to designing how copiers are understood and used, Xerox was able to create positive copying experiences for office workers.

5. From products narrowly construed to a total Xerox experience. The team did more than design copiers, they designed an overall Xerox "look and feel" for Xerox products, Xerox product interaction styles, and Xerox as a company. Realizing that an interaction with a copier was actually an interaction with a copier company, Xerox was able to adopt a much broader design perspective and use this perspective when communicating in the market.

6. From organizational structure to organizational learning. Traditionally, organizations change through formal restructuring. Xerox found that it was also possible to change through organizational learning, and that the changes accomplished through organizational learning were more positive and longlasting than those accomplished by juggling players in management hierarchies. One of the most positive outcomes of the Xerox usability project was the enhanced sense of discovery and increased communication within and among development and management teams.

Further Reading

The work of many people has contributed to these results. Since this chapter is a case study, we have stressed the real-world significance of the ideas. If the reader wants to go further with these concepts, we would recommend the following:

Alexander, C. (n.d.). *The Nature of Order.* Unpublished manuscript.

Barwise, J., and J. Perry (1983). *Situation and Attitudes.* Cambridge, Mass.: MIT Press.

Polanyi, M. (1967). *The Tacit Dimension.* Garden City, N.Y.: Doubleday Anchor.

Schön, D. A. (1983). *The Reflective Practitioner.* New York: Basic Books.

Wenger, E. (1990). *Toward a Theory of Cultural Transparency.* Ph.D. Dissertation, University of California, Irvine.

Acknowledgments

We would like to recognize the working contribution made by the staff at Xerox, who both inspired the work and continue to labor through implementation. We are particularly indebted to the willingness of researchers at Xerox PARC (with the leadership of John Seely Brown) and Webster Research Center (with the leadership of Mark Meyer) to help us grapple with the real-world issues discussed in this chapter.

We owe special thanks to a legion of Xerox and FRS practitioners who actually produced the results we describe in this chapter. We regret that there is insufficient space to cite their individual contributions.

CHAPTER 3

Designing Effective Systems: A Tool Approach

CHARLES D. KUKLA, ELIZABETH ANNE CLEMENS,
ROBERT S. MORSE, AND DEBRA CASH

Successfully designing large, complex systems requires including people and organization as elements in the system. Many current design approaches consider only the system's technical aspects. We need an expanded approach to system design that incorporates the insights from each of three disciplines: system engineering, human factors, and organizational design. Only in this way can we address the dynamics of technology, people, and organizations in a single, coherent approach.

The need for a new design strategy is magnified by the accelerating rate of change in the business and technology environment. System design efforts are often stymied by the fact that manufacturing businesses have constantly changing needs and requirements. Companies constantly need to shift the balance between quality, cost, and manufacturing capacity to meet evolving market goals. Moreover, these operations have to consider competitive pressures for the control of cost and schedule, rapidly changing product technology, changes in worker demographics, worker skill, and education, and regulatory pressures. The mission of a plant changes over time.

Based on the notion that truly effective systems must offer tools for skilled work, our approach to system design offers an alternative to standard automation strategies, one better able to deal with this context of change. Systems designed as tools for skilled work can help organizations take full advantage of the investment they have already made in people, preserve the tacit knowledge and judgment that cannot be automated, and enable workers to solve problems and improve operations. These tools can help to expand the way existing data are used to help identify and solve problems. They can optimize the effectiveness of existing production processes. They do not constrain the workers by demanding that they follow strictly prescribed sequences, but instead enhance the workers' ability to respond quickly and effectively to constantly changing combinations of events, to allocate and coordinate limited human resources and materials, and to work together more effectively through ongoing, company-wide collaboration.

The purpose of this chapter is to describe some key elements of an expanded approach to system design. We first discuss the foundations, perspective, and techniques of our approach to system design. We then present a case study that illustrates a successful application of this approach, and conclude by presenting a summary of the insights derived from our use of this approach for the design of tools for skilled work in operational, real-time systems.

EXPANDING THE APPROACH TO SYSTEMS DESIGN

Consider U.S. industry's experience with computer-integrated manufacturing (CIM). CIM research has resulted in the development of a number of sophisticated automatically controlled manufacturing plants, up to and including "lights out" robot-populated factories.

These systems have been a disappointment. Despite promises to the contrary, most so-called CIM facilities are characterized by "islands of automation" that focus on discrete areas of production that cannot work in concert with other plant operations. Many of the facilities are inefficient and costly to run. Others have alarming safety records that can be traced almost entirely to poor system design, although most of the accidents are attributed to "human error." These limits have been well publicized, and commercial manufacturers have been reluctant to make the multimillion dollar commitments these systems require.

More important for our discussion, the automation strategies for these plants "freeze" both the production processes and the division of labor within the organization, making it difficult if not impossible to improve the system or adapt it to changing needs and system requirements. This has not gone unnoticed: Some observers (Noble, 1987) suggest that rigid technical systems can be "balanced" by "adaptive work strategies" that try to preserve the system by asking the workers and their organizations to be as flexible as possible. There is nothing wrong with establishing flexible organizations, but a more promising solution would be to design integrated systems that do not have to be propped up and fixed constantly.

Current approaches to the design of manufacturing systems are limited in their ability to solve such problems, because:

1. They use narrow, static definitions of problems, definitions that do not realistically represent the problems workers must solve.
2. They use design approaches that focus too narrowly on the material trans-

formation process, always leading to automation whether or not it is appropriate.

3. They do not consider the importance of the workers and their specific skills in designing systems.
4. They do not consider the characteristics of the organization in which the system will be used, how the system may or may not fit in with the organization, nor how the organization might need to change in order to implement the new tools effectively.

To be effective, systems design must consider the people and the organization as well as technology. In trying to take all these factors into account, however, the system designer is faced with a very complex design problem. As J. Christopher Jones points out, there is "greater uncertainty and instability of design problems as they include more of life" (Jones, 1984). Such complex problems can become extremely difficult to describe completely and accurately, and therefore can become extremely difficult to solve. The design problems thus often fall into a class of problems that have been called "wicked problems" (Rittel and Webber, 1984). These wicked problems have the following characteristics:

1. There is no definitive formulation of the problem. Because these systems are large and constantly changing, the person solving the problem does not have all the information needed to understand the problem fully.
2. There is no stopping rule to tell when the problem is solved. The problem solver can never conclusively answer the question "Have I done enough?"
3. There is no immediate nor ultimate test of whether the system design is successful. The system design process has unbounded consequences, and there is no way to conduct comparative analysis.
4. There is no single, identifiable "cause" of a problem. The problem may be a symptom of other problems, and the solution will change depending on how the problem is formulated.

To equip us better to tackle such problems, we have expanded our approach to system design in a way that calls for intensive, ongoing interaction among system engineers, human factors engineers and organizational designers. Our approach addresses problems in their practical context; we recognize the importance of the users and organizations as well as technology in the design process.

Defining the Criteria for a Successful System

The first step in expanding the approach to system design is to redefine the criteria for the success or failure of a system. Current models of manufacturing system design have a single criterion for success: technical efficiency. In business terms, a successful system must reduce costs, increase the ease of operation, or increase the productivity of a process. But when technical efficiency is the only criterion for systems success, the needs of the users of the system are neglected, and the broader set of needs of the organization in which the system will operate are ignored. Although the system may solve the specific operational problems for which it was designed, by ignoring these other considerations, the conventionally designed is likely to create problems of its own.

In order to ensure a better outcome in the design of a new system, we must expand our criteria for success. A successful system must be:

1. Technically efficient—it must reduce costs, increase ease of operation, or increase the productivity of a process.
2. Easy to use—the people who will be using or operating the system must be able to focus on their work, not on the technology.
3. Useful to its operators—it must provide its operators with a new or better way to do their job, or one at least as good as the existing method.
4. Adaptable to the changing organization and business conditions—it must be able to adapt to the evolving priorities and constraints of the business and organization structure in which it is placed.

Using all four of these criteria to define the success of a manufacturing system rather than technical efficiency alone makes individual and organizational issues visible for the system designer. System engineering requirements ensure that the system will be technically efficient; human factors requirements ensure that the system will be easy to use and useful to its operators; and organizational requirements ensure that the system can deal with changing conditions.

Understanding Users

To ensure that a system will be easy to use and useful to its users, it is necessary to understand the needs of those users, and to this end it is necessary to involve them in the design of the system. No one understands human behavior well enough to be able to predict how a new computer system will be used. General guidelines may provide a basis for design, but the usability of the system must be verified in a practical context.

To gain an understanding of users, our approach to design relies on human factors analysis. Human factors engineering has developed as a key discipline in the development of computer systems. In the early days of computers, computer systems were designed by engineers for engineers. Engineers understood many of the needs of the users because the designers were themselves the users of these systems. As the use of computer systems began to expand into areas where users no longer had a working knowledge of computer systems, human factors engineers were brought in to help identify and answer questions about who would be using the computer, what the computer would be used to do, and how it would be used.

While the existing body of human factors knowledge provided a starting point for system design, it was not enough to ensure that a finished system would be easy to use. Human factors engineers have therefore recognized the importance of conducting usability tests of systems as they are being developed. In a usability test, users of a system are asked to use a prototype of that system to perform a number of tasks. The users may be observed, videotaped, and interviewed while using the system, and their performance may be measured. By conducting such usability tests, problems in the usability of the system can be identified and eliminated. Ideally, usability testing should begin early in the system design process and continue iteratively as the system is being developed.

In addition to conducting usability testing, an essential element of human factors engineering is studying users in the context of their work environment. While usability testing provides valuable input into the design process, it is often conducted in a laboratory setting, and may not accurately represent how a system is used in the work environment. To understand users fully, human factors engineers conduct observational studies, observing and interviewing users on the job. Such contextual research offers a much more complete understanding of how users do their work. During an interview it is often difficult for users to articulate the details of how they do their jobs, the problems they encounter, and how their work could be made easier. However, in the context of their work, it is easier for users to show how their jobs are actually done, and for an observer to see the problems they encounter and suggest solutions to these problems. As John Whiteside put it, "The purpose of contextual research is to reveal the product from the user's point of view. Users will view the product through the needs of their work" (Whiteside et al., 1989).

Along with studying users in a work context to identify their needs, it is also important to test mockups and prototypes of the system on the job. Placing an early version of the system, which can be anything from a paper mockup to a working prototype, in the workplace allows users to comment on and improve the system, as well as to become gradually acclimated to the changes that will occur when the new system is implemented. The user input throughout the development period encourages the system's later acceptance (Ehn, 1989).

Understanding the Organization

For a system to be successful, it has to be useful not only to those who are going to operate it but to the organization as a whole. Operational systems and organizations are interdependent. Any change in one part of the system will have ramifications throughout the enterprise.

The system designer must understand the formal organizational structures of the business. These formal structures are chartered with coordinating the key functions of a business. This formal organization does not, however, fully represent how people in that organization work. People also interact with one another in informal ways. Many times these patterns of interaction are invisible or "second nature" to the workers themselves, but they should be captured and analyzed through careful study and modeling techniques. We have found that neglecting to identify these informal patterns of interaction in the design of operational systems results in incomplete or even useless technological solutions.

PERSPECTIVE AND LANGUAGE IN DESIGN

Because of the limited effectiveness of traditional approaches to system design in dealing with complex, dynamic environments, it is necessary to expand the criteria for a successful system and include human factors and organizational design in the system design process along with systems engineering. However, to work together effectively, these three disciplines need some common ground from which to view the design problem. An explicit design "perspective" can provide this common ground.

Each actor in the design process approaches it from some perspective, and different actors often approach from different perspectives. Usually, these perspectives are not clearly defined nor consciously chosen, but arise from the background and experience of those formulating the problem. As Winograd and Flores argue in a discussion of the importance of perspective in design, "A perspective does not determine answers to design questions but guides design by generating the questions to be considered" (Winograd and Flores, 1986). A carefully chosen, commonly agreed upon design perspective is needed to tie together the disparate approaches of human factors, organizational design, and systems engineering to a design problem.

We have found that language provides the key to creating this common perspective across the three design disciplines. As Winograd and Flores point out, people act through language: "The lifeblood of an organization is not data or computation, but interaction. People working with computers get things done by placing orders, requesting and producing reports, and releasing products, not by processing information. Work is organized as a network of interlinked actions that are embedded in language. The ability to affect and anticipate the behavior of others through language is an important condition of human action" (Winograd and Flores, 1986). By focusing on language, it is possible to create a common representation of the work environment and reveal often invisible patterns of communication and decision making.

Combining these two ideas—the importance of perspectives and the role of language—we describe our approach as a "language perspective." Such an approach to system design offers two key benefits. First, it focuses our attention on how people from various disciplines and organizations establish a shared description and understanding of the environment under analysis. It highlights the importance of, and clarifies the process whereby, words with vague meanings are clarified; terms that are used in different ways are harmonized; specialized terms and technical jargon from one context are explained and either adopted by the broader design team or replaced with a more global term.

Second, analyzing the language that people use can illuminate the relationships between people and between people and the technical processes. This is crucial because many of these relationships are often tacit, and it is difficult for the people involved in these relationships to describe them.

To understand the language that is being used in the work environment fully, one must understand both the interactions and the context in which those interactions take place. Winograd and Flores identify "conversations for action" as the most important in accomplishing cooperative work, and therefore the most important in designing computer systems to support collaboration: "Conversations for action are the central coordinating structure for human organizations. We work together by making commitments so that we can successfully anticipate the actions of others and coordinate them with our own. The emphasis here is on language as an activity, not as the transmission of information or as the expression of thought" (Winograd and Flores, 1986).

Model Building

The language perspective provides a useful foundation on which human factors, organizational design, and systems engineering can effectively cooperate in the design of a manufacturing system. To support this approach, it is necessary to represent the plant and its operations in a manner that can be interpreted consistently by all parties involved and that provides a shared understanding of the domain. The representation itself must be concise and explicit. It must identify interdependent aspects of the plant and establish the project's boundaries. Model building provides a basis for this shared understanding.

Some engineers use the word *modeling* to mean the creation of some abstract description of the system. Because traditional engineering approaches usually start with functional specifications, they never fully articulate their implicit model of the real world. In our work, we have followed the lead of Sally Shlaer and Stephen Mellor of Project Technologies, Inc., who define a model as an abstract description of some aspect of the real world—such as a manufacturing plant and its operations—in words and images (Shlaer and Mellor, 1988). The object-oriented analysis that Shlaer and Mellor have pioneered isolates the elements of the manufacturing process. It differentiates what the process is from what the process does. The object model—the model of what a certain manufacturing plant is, for instance—defines the data and those data's essential relationships. It identifies dependencies within the system and establishes system boundaries. This model provides an abstract description of the real world that provides the context for functional specifications. In addition, it provides a strategy for partitioning system problems into discrete, workable pieces.

Scenarios

To help capture and explore aspects of interactions among people in different settings and situations, our design approach relies on scenarios generated in collaboration with the users. Initially, descriptive scenarios are generated to help us explore specific aspects of the environment. More extensive scenarios are then generated as important and recurring aspects of the domain are revealed. Finally, scenarios are useful for exploring how work would be changed if new technology were introduced.

The scenarios can be represented in different ways, but all have these common characteristics:

1. A description of the surroundings and the setting: the physical location, function and purpose of the building, the technology in place and how it is used, communication technology such as phones and radios, time of day, current state of the manufacturing process, history of the process, projected plans, etc.
2. A description of the situation: a description of the initiating event and the pattern of events that follows in the form of a narrative and an explanation of why this situation was important.
3. A description of the participants.
4. A description of the activities and interaction of the participants.

Using Mockups and Exploratory Simulations

Testing the accuracy of models and the usefulness of a proposed system calls for capturing the actual dynamics of work. Developing a mockup of a proposed system and a simulation strategy to allow users to interact with it allows systems engineers, human factors engineers, organizational designers, technologists, and users to work together to design useful systems. This strategy significantly reduces the risk associated with blind technical development. Developers' expectations about how users will use a system are often incomplete. Users often use various tools and interfaces in completely unforeseen ways—and in many cases better ways—than those intended by the designers.

Mockups must be flexible, inexpensive, easy for users to interact with, and designed to enhance their imagination. Like the proposed solution itself, the mockup must be relevant to the users' work. Mockups can be made from a number of materials: paper "post-its," projected slides, boards, and magnets. Mockups for computerized systems are not an early version of the proposed software—mockups and prototypes serve different purposes (see the following). It is important that users perceive the mockup not as a final solution, but as a proposal of what the finished solution could be.

Once a mockup has been designed, a group of users can be gathered for an exploratory trial. Although its ultimate purpose is serious and may have important implications for a business, this "design game" must be fun and engaging. Pelle Ehn, whose research has involved the most thorough application of a game-playing strategy for design, points out that such simulations allow the users to describe their needs in terms of a real problem instead of through the review of often intimidating and arcane engineering documents (Ehn et al., 1989). Exploratory trials also illuminate the ways any proposed solution will affect the relationships between various jobs, and make visible the impact the solution will have on existing organizational structures.

Prototyping

Obviously, it is possible to contemplate some system solutions that cannot actually be developed due to the limitations of technology or the costs of implementation. Prototyping the design scheme suggested by the user exploratory trials helps a developer test and evaluate any high-risk portion of the technology's implementation. Also, it provides immediate feedback from the users as they see how to use the technology to complete their work. At the same time, the prototype ensures that limitations imposed by the technology will not affect the solution's ultimate usefulness. The prototype must be complete enough to be applied in a realistic setting. The mockup used during the trials is a good starting point to define the prototype's minimum functionality.

Yet prototyping holds significant risks that are not well understood. Many developers view the prototype as an early version of the final system and look at evaluation as a proving trial. Prototypes are often rushed into operational use before their usefulness is really defined and established. Moreover, personnel are often not properly trained to use the technology, which affects their ability to complete their work. Managers become disappointed with both the technology and the user participation process, and may feel that creative solutions do not "pan out."

Prototypes of a proposed system are also useful in addressing organizational issues. A prototype can be helpful in the following ways:

1. It can demonstrate the usefulness of the system to an organization.
2. It can provide insight into the changes the new system will cause and how they will propagate throughout the organization.

3. It can provide an understanding of the effect the technology will have on the workforce, including the direct effect it will have on specific work roles, and the need for new work roles it may create.
4. It will demonstrate the ability of people to use the new system, and help in understanding employee selection and training requirements. In addition, the prototype itself may be used as a training tool.

CASE STUDY

This case study presents work done at a Monsanto Chemical Corporation plant. We will describe our analysis of the plant and how we derived a set of design requirements for software tools that would enhance plant performance. The study illustrates how human factors and organizational design can contribute to the system design process, and provides examples of model building and the use of a language perspective.

In 1987, Digital Equipment Corporation participated in a joint project with Monsanto Chemical Corporation and Fisher Controls, Inc., to investigate and apply modern information technology to Monsanto's integrated nylon facility in Pensacola, Florida. The goal was to optimize the use of raw materials and energy throughout the facility.

The initial design strategies were conventional ones. A vision was articulated, along with a mission statement, charter, and formal objectives for the engineering team. We described the plant in terms of functional models, incorporated newer object-oriented analysis techniques, and justified the various solutions in terms of cost–benefit ratios.

Despite these diligent efforts, these techniques failed to offer real insight into the plant's needs. Over time we came to recognize that these techniques alone could not capture the information needed to develop an effective system solution for this complex, real-time operational environment. The traditional methods of designing systems focused on how systems were supposed to work and how the different pieces of the system were connected, but they could not characterize the work in which the people at the plant were engaged each day. They could not help us assess if the proposed technology would be appropriate in that environment.

We found that to design a useful system at Monsanto, we would have to understand both the production process and the ways people worked. Keeping a complex manufacturing operation running smoothly and safely calls for a great deal of skill and judgment on the part of the people working there. Every day offers different challenges, and calls for different solutions.

We determined that instead of trying to automate any given process or subsystem within the facility to optimize the use of energy or other resources, we would develop tools that would take advantage of the skill of the workforce. This goal did not contradict Monsanto's original management objective. We were convinced that improving communication, coordination, and collaboration among workers would improve overall organizational effectiveness, lead to better utilization of limited resources (including skills), and help to empower the people to identify new opportunities for improvement.

To accomplish this goal, we undertook an analysis of the existing manufacturing system at the plant, with the intent of using this research as a basis for developing software tools designed to coordinate activities within the plant's real-time manufacturing environment. We analyzed the existing manufacturing system, including people, organization, and technology. Our focus in the study was not on the specific details of designing a particular control room, but on the best way to integrate the people and the process, and to enhance communication and collaboration throughout the plant. An additional goal of this study was to use this plant as a test case to develop a more effective strategy for designing systems for manufacturing environments.

The study was conducted in two phases. In phase one we conducted interviews and observations within the plant in order to characterize the users in the plant and the work they do, understand the plant organization and the manufacturing process, and identify human factors issues and problems in the current system. In phase two, we gathered detailed information on the people, process, and communication within one area of the plant. We used this information to construct models of events, conversations, and processes within that area of the plant. These models were to be used as a basis for developing software tools for use within the plant.

In order to focus our resources, this study targeted operations in one of the five areas of the plant. We chose an area in which the operators were using computers to help them control their part of the chemical process. By working with operators who were familiar with computer systems, we were able to talk with them about how their job roles had changed when computer systems became available. We were also able to discuss with them their likes and dislikes in using the computer systems as they worked.

The operators in the target area were very experienced, each averaging 20 years at the plant. As control room equipment had become more sophisticated over the years, the number of operators had decreased. However, the complexity of the process had not been reduced. These operators were responsible for monitoring and controlling an overwhelming amount of information in order to keep the plant operating optimally. Their ability to do this effectively was based on their extensive practical experience, which gave them the skill to make quick judgments regarding complex situations.

PHASE ONE—INTERVIEWS AND OBSERVATIONS

In the first phase of the study, our goal was to develop a detailed description of the environment and the structure of work within the plant. We needed to characterize both the users of the system that we were designing and the organization in which it would be placed. We did this by collecting information on the following five areas:

1. Employee profiles: this included user experience (in terms of number of years on the job and skills), job responsibilities, job design, employee interaction, and training.
2. Employee organization: this included organization reporting structure, job titles, styles and methods of employee interaction, and job responsibilities and communication within shifts, between shifts, and between different areas.
3. Production process: this included the operation of each part of the material transformation process and the interaction between the different parts of the process.
4. Operator control of the process: we studied the tasks involved for operators in the control of the process, how users think and talk about their work environment, and how the control rooms interact with one another.
5. Problems in the existing system: we studied problems with the current user interface and provided recommendations in order to make the user interface more useful and to avoid similar errors in subsequent designs.

To collect this information we conducted interviews and observed people as they worked. One-on-one interviews were conducted with supervisors, engineers, and trainers, and group interviews were conducted with control room operators. In the interviews, people were asked to describe their jobs, work experience, the routine and unexpected tasks they performed on the job, their understanding of how the control room equipment worked, the ways in which they communicated with their colleagues, and how they were trained. In addition, supervisors were asked to describe the work flow in the control room, engineers were asked about their involvement in designing the display consoles, and trainers were asked about educational activities in various areas of the plant.

We then conducted detailed observations of activities in the target area control room over a 3-day period. Our goal was to characterize the control room environment by collecting quantitative data on the tasks performed there. To collect these data we categorized each task conducted in the control room—monitoring, controlling, communicating, logging data, inputting information, and receiving information—and tracked the frequency of each task. We also took an inventory of the current user interfaces in the control room, identifying the type of user interface, where necessary information was located (manuals, logs, etc.), and the physical location of people and equipment.

During the observations, one observer recorded the general flow of events and conducted informal, on-the-spot interviews with control room operators to clarify what they were doing and what was happening. At two-minute intervals, the other observer recorded what was displayed on each console screen, where each operator was positioned, and what each was doing. The observations took place at various times during a 64-hour period so that they included different shifts, shift-to-shift changes, and activity levels during the day, afternoon, and graveyard shifts.

Results

Through the interviews and observations, we found that at any given time an operator's attention is divided between a number of tasks. It was common for an operator to be controlling information from the console as he or she was answering alarms, monitoring levels in plant-floor equipment, talking to field operators, and talking to another person in the room. In general, we found that the control room environment was very dynamic. It required a great deal of coordination of resources and activities within and between control rooms to keep the plant running optimally.

We characterized the environment thus:

1. While the majority of the operators' time (51%) was spent monitoring the system (watching the displays to ensure that things were running smoothly without taking any action), communications (accounting for only 10% of their time) were very frequent. Although these interactions were brief, they often required direct action (such as coordinating the shut-down and start-up of equipment between areas or scheduling maintenance to repair broken equipment).
2. Understanding the overall process is important in operating the process. Due to the interactive nature of the nylon process, it is not enough for operators to focus on only the part of the process for which they are responsible. Often, troubleshooting requires two or more operators as well as other non-control-room personnel.
3. Operators often are not able to identify the cause of an upset in the process immediately, nor to distinguish between the breakdown of equipment and an interruption in the flow of a utility. They rely on each other's experience and the process of elimination to get to the root of any given problem.
4. It takes years of experience to be able to deal with the frequent, unexpected events that occur during the day. Operators are not able to perform their jobs by following a routine set of procedures.
5. There is a need for a consistent user interface in the control room. At the time of this study, operators were required to know how to use three or four different user interfaces to complete their tasks. Operators noted that they would rather focus on controlling the process than on using the system.

6. Since operators do not have experience with systems other than the ones that they are currently using, it is hard for them to articulate ways in which to improve the displays and the system.

In addition to these general results, we were able to provide specific human factors recommendations for improving the ease of operations. These covered topics such as the design of console displays, methods of troubleshooting, and alarm management.

More important, we noted discrepancies between, on the one hand, what was told us in the interviews and the models of how the process worked, and, on the other hand, what we actually observed. The manufacturing of nylon is based on process technology over 30 years old, implemented in a highly mechanized continuous process. While at first sight the operation appears to be routine and repetitious, the results of our observations proved it to be otherwise. Even though a conventional model of the production process would present the process as routine, the control room environment itself was dynamic and highly interactive. There were simultaneous phone and radio communications between operators, field personnel, engineers, and other control rooms, numerous conversations occurring in the control room, people moving about to look at displays on other terminals, and many people entering and leaving the control room.

Based on these observations we decided to examine the data in the study in light of this situation. Four themes emerged from our examination:

1. Work is collaborative. To achieve any particular objective required coordinated interactions among many different people. Troubleshooting a process problem always involves the control room operator working in conjunction with the field operator and other control room operators. It may also include interactions with engineering, maintenance personnel, and people in other control rooms, depending on the extent of the problem.
2. Operators use many types and levels of data:
   a. Operators in the control room deal with data from a variety of sources: field operators, control system displays, and their own skill, knowledge, and experience.
   b. Operators deal with various displays showing different levels of detail about that portion of the process.
   c. Data about interdependent areas of the process are obtained from other operators, and the operator has to get up and physically go to see the other displays.
   d. Other information is obtained over the phone, radio, or delivered on paper.
3. The operator's knowledge and understanding of issues of safety and reliability, quality and yield, what happened on the previous shift, and today's plans all influence his eventual course of action.

4. This information is not all available simultaneously. It may be known somewhere, by someone in the operation, but be beyond reach. In one case, the knowledge and skill of one expert was on site, but unavailable to the operators who had to make a critical operation decision. The result was a costly shutdown.
5. Orientation is critical. Since work involves interactions among people, any time a new person joins that team, that person must become oriented to the situation quickly. The orientation problem is most critical at the change of shift, where the new shift has to gain not only an understanding of overall operations and the plans for that shift, but exchange places in these ongoing, interactive problem-solving teams. Often a new shift begins by making a paper copy of every display.
6. The control room is a clearinghouse. The control room seems to act as a clearinghouse where information is collected and disseminated, plans formulated, and actions coordinated.

PHASE TWO—CONVERSATION MODELING

As a result of the first phase of the study, we identified three questions that needed to be addressed to help define the software tools for this environment. These questions were:

1. How can we add data and applications to an already busy control room in a manner that control room operators will find useful?
2. How can we help resolve conflicting goals and competition for limited resources among control rooms throughout the plant?
3. How can we coordinate activities between control rooms throughout the plant in a dynamic environment?

To answer these questions, we analyzed and modeled how people interacted and how they communicated within this environment. Specifically, we focused on modeling the structure of conversations within the plant. We defined a "conversation" to be any oral, written, or electronic exchange that requests information, confirms a commitment, or requests or fulfills requests for information. Our goal in this phase of the study was to model the organizational structure of the plant, the links of conversation between personnel in the plant, and the method (i.e., phone, radio) and the topics of conversations, and to collect qualitative information on these conversations.

We viewed the manufacturing operation from both the perspective of the material transformation process and how people worked. The formulation of each perspective was broken down (partitioned) into well-defined parts. It was essential to ensure that the representations could be interpreted consistently by developers and users alike. The models would serve not only as necessary design elements but as a critical communication vehicle: They represented the common ground on which all the disciplines could be engaged in a discussion about potential solutions.

It is important to appreciate that formulating a problem from many different perspectives and getting different disciplines to agree on a model is a difficult, time-consuming task. Constructing models is not a straightforward, deductive activity. We understand the world through language, and each person uses language differently. For example, a term like *error recovery* is used differently by software engineers and production supervisors, and many of the problems we faced in building our models could be traced to the confusion between these conflicting definitions.

We found it helpful to use scenarios as way of describing activity in the plant and to create a context for our model building. To develop scenarios we interviewed operators and asked them to "tell a story" about their work so that we could partition the system in terms of how it would be used in any given circumstance. This method had powerful results, because it ensured that the technical system was never artificially detached from its use. The models we created ultimately distinguished the plant's control and communication technology, the existing organizational structure, the underlying process technology, features of the physical plant, and the pattern of interactions and conversations taking place during the work day. We also distinguished data and data flows.

As an initial step in building the conversation models, we conducted interviews with personnel from all areas of the plant. The purpose of each interview was to determine with which areas of the plant the interviewee had conversations, what those conversations were about, and how often they occurred. Participants were asked to provide us first with some background information (job title, etc.) and then they were asked to go through the list of areas of the plant and identify each area with which they conversed. For each area they identified, they were asked to specify the topics, method, and frequency of conversation with that area. After the list had been completed, each participant was asked to identify any written reports that they wrote or read on a regular basis, and any computer conversations they had on a regular basis. At the end of the interview, participants were asked about problems they had in pursuing conversations with other areas of the plant, and about topic areas in which they felt that there was a need for additional conversation or for fewer conversations. As a result of these interviews, we identified the areas of conversation most appropriate for modeling and provided a list of recommendations on conversation within the plant.

Based on the first set of interviews, we chose three areas of operation in the plant among which there was a need for frequent coordination and communication. We then constructed three models of interaction between the selected areas: a process model, an event model and a conversation model. We defined the models in the following way:

1. The process model identified the process connections between the areas.
2. The event model identified events that initiate conversations between the areas. Events included equipment failures, computer failures, material shortages, etc.
3. The conversation model identified conversations that occur as a result of initiating events, including initiation, content, and means of conversation.

To develop these models, we first had to identify the events that initiated interaction between the three selected areas of the plant. To do this, we conducted a joint meeting with engineers from each of the areas. In this meeting, we asked the engineers to identify all of the utilities and materials produced within their area and to identify where the utilities and materials were sent from their area. Each of the engineers was then asked to discuss management of these utilities and materials in more detail. Specifically, we asked them to talk about how a change in the supply or demand of utilities and raw materials would affect their area. We then compiled a list of utilities and raw materials for each area, and identified what materials they produced. This list was essentially a list of topics of conversation between areas, since most conversations between areas involved management of utilities, raw materials, or products.

These lists were the basis of detailed interviews with operators in each of the three areas. The purpose of these interviews was to understand the initiation and content of conversations between areas. Each interview began by asking the participants background questions about their job title, work area, and job description. Participants were then asked to describe what happens in the process when there is a change in the supply of a given utility or material. They were asked to explain both the short-term and long-term effects of a change. They were also asked to explain the actions that take place when a change occurs, focusing on what people do, to whom they talk, and what they discuss. In the last part of the interview they were asked to explain what might cause a change in supply of a given utility or material produced in their area. From these data, we were able to construct process, event, and conversation models for each area.

Results

Through our interviews and observations, we identified seven types of conversations that were used in controlling operations in the plant. These types of conversations were defined by their content focus:

1. Process operation conversations occur in the course of normal operation of a process.
2. Event coordination conversations coordinate events between two areas of the plant.

3. Problem reporting conversations report process problems within an area or throughout the plant.
4. Resource coordination conversations seek to coordinate the allocation of resources within an area or throughout the plant.
5. Internal troubleshooting conversations seek to identify a problem within an area.
6. External troubleshooting conversations seek to identify a problem between two areas.
7. Social conversations do not relate to conducting work.

These conversation types provided a structure that allowed us to define and categorize the conversations that we studied. From the data collected in the detailed interviews with control room operators, we constructed process, event, and conversation models for raw material, utility, and product links between areas of the plant. To represent interactions among areas better, the event and conversation models were consolidated into a single diagram showing the initiating events and resulting conversations for each topic of conversation. Figure 3.1 shows a part of such a diagram.

DESIGN OF SOFTWARE TOOLS

The models we constructed provided valuable insight into the needs of the users of the organization. The models reflected and illustrated our understanding of the dynamics of work in the plant and allowed us to identify opportunities for new tools to support that work. By studying the models, we were able to see where conversations in the plant were most important and identify areas where additional support for conversations was needed. This led us to ideas for software tools that could facilitate key conversations.

At the simplest level, the models showed where communication links were missing or were not very robust. For example, conversations between control rooms and the central laboratory often involved a combination of phone calls, computer reports, and handwritten data. Often, laboratory results would be received on one computer system, written by hand into a log book, and then typed into a second computer system. One of the tools we suggested was a Shared Data Window, which would let users easily send each other data and transfer data from one application to another.

The area in which the majority of conversations took place throughout the plant was between control rooms. Operators in different control rooms frequently communicated with each other concerning supplies of raw materials and utilities, to find out about problems in other areas of the plant, and to collaborate on tasks that required cooperation between areas of the plant (such as the transfer of chemicals from one area to another). The frequency of conversations between control room operators led us to design two tools to

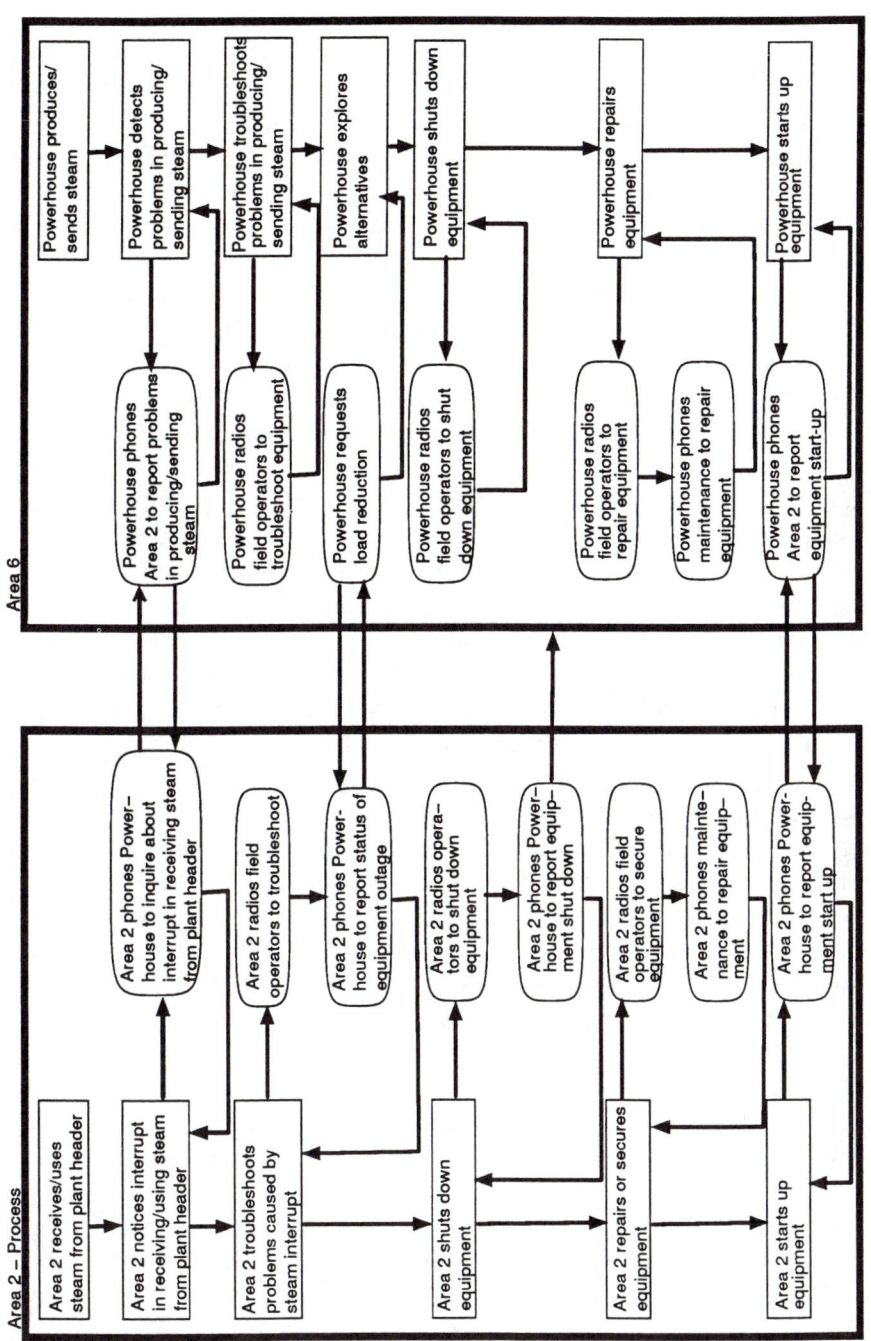

Figure 3.1. Simplified steam event/conversion diagram for Process Area 2 — and Area 6 — Powerhouse.

support these conversations. The first tool we designed was a Conversation Management tool to facilitate these conversations. This tool stepped people through repetitive conversations and transferred data automatically; it thus allowed them to focus on their work instead of concentrating on the process of the conversation. To help control room operators understand and troubleshoot problems in different areas of the plant, we created a Remote Window Viewing tool, which allowed a control room operator in one area to send a picture of a display to a window on an operating console in another area.

Another area in which the models showed an opportunity to enhance conversations was between the control room and the field. The control room operators needed to know what was happening in the field, but their only means of doing so was by radio communication with field operators. To assist in this area, we designed a Video Observation tool, which would use a camera in the field to display a live video image in a window on the control room operator's workstation, increasing the fidelity of information received from the field.

The models also illustrated the need for improving conversations between the control rooms and the centralized areas of the plant such as safety, central engineering, and plant management. Conversations between these groups needed to be improved in both directions. The central areas of the plant needed a way to get plantwide information—such as changes in safety procedures or process operations—to all of the control rooms quickly and easily. The control rooms needed more immediate feedback from central engineering and management on production goals and operating efficiency. To make it easier for the central areas of the plant to distribute information to the control rooms, we designed a Plant Information tool. This tool provided a centralized bulletin board and videotext service to which all areas of the plant would have access, allowing the central areas of the plant to distribute information to all of the control rooms quickly. To give the control room operators better feedback on the efficiency of their processes, we designed a System Performance Monitor tool. This tool gave the control room operators continuous, clearly displayed information in about the overall operating efficiency of their process, helping them to adjust the process to run at peak performance.

The last area in which the models showed a need for expanded conversations was between the control rooms and staff such as the process engineers and the plant shift supervisor. The supervisory and engineering staff needed information about operations in the control room in order to coordinate activities throughout the plant and help the control room operators troubleshoot problems. The only way they could get this information was by calling or visiting the control rooms, which was time consuming and at times interrupted the control room operators. We designed two tools to help eliminate this problem. The first was a Plant Overview tool, which provided a number of overviews of particular aspects of plant operations, such as maintenance activities, utilities management, and raw materials supplies. By using these overviews, process engineers and the plant shift supervisor could get a picture of activities throughout the plant without having to contact each of the control rooms. The second tool was a Monitor Display, which made it possible to view (but not modify) a control room display from a remote location. This would allow process engineers to see what was happening in a control room and to help troubleshoot a problem without having to be in the control room.

We have found our process of modeling and analysis to be extremely valuable in our work at Monsanto. It allowed us to envision how workstation video and windowing technology would enhance communication and the sharing of information at all levels of the plant, and would allow the plant organization the flexibility to grow and change. The envisioned software tools would make information more widely available, allowing workers in the plant to collaborate effectively, and extending the use of existing technology.

After designing these new tools, it was necessary to demonstrate how they would work and how they would be used, in order to allow users in the plant to understand, modify, and improve them. To do so, we constructed a mockup of the tools. This mockup consisted of full-size drawings of each of the tools as a series of workstation windows. These drawings were mounted on magnetized boards so that the use of the tools on the workstation could be illustrated, and user trials with the mockup could be conducted.

To support the idea that users need to discuss solutions and alternatives to existing problems in the context of their work, the software tools mockup will be used for a user exploratory trial with the operators and developers of these tools. The trial will provide user interface requirements, and, along with the definition of applications and the system architecture, will provide a basis for developing prototype software tools. These prototypes will then be evaluated in the working environment.

To develop an innovative user interface to enhance coordination and collaboration throughout the plant, information must be standardized throughout the plant, but tailored to the needs of the different users (operators, engineers, etc.) in response to the suggestions of the users themselves. The information should be designed with multiple users and multiple applications in mind. Such an interface will enable users to take advantage of available knowledge to assist them in running operations smoothly and effectively.

ASSESSMENT OF OUR EXPERIENCE

When we originally began our work at Monsanto, we believed that a conventional approach to system design would adequately address the plant's needs for new systems to meet the company's business goals. When we found this not to be the case, we had to re-examine our premises. Monsanto's managerial commitment was not the problem—the company was committed to improvement and had authorized the appropriate funds. Nor was technology the problem—and the market was full of technology that promised to solve the kinds of problems Monsanto faced.

When confronted with the challenge of defining a design strategy to address the dynamic problems of real-time operational environments, we recognized that the control room work environment is not static and repetitive, and therefore its operations could not be modeled as a fixed set of procedures. Our designs needed to support workers' activities by allowing them to coordinate their activities and collaborate in solving operational problems.

Our work leads us to a number of tentative generalizations about the characteristics of the manufacturing environment and issues in the design of systems for such organizations.

Characteristics of the manufacturing environments we studied:

1. There are unanticipated combinations of events occurring at any point in time.
2. Resources (people, equipment, and materials) are limited and committed.
3. There is severe time pressure on many tasks.
4. Workers' reactions are based on intuition and experience, not rote actions.
5. The need to attain maximum operation efficiency must be balanced within fixed boundaries of safety and reliability. This safety and reliability envelope creates constraints on the system design.
6. There are high risks associated with catastrophic failure. This means that the key functions of the system need to be overlapping and redundant.
7. There are health and environmental laws and regulations that must be considered in the system design.

Software tools for such manufacturing environments must be able to:

1. Support and enhance all seven categories of conversation;
2. Aid users in collaborating and in coordinating work;
3. Coordinate and commit resources in a dynamic environment;
4. Respond effectively to unanticipated events;
5. Share and exchange information in order to generate options for further action.

Collecting data from users:

1. Traditional human factors evaluations need to be supplemented by first-hand interviews within the manufacturing environment to analyze how users work and interact on the job.
2. Users cannot easily articulate the details involved in performing their jobs, but they are good at answering specific questions and demonstrating what they do.

3. Users have difficulty proposing solutions to problems they encounter in their jobs without understanding the technology available to solve these problems. Mockups and simulation strategies can help them to understand and choose from available technological solutions.

A STRATEGY FOR DESIGNING EFFECTIVE TOOLS

Traditional automation strategies cannot address the problems associated with unanticipated combinations of problems and unforeseen circumstances—the essence of work in a modern manufacturing environment where, "learning is never complete, as new data, new events, or new contexts create opportunities for additional insight, improvement, and innovation" (Zuboff, 1988).

The key elements of our expanded approach to design for manufacturing environments are:

1. A perspective that links human factors and organizational design with system engineering;
2. Use of modeling to analyze the environment in which the system is going to operate;
3. Modeling of the manufacturing process by focusing on conversations;
4. Engagement of a multidisciplinary team that includes users throughout the analysis, modeling, user exploratory trials, and prototyping phases of design.

Design approaches that focus only on the underlying material transformation process result in a solution that is blind to the role of people, skill, intuition, and experience. We create tools for skilled work by providing:

1. Tools to facilitate coordination so that decisions can be acted on appropriately;
2. Tools that facilitate collaboration—developing new possibilities and hence improvements in system performance;
3. Tools that allow people to work together over a wide area, putting people where the work is rather than continuing to centralize operations;
4. Tools that can characterize with sufficient fidelity a hazardous operation from a safe distance (through audio and video technology);
5. Tools to share knowledge and skill to train new workers.

Developing tools for skilled work fills a significant gap left by most automation projects. Because such a design strategy does not seek to mechanize the skill and knowledge of the operators, and because it does not assume that the designer has uncovered all possible combinations of events, the systems that result from such a strategy can support workers as they adapt to unforeseen circumstances and an ever-changing business environment. The flexibility of such tools makes them very appropriate as training vehicles. Workers can enhance and improve the system themselves, in ways that will help them do their jobs more effectively.

Tools designed in cooperative sessions with users and technologists also offer the promise of true "transparency." These systems are designed to fit into the real work environment, rather than in the imagination of the isolated system developer. This helps ensure that workers can concentrate on their jobs, rather than wrestling with the constraints of the technology itself. At Monsanto, the ability to coordinate activities electronically allows process engineers to respond in real time to a problem in another part of the plant without leaving the control room.

A tool perspective is the logical result of a concerted effort to take technology, human factors, and organizational design into account when a system is designed and implemented—in a manner that does justice to the concerns raised by each discipline. Our commitment to designing systems that support skill, encourage cooperation, and enhance collaboration, offers a path towards a more humane and productive future for workers and the societies in which they live.

Acknowledgments

We would like to thank Gil Steil for his contributions on organizational design issues. We also appreciate the comments from our reviewers. We thank Charles Abernethy, Michael Good, and George Casaday.

REFERENCES

Ehn, Pelle (1989). The art and science of designing computer artifacts. *Scand. J. Inform. Sys.* **1,** 21–42.

Ehn, Pelle, Bengt Molleryd, and Dan Sjogren (1989). Playing in reality.

Jones, J. Christopher (1984). How my thoughts about design methods have changed during the years, in Nigel Cross (ed.). *Developments in Design Methodology.* New York: John Wiley and Sons, pp. 329–36.

Noble, David (1987). Command performance: A perspective on military enterprise and technological change, in Merritt Roe Smith (ed.), *Military Enterprise and Technological Change—Perspectives on the American Experience.* Cambridge, Mass.: The MIT Press, pp. 329–46.

Rittel, Horst W. J., and Melvin M. Webber (1984). Planning problems are wicked problems, in Nigel Cross (ed.), *Developments in Design Methodology.* New York: John Wiley and Sons, pp. 135–44.

Shlaer, Sally, and Stephen J. Mellor (1988). *Object-Oriented Analysis: Modeling the World in Data.* Englewood Cliffs, N.J.: Prentice–Hall.

Whiteside, John, John Bennett, and Karen Holtzblatt (1988). Usability engineering: Our experience and evolution, in M. Helander (ed.), *Handbook of Human–Computer Interaction.* Amsterdam: North-Holland: Elsevier Science Publishers.

Winograd, Terry, and Fernando Flores (1986). *Understanding Computers and Cognition—A New Foundation for Design.* Norwood, N.J.: Ablex.

Zuboff, Shoshana (1988). *In the Age of the Smart Machine—The Future of Work and Power.* New York: Basic Books.

CHAPTER 4

Skill-Based Design: Productivity, Learning, and Organizational Effectiveness

HAROLD SALZMAN

The effective implementation of new technology, particularly computer-based systems, typically requires more, not less worker skill and judgment (Adler, 1986; Hirschhorn, 1984; Jaikumar, 1986; Majchrzak, 1988; Walton and Sussman, 1987). While a considerable body of evidence has accumulated in support of this proposition concerning technology implementation, we know much less about what this implies for technology design. In this chapter, I argue that an effective technology strategy needs to include new principles for the "skill-based design" of technology. These principles of skill-based design go significantly beyond considerations of traditional human factors and ergonomics to encompass both the process of designing systems and specific design principles, including features and functions of the technology.

More generally, I submit that technology design is always explicitly or implicitly based on social as well as technical assumptions. This chapter will show how the social assumptions regarding human capabilities and motivations that underlie the dominant design principles, including those embedded in the seemingly objective calculation of economy and efficiency, are not optimally suited to current production requirements. The key social assumptions affecting cost–benefit assessments concern the nature and degree of workers' involvement in production, specifically the assumption that worker activity is typically limited to the exercise of a few manual skills, and the assumption that production systems can be understood as mechanistic interactions of these limited skills with the installed technology. Since workers' activity is assumed to be limited to the exercise of rote manual skills and to be based on limited production knowledge, workers' participation in production problem solving or performance of skilled work is not valued. On the contrary, worker involvement is seen as an unquantifiable "risk" to system performance. Complex and costly equipment designs are therefore adopted to try to eliminate human intervention.

The first part of this chapter suggests a contrast between two technology design philosophies: the traditional technology-based approach and the emergent skill-based approach. The second part examines the social assumptions underlying engineering design approaches through a review of books on the design of mechanical and electro-mechanical manufacturing equipment. In this review, we find the technology-based approach ubiquitous. These texts are typically based on the assumption that the value added contributed by workers is limited to versatile, but recalcitrant, physical exertion. The dominant design approaches therefore assume that effective designs should minimize both labor force skill requirements and the degree of worker initiative possible in production. These design principles, I suggest, conflict with production strategies for increasing quality, productivity, and overall performance, since these strategies require greater worker involvement (e.g., Skinner, 1986; Salzman, 1989). To explore these issues in greater detail, the subsequent sections discuss the results of a survey of manufacturing equipment design, and then four case studies that illustrate different types of design strategies and practices. A conclusion summarizes some principles for effective technology design.

SKILL-BASED VERSUS TECHNOLOGY-BASED DESIGN

Before launching into the details of our results, this section sketches some of the salient contrasts between skill-based and traditional, technology-based design approaches. These contrasts are nicely illustrated in the design of machining centers in two companies we studied. In the first company, the machinists and operators were involved early in the design process and in the selection of equipment. The machines purchased were designed to be operator programmable, and operators were expected, within their ability, to make program modifications to ensure high-quality output. In the second company, the machining center was designed without worker involvement because machinists were thought to have little to contribute to engineering design decisions. The system was designed for centralized control of all programming, and the machines selected did not allow for operator programming. In both cases, implementation led to changes in traditional machining skills. Specifically, there was a loss of manual machining skills since the tool control task was automated. But beyond this similarity there were some striking contrasts.

In the second company, the centralized communication linkages did not work properly and routine modifications of the part programs caused a backlog in the programming department. Eventually, operators were allowed informally to make changes in programs at the machines. This proved cumbersome, since programming changes had to be made in machine code. In the first company, the operators were encouraged to make all necessary changes for which they had the skills, and these changes were easier to effect since the machines were designed to provide aids to operator programming such as graphical displays of tool paths. The operators, who had no previous programming experience, were soon able to make most program modifications, reducing the need for part programing staff by 50 percent.

As these cases illustrate, skill-based design does not necessarily mean design based on an unchanged set of skills. In more routine processes, skill-based designs can result in the complete elimination of worker involvement in the actual fabrication operation, but it will provide operators with production information that allows them to control the process effectively and to respond competently to problems. For example, in one highly automated steel plant we have studied, operators had access to process controls and were provided electricity consumption information to encourage them to make modifications that increased energy efficiency. In contrast to skill-based designs, traditional designs typically provide little more than warning lights and stop buttons, since such a design assumes that the operator should act only as a monitor and should, when faced with a problem, halt the process and summon a technician.

In skill-based design the designer sees the elimination or simplification of the more routine and rote tasks as an opportunity for the worker to assume a broader role in the production process, although it may involve a shift in types of skill used. Skill-based design thus requires a fundamentally different conception of technology, engineering, and the role of workers in production.

The research reported in this paper builds on the human-centered and skill-based design approaches that have been developed in Europe and Scandinavia (Brodner, 1986; Ehn, 1989). In these approaches, however, we find a tendency to overrate the importance and feasibility of preserving workers' current skills. Moreover, these approaches often rely on a moralistic call upon individual designers to be more "humanistic" in their design philosophy. While agreeing with the general proposition that automation requires skilled users, I submit that preserving existing skills may not lead to the best utilization of human labor. I would also argue that new design approaches are not likely to be widely adopted as the result of individual injunction, at least in the United States, unless driven by structural and technological changes in production strategy.

A SURVEY OF TEXTBOOKS

The first part of our investigation into principles of design involved examining the assumptions concerning the role of workers in both the equipment design process and the manufacturing process. Restricting ourselves to books published between 1938 and 1989, we reviewed over 100 books on equipment design in the Boston University Science and Engineering Library and 100 textbooks used in engineering courses, and found only 42 books that made any mention of workers' roles. These 42 books were identified by a search of tables of contents and indexes for any mention of human factors, ergonomics, safety, skill, or the names of any management theorists such as Taylor or McGregor.

These 42 books all present a view of the role of people in production as subordinate if not marginal. We categorized the themes of these books as primary and secondary. We found that primary considerations included factors such as machine performance (measured by variables such as cycle times and throughput) and economic efficiency. Discussion of the potential for deliberate operator action to promote systems performance rarely ranked as even a secondary theme. Discussion of the possible advantages of user involvement in designing systems was entirely absent.

A typical discussion of the general principles guiding the consideration of humans in design can be found in *Systems Philosophy* (Ellis and Ludwig, 1962): "The optimal performance of the element 'man' in man–machine control system performance can be obtained only when the mechanical components of the system are designed so that the human being need only act as a simple amplifier." A more recent formulation of systems engineering principles stated the primary personnel objective as eliminating people; when people are required, "skill level requirements should normally be minimized," and jobs should be designed on the assumption that workers are "able to follow clearly presented instructions where interpretation and decision making are not necessary [and] will normally require close supervision" (Blanchard and Fabrycky, 1981). Another author began a section on "Human Factors" with the reminder that: "The engineer must never forget that whatever he designs is meant to be used by human beings. . . . Unless the designer goes to apparently absurd lengths to prevent it, people will operate the device incorrectly" (Gibson, 1968).

In the minority of books discussing explicit design principles relative to workers, the most frequently cited author is Taylor, followed by Gilbreth. These discussions cover the essentials of time and motion studies, such as, "In order to increase productivity, a worker should be paid per unit of production rather than on an hourly basis. . . . [This] is called time study"; and "Quite often a scientifically trained engineer can study the way a worker goes about his job and suggest a more convenient arrangement of work space and a more efficient series of motions of the worker. . . . [This] is called motion study" (Gibson, 1968). Translating time and motion study principles into design principles involved generally broad precepts such as "minimize the total number of motions required," or "work should be distributed as equally as possible over the two hands and two feet."

The tenor of these human factor considerations was illustrated in an example of designing a workbench for installation of electrical resistors. This assembly process required that after determining the "good" and the "bad" resistors, the worker would deposit them in different bins:

Paint the good hole edge [of the bin] green, the bad hole edge red. The girl should not read a meter. She should not be told what an ohm is. She should not be asked to make difficult borderline judgments. A green light should go on if the resistor is good and a red light if it is bad. . . . The foreman should make the set up and test it before turning it over to the girl. Any adjusting of the test procedure may upset the girl, and any slight gain in efficiency will be lost by retraining time. Note that the job of converting the actual quantity under test to a simple binary decision is done by the industrial engineer in designing the test circuit, not by the girl. . . . Theoretically it would be possible to let the girl watch the dial on an ohmmeter [and decide if the resistor was good]. For the highly trained technician in a laboratory this is perfectly satisfactory, but not for girls on an assembly line for whom the procedure should be wholly automatic (Gibson, 1968).

The authors of the previously mentioned book on systems design concluded their chapter on "Human Subsystems" with the following summary: "Having indicated some of the problems associated with human subsystems . . . and having compared certain characteristics of men and machines, we may well raise the question of why human subsystems should be utilized at all in systems design" (Ellis and Ludwig, 1962). The reason the authors give for using human subsystems is that few automated systems can run entirely without human intervention, and, "more practically, as has been humorously pointed out by many, man represents a fairly high capability control element, already inexpensive in mass production and producible by inexperienced labor."

If we turn from general considerations to specific recommendations, we find more frequent but still brief discussions of safety and traditional human factors/ergonomics. In the mid- to late-1960s, safety became a more prominent concern in design books, presumably as a result of Occupational Safety and Health Administration standards. Consideration of safety requirements leads to an important shift in philosophy because safety benefits the human operator rather than machine performance. Brief lists of safety considerations appeared in most books written after the mid-1960s, and most of these books advised the designer to consult the applicable safety codes of his or her state, industry, or professional association. Most of the discussions were brief, and reminded the designer that safety should be considered along with the "primary" criteria of good machine design.

Ergonomic considerations focused on the physical capabilities and limitations of humans and the designs needed to obtain optimal machine performance (rather than any instrinsic value to the operator). The discussions of machine–human interface design typically focused on designing for the 95th percentile of height, reach, and similar physical properties. Many books included charts detailing average lift capacity, grip strength, reach, comfortable seat height, reaction times to sound, sight, smell, touch, and temperature.

One text noted that understanding the limits of human capacities is important because "Requirements outside of these recommended limits will result in operator inefficiency and system failures" (Blanchard and Fabrycky, 1981). An example of the significance accorded such issues can be found in a study of the effect of noise on performance. This study concluded that steady noise is less distracting than intermittent noise, even at high levels, and that "an individual can adapt to it and work efficiency may not be significantly compromised." The authors do note that "if the noise level is too high (even though steady), the individual will probably experience permanent injury through loss of hearing," but, "on the other hand," intermittent noise, although less likely to cause injury, is distracting and does result in a loss of job efficiency. Thus, the "noise generated by the system must be maintained at a level where human efficiency is maximized" (Blanchard and Fabrycky, 1981).

Ergonomic considerations were generally limited to one or two paragraph overviews of ergonomic concepts. One book concludes a brief section on human factors by noting that, although the "numerosity of designs requiring consideration of human factors is extensive," the "competent designer handles these with little but careful deliberation and judgment" (Vidosic, 1969). In general, when human factors need to be considered in greater depth, most books advise the designer to consult the human factors specialist much as they would consult any other engineering specialty for expertise on a part or material with which they were not familiar. However, since human factors engineers are only 0.2 percent of all engineers, they are not likely to be involved in a typical design project. Moreover, when design engineers do consult human factors texts, they find that the role of the worker in production is discussed very mechanically, in terms of the physical properties of human "material" as it needs to be used as part of the equipment. Human skills are identified with specific motor and perceptual capabilities, and sometimes with passive "information processing" capabilities.

This brief review reveals the assumptions embedded in the traditional design approach's concerning the nature and limitations of worker abilities and workers' contributions to production performance. The goal of traditional design is to create a system in which workers perform prescribed instructions rather than taking independent action or analysis. No consideration is given to the idea that reducing the complexity of some tasks might allow the operator to engage in other activities that could enhance system performance. On the contrary, the less complex the task, the greater is assumed to be the need for supervision, either because the job would be staffed by someone less skilled and therefore less capable of reliably performing their tasks or because management doubts workers' willingness to perform these tasks. The "scientifically trained engineer" is—and the worker is not—trained and willing to identify improvements for work efficiency. As in the example of designing a work bench, the goal of making the task as automatic as possible is assumed to require maintaining workers' ignorance about the task. No consideration is afforded the idea that some additional knowledge and an ohmmeter might not "upset the girl" but instead allow her to make suggestions for increasing efficiency, to conduct the setup herself instead of relying on a foreman (also increasing efficiency), and to provide feedback on the magnitude of error and margin of quality in the resistors.

In our literature review, we found no appreciable change over time in the nature of these assumptions concerning the human role in production or in its importance as a design criterion. The more recent books tended to mention human factors or the "machine–human interface" to a greater extent than the earlier books, but the discussion is still quite limited (e.g., Rouse and Cody, 1987). A 1983 machine design book of 642 pages is typical in devoting two paragraphs to human factors engineering, stating, "human factors engineering is concerned with all aspects of the man–machine relationship," and then listing all those aspects as "safety, comfort, and efficiency" (Hindhede, 1983).

Although management theory has evolved during the post-war period, design principles do not appear to have undergone a similar development. Engineering design, as indicated in the books reviewed, proceeds with the same basic understanding of the human role in production as first articulated at the beginning of the twentieth century.

While our review and this chapter focus on equipment design, we should note that the software design literature is in general more advanced in its recognition of the cognitive dimension of humans and the role of users in design. The cognitive psychology models used in systems design are, nevertheless, also open to criticisms of being mechanistic and deterministic models of human functions (Coulter, 1979, 1983; Dreyfus, 1979). And the recommended user involvement approaches ignore the problems of conflicting user needs and the way organizational structure and power differentials among users bias the determination of requirements (Hedberg and Mumford, 1975; Bjorn-Andersen and Hedberg, 1977; Markus and Pfeffer, 1983).

Our findings in the review of equipment design are consistent with other researchers' studies of engineering. David Noble has suggested that the values of the engineering profession reflect those of management, since engineering has developed within the confines of industry and thus tends to be subservient to management. In addition, he argues that these values reflect a set of distinctive professional values. He found among engineers "a delight in remote control and an enchantment with the notion of machines without men . . . a general devaluation of human skills and a distrust of human workers and an ongoing effort to eliminate both" (Noble, 1984). While factors other than the ones listed by Noble may underlie this ideology in engineering, our review of recommended design approaches is consistent with his characterization of the prevailing attitude.

Perrow's (1983) study of human factors engineering found that even basic human factors considerations were marginal in engineering design. He attributed the neglect of human factors principles to "top management goals and perspectives, the reward structure of the organization, isolation of design engineers from the consequences of their decision, and some aspects of organizational culture." In essence, the organization of engineering practice leads to designs that are not engineered with regard to human factors. Moreover, even when human factors engineers do get involved in design, there is little consideration of the social consequences of design choices. According to Perrow, human factors engineering itself, while focused on the "human subsystem," is based on a rationalistic, biological, and mechanical view of humans. Human factors engineers share with their engineering colleagues a view of the human as an information-processing system that responds predictably to positive and negative sanctions. Workers are seen as "transfer devices" in the automation loop—subsystems that are used "for want of a robot."

In an extensive review of technology design models, Blackler and Brown (1986) noted that ergonomics, sociotechnical theory, and the theory of participative management have had limited impact on design because the "climate of opinion" is not receptive to such theories. To influence technology design, they suggested greater "intervention" in design by social scientists, and by psychologists in particular, to "help different groups within organizations to recognize and implement new approaches to technological innovation." Mumford, in an historical review of sociotechnical theory (1987), noted that very little of the research in this stream addresses technology design and suggested that one reason for the omission may be the lack of engineering expertise by sociotechnical researchers (see also Cherns, 1987).

Although the factors discussed in these studies are undoubtedly important in accounting for the persistence of design perspectives that disregard the human dimension in production, I submit that traditional engineering design also reflects traditional production strategies. Since at least World War II, the dominant pattern in U.S. industry has been standardized production for expanding mass markets, a perception of direct labor as the major cost reduction opportunity area, and antagonistic labor–management relations. The traditional design approaches, it should be conceded, were functional for this traditional model of production.

THE VIEW FROM INDUSTRY

The current turbulent changes in the economy, global competition, and consumer markets have led some U.S. companies to seek new management formulae, new technologies, cheaper sources of labor, and new ways to organize production processes. One increasingly popular strategy for improving quality and productivity relies on greater worker responsibility and involvement—which, as I have argued, could be enhanced by skill-based system design.

To assess the extent of change in design practices and identify particular design approaches that might be successful, we undertook a survey of design practices and principles in computer-based manufacturing systems in the metal-working industries. (A parallel study, not reported here, focused on software design. Detailed reports on both these studies are in Rosenthal and Salzman, 1989, and Lund, et al., 1990.)

Methodology

The first stage of this survey consisted of a telephone interview using a semistructured questionnaire, and the second stage consisted of a series of in-depth case studies. We interviewed senior executives in 63 manufacturing firms. The case studies involved on-site interviews and observation, as described in the following. In this section I will discuss the survey results, and in the next section I describe some of the cases.

The companies in the survey were selected from the largest companies in the metal-working industries, (SIC codes 34, 35, 36, 37, and 38). They produced a wide range of products, including automobiles, aircraft, machinery, photographic equipment, engines for aircraft, locomotives, and tractors, razors, computers, and air conditioners. Half of the companies were the largest manufacturer in their industry, and another 27 percent were the second or third largest in their industry. They were therefore large companies, with median sales of over $800 million and median employment of 10,000 employees.

Most of the companies had a substantial or dominant share of their product market: nearly a quarter of the companies held more than 50 percent of their markets. Their industries were highly concentrated, with over half (57 percent) of the companies in markets in which five or fewer firms controlled 75 percent of their product market. Nonetheless, 94 percent of the respondents reported that there was strong competition in their market area.

The companies varied widely in the percentage of their production equipment that was computer based or programmable. In 18 percent of cases, over 75 percent of the equipment was programmable or computer based; in another 18 percent the ratio was one-half to three-quarters; and about two-thirds reported that up to 50 percent of their equipment was computer based or programmable. All companies had made substantial investments in new equipment in the 3 years prior to the survey, with a median investment of $3 million (see Table 4.1).

Design Policies and Practices

The survey focused on the role of workers and of assumptions about workers in design policies and practices. We thus examined the impact on equipment and process designs of assumptions concerning workers' skills, capacity to

Table 4.1. Sample Description

Company background	Number of companies	Percentage
Sales		
Less than $100 million	8	12.9
$101 to $300 million	9	14.5
$301 to $800 million	13	21.0
$801 million to $1.5 billion	13	21.0
More than $1.5 billion	19	30.6
Total	62	
(In millions)	3052	
Median	829	
Employees		
Under 1,000	7	11.1
1,000–25,000	24	38.1
26,000–50,000	15	23.8
51,000–75,000	10	15.9
76,000–100,000	2	3.2
More than 100,000	5	7.9
Total	63	100.0
Mean number of employees	104,000	
Median number of employees	10,000	

Market characteristics	Frequency	Percentage
Market share		
<25%	18	32.7
26 to 50%	21	38.2
51 to 75%	15	27.3
75% +	1	1.8
Total	55	
Perceived competition		
Strong	59	96.7
Moderate	2	3.3
Total	61	
Concentration ($\geq$75% of product market)		
4 or fewer firms	36	58.1
5 to 10 firms	19	30.6
More than 10 firms	7	11.3
Total	62	
Market growth		
Growing market	30	50.0
Stable market	19	31.7
Declining market	11	18.3
Total	60	
Product life cycle		
3 years or less	11.1	
4 to 10 years	38.1	
More than 10 years	50.8	

Table 4.1. Sample Description (*Continued*)

Production equipment	Number of companies	Percentage
Programmable equipment (as percentage of all production equipment)		
1 to 25%	19	30.2
26 to 50%	22	34.9
51 to 75%	11	17.5
75 to 100%	11	17.5
Total	63	
Mean	47%	
Median	43%	
Investment in production equipment, previous 3 years		
Under $10 million	2	3.4
$11–25 million	18	30.5
$26–50 million	9	15.3
$51–75 million	15	25.4
$76–100 million	5	8.5
Over $100 million	10	16.9
Total	59	100.0
Mean (in millions)	139	
Median (in millions)	26	

learn, the autonomy necessary to exercise skill and judgment, and workers' roles in improving production effectiveness.

The first task in our research was to determine the range of policies companies were using in the design process, including design specifications used for procurement. In doing so, we distinguished between equipment design policies and more general policies relating to the organization of work. Equipment design is only one of several factors shaping work organization policies. In fact, company policies in the two areas often were not compatible.

We distinguished two broad areas of interest: first, the role of workers in the design or procurement process and, second, the criteria used for design specification. In the first area—the design process—we asked about policies regarding (1) worker participation in the design or selection of new equipment and (2) worker involvement in modifying equipment and process design after installation. In the second area—the design criteria—we asked about design policies regarding (1) the provision for feedback of production information to the operator, (2) the operator's ability to modify the operation of the equipment and process for optimal production (for example, by changing tool paths), (3) the operator's control of the process and the degree of centralization of process control (for example, the pacing or sequencing of work), and (4) the skills and the role of workers in equipment operation (for example, whether designs should encourage skill upgrading or reduction). I first discuss the overall responses to the questions and then the comments of interviewees.

Policies

Policies regarding worker participation in the design process and in the postinstallation process changes ranged from informal, ad hoc, worker consultation on a project-by-project basis to formal policies requiring committees for the design and selection of new equipment and specifying worker membership in such committees (see Table 4.2).

Most companies did not have an explicit policy specifying worker participation in the design process or worker involvement in the postinstallation modification of the process. Thirty-two percent of the companies had only informal procedures or opportunities for such worker input, and only 8 per-

Table 4.2. Manufacturing Equipment Design Survey

Design process

Worker participation in the design process:	
No policy (no regular participation)	59%
Informal participation	33%
Formal participation	8%
Postinstallation participation in design changes:	
No policy (no regular participation)	78%
Informal participation	15%
Formal participation	7%

Design content

Information/feedback to workers:	
No policy	68%
Production information (SPC or QC)	25%
General production information	7%
Process/equipment controls designed with regard to worker modification of process:	
No policy	56%
Lockout/prevent worker process modification	22%
Controls designed to allow/facilitate modification	22%

Maintenance

No policy	53%
Prevent operator maintenance	17%
To allow/facilitate operator maintenance	31%

Skill

No policy	69%
Informal consideration of skills	20%
Formal policy	11%
Lockout/deskill	5%
Utilize worker skill	6%

cent formally required worker participation in equipment selection and/or design committees. Postinstallation worker involvement was informally allowed in 15 percent of the companies, and explicit policies prescribing this involvement were present in only 7 percent of the companies.

Policies specifying design criteria were examined in four areas: feedback of production information to the operator, modification of the process by the operator, maintenance by the operator, and consideration of operator skills.

To implement modern quality control methods such as statistical process control, the operator needs information about the immediate production process. Yet over two-thirds of the companies did not have an explicit policy regarding feedback of information to the operator. Only a quarter of the companies had a policy of designing equipment or processes to provide production information for purposes of statistical process control or quality control. Another 7 percent had policies encouraging the distribution of more general information about production.

Twenty-two percent had policies specifying designs for operator-controllable processes, while another 22 percent had policies specifying equipment designs to "lock out" any type of operator intervention. Most of the remaining companies did not have an explicit policy.

Most companies (53 percent) did not have any policy regarding design for operator involvement in maintenance. Seventeen percent reported a policy specifying designs that would not allow operator maintenance. Thirty-one percent specified that equipment should be designed for operators to be able to do first-level maintenance. Designing for operator maintenance might involve creating modular components that operators could replace or locating parts to be lubricated, adjusted, or changed in places accessible to operators. Designs to prevent operator maintenance (as to prevent other equipment adjustment) might involve placing parts in inaccessible locations (such as behind bolted panels) or requiring special tools.

The issue of skill considerations in design was addressed by an open-ended question about whether there was any policy requiring engineers to design equipment with worker skills in mind. Only 20 percent said that skill issues were a "consideration," and 11 percent said they had an explicit policy relating to skills. In most cases, the policies were to reduce labor force skill requirements. Only 4 companies (6 percent) reported having design policies that were oriented towards utilizing and enhancing worker skills. Two of those companies focused on reducing manual and machine-operating tasks so that workers could assume a broader role using their analytic skills and judgment for process and/or system improvements.

Interview Comments

In many companies without formal policies, interviewees nevertheless identified various relevant design practices. The following comments summarize the notes we took in interviews covering both policies and practices. In most areas, over 80 percent of the interviewees commented on design practices because there was no policy.

The policies and practices governing worker involvement in selection, design, and postinstallation modifications were primarily informal in nature. In a few companies, they were required by union contract. At one company, "once the functional specification is put together by manufacturing engineering, they will review them with the people who run the process. The engineers will preselect three good vendor companies and then the people who run the process participate in the review." Several interviewees from other companies felt that worker participation was vital, and required such participation even in the absence of contractual obligation. In the words of one interviewee, "otherwise we don't get specifications that are needed and the operators have a negative reaction"; as a result of this participation, "workers now propose new equipment."

Worker involvement in postinstallation modification was more frequent, but policies supporting it were also generally informal. Many companies had nonfunctioning suggestion systems; in practice, there was little active participation by workers and minimal followup by the manufacturing engineers. Postinstallation involvement appeared to be most effective in companies that required some type of formal participation system or had other types of programs that included workers. Companies using statistical process control and quality circles found the workers often addressed equipment and process design as one way to improve quality. Overall, however, there was little recognition of the value of worker involvement either before or after design and installation.

Companies often sought to minimize maintenance by operators because management viewed maintenance as a higher-level activity outside the scope of operator responsibility and/or capability. Union contracts sometimes reserved this activity for higher-paid workers. In a few companies, however, workers were encouraged to perform routine maintenance on the equipment with which they worked. Such operator maintenance was typically a relatively new policy in these companies and was implemented with the goal of reducing the number of job classifications or of increasing worker "ownership" of the process. This approach was often a job design policy rather than an equipment design policy: It rarely led to any reconsideration of equipment design.

In only a few of the companies were there efforts (and in none were there policies) to source or design equipment that provided diagnostic information or greater access to facilitate operator maintenance. One company was only beginning to design "smart panels" that diagnose problems and issue voice commands to guide the operator in fixing the problem. Another company was trying to design equipment in modules that could be replaced by the operator. One of the reasons cited for this effort was to "minimize dispute-related maintenance issues among certain areas such as electrical, plumbing, etc.," since the replacement of modules, as distinct from repair, was not a procedure under the jurisdiction of a trade.

Companies in the survey took divergent approaches to achieving their goals of improving product quality and process reliability and efficiency. The predominant approach (although not always a policy) took the perspective that full automation entails "locking out" direct human intervention in the production process. One manufacturing engineer stated that his firm used "standard industrial engineering operating policies: keep the operator away from the controls; the machine controls quality and the operator only loads and unloads the machine." Companies following this approach typically had a policy that programming would be done by a salaried group of technicians and kept off limits to operators.

In this dominant approach, to allow operators any control would increase uncertainty in the process. One manufacturing engineer from a company where operators did not have access to the controls said, "If the knobs are available to the operator, he will do what he wants." He argued that the operator would vary the process in nonstandard and unpredictable ways, and in the words of another manager, "bastardize the process." One engineering manager proffered, "Designs need to minimize the 'creativity' of the operator." Another claimed, "Less human control leads to more production." One interviewee said, "Operators are just that and rarely program; we discourage operator control and want central control." This approach was characterized by one engineer as making sure the system was "Murphy-proof."

Some managers viewed process control as a labor–management issue. One said that although "greater human interaction may be more self-fulfilling for the operator . . . they feel they can usurp the engineer's role, overstepping their bounds of knowledge. This is especially true when there is a union." This opinion was echoed by another interviewee, who stated his policy as "removing human control; let people be parts feeders or material handlers where they cannot affect outcomes. We won't allow the union to shut us down!"

In other companies, the human dimension of production was viewed more positively, and operators were regarded as "owners" or "managers" of the production process directly under their purview. Companies that designed equipment or systems to provide operators with production information were generally using statistical process control (SPC) or other quality procedures. Companies designing equipment for information feedback to operators did not necessarily, however, design equipment for operator control or modifications: The information from this equipment could be used either passively or actively. In a passive approach, operators monitored and recorded production activity and referred noted problems to technicians (with operators themselves locked out). In an active approach, the information was provided for corrective action by the operator, and, in more advanced companies, the equipment was designed to facilitate operator modification of the process.

Although operator participation in setting machine controls for process operation was a policy or practice in some companies, even here workers typically had little flexibility. One company was implementing SPC and designing and retrofitting work stations with computer terminals that provided operators with necessary SPC data, but they carefully regulated manual overrides by operators and required overrides to be reported to supervisors. Nevertheless, these companies found significant benefit in providing production information to operators. One company discovered it allowed "real-time verification of specifications, finding defects, and [it] results in first-time quality with no rework." In the companies that regulated worker responses, information provided to the operators was used passively by the operator to monitor the process but not to make adjustments. Adjustments were referred to the programming staff or made under the direction of a supervisor.

In a small minority of companies, operators were expected to participate actively in the production process, and information was provided to assist them. The processes in these companies were often referred to as "operator owned" or "operator managed." In them, as one executive explained, "Operators are trained to be self-sufficient and to work generally without supervision to do what is necessary, including adjustments if the job calls for it." Other companies had policies based on the perspective that "the system is the operator, and each is responsible for operation of the system" and that the "operator should almost always be permitted to override; each individual operator is responsible for quality." They emphasized "developing designs that allow the operator to modify controls once sufficient information is available to know how to do it effectively, [and thus] to give operators SPC information on line."

A few companies were actively training their operators to run the production process with minimal supervision. One manufacturer of system controls "trains operators in problem solving and expects them to do so when needed, within specified boundaries." In perhaps the most far-reaching policy of this nature, one company designed a variable-speed assembly line that was directly controlled by an operator chosen each week by the entire group of operators. Combined with an incentive pay system, this policy achieved a line speed of 110 percent of the base rate within the first week of implementation. In a different area of this company, operators were provided only a recommended method of operation that they could modify as they found necessary.

In all the companies surveyed, design approaches to worker skills were consistent with approaches in the areas of control and maintenance. The most typical approach was to "simplify the machines to lower the skill required" of the labor force; "automate to remove worker influence in order to improve consistency"; "centralize control" so there is "no operator modification of the process"; "lock out the operator so he only *monitors* speeds and feeds" and the "programming unit has control of the machines"; and develop a "policy to make the process as independent of people as possible." The ideal in design was stated by one manager as "automating as much as possible—if you have an operator interacting with the process to keep it going, it causes problems. When there are problems, call in skilled people to maintain the system; keep it automatic without direct labor interacting."

A small minority of companies took design approaches that consciously relied on the use of worker skills, sometimes new skills. One company claimed to use automation to "eliminate the boring, repetitive, unsafe jobs so we can get broader worker involvement and skills." And another also tried to reduce the importance of "manual dexterity [in order to] increase judgment-based work using statistics, understanding the information on the computer screens." One company invested heavily in complex manufacturing and assembly equipment to yield the greatest possible productivity improvements, and found that its approach required much greater skill on the part of operators since they were expected to learn about SPC, the operation of computer-based equipment, and robotics programming (particularly on the evening and night shifts, where such skills were needed in order to keep programmers from being called to work in the middle of the night). In general, the firm found that workers had to understand, operate, and adjust more complex equipment.

One hypothesis that might explain the prevalence of policies and practices that minimize worker involvement is that of "deskilling": If automation were most efficient when it reduced skill requirements and was used with less skilled workers, then skill-based design would be of little benefit to the company. A section of the survey therefore asked respondents about automation's impact on skill requirements. However, few respondents reported any reductions, and many reported an upgrading of the skill requirements of operators, mechanics, and technicians working with the new equipment. For all three groups, skill levels and pay rates remained the same or increased in two-thirds to 90 percent of the processes. For operators, 48 percent remained at the same skill level, and 41 percent saw an increase in their skill level, although only 27 percent also had a pay increase. As might be expected, skill requirements of mechanics and technicians went up more than those of operators, but fewer of them had increases in pay rates. Specifically, nearly two-thirds of mechanics and technicians experienced an increase in skill requirements, but only 10 percent of mechanics and 17 percent of technicians saw increases in their pay rates.

A second hypothesis that might explain the prevalence of skill-minimization policies is the "job loss" hypothesis, which holds that if automation were accompanied by job elimination, worker participation to increase efficiency might be difficult to encourage. The employment impact resulting directly from the introduction of these new processes was difficult to assess. Overall, a substantial number of companies reported decreases in operator employment levels in the particular area of the new process. There were job losses in the area where new equipment was installed in 53 percent of the cases, although job losses for mechanics occurred in only 10 percent of the cases and for technicians, in 16 percent of the cases. However, in many of the cases, the employment change was not due primarily to productivity changes in the equipment. Companies often reported that changes in their production processes occurred during a downturn in their sales. The employment changes were due primarily to the decline in sales, and many claimed the introduction of the new process, which improved quality and productivity, allowed the company to stem further declines in sales. In other words, the new process was considered to have saved some jobs. In nearly all cases, displaced workers were transferred to new jobs within the same company.

CASE STUDIES

In order to pursue further our investigation of design practices, we also undertook several case studies. Discussed here are findings from four of these case studies. The first case was an optics manufacturing company known for its progressive approach to personnel management. The second company was in aerospace and had indicated in our survey that it was using innovative design procedures. The third case was a machining shop in a large diversified manufacturer. The fourth case was a steel plant that was a division of a large manufacturing company. These cases were selected to illustrate different design approaches and outcomes.

Optics Manufacturing

The manufacturing process examined in the first company was for the assembly of an optics subassembly in which several lenses were placed in a plastic housing in a complex arrangement with critical tolerances. The design of this process illustrated well the problems with the prevailing engineering approach to automation and attempts to "lock out" and deskill workers.

The process was first designed with extensive human labor involvement, in part because the company did not think it could justify advanced automation equipment with traditional financial criteria. However, the company changed the initial design to that of a fully automated assembly line utilizing eight robots because of a policy decision not to increase the size of its labor force. The company had a no-layoff policy and did not think it could absorb any additional workers in the future when they finished production of this part. In addition, the president of the firm issued an edict to adopt "cutting-edge" technology. Although the robotics technology was new to most of the engineers, they welcomed it not only because it brought in "modern technology," but, as explained by one engineer, it would allow them to advance toward the goal of laborless production. This engineer described his ideal system as one where a "guard walks to the edge of the plant, turns a key, and the process starts and runs completely automatically."

The line was designed as an elegant "walking beam," with 11 linked work stations or modules each 3 to 4 feet long. Lens insertion, plastic cap assembly, and lens adjustment were all done automatically by robots and fixed automation equipment. As designed, humans were required only for three functions: loading the plastic housing from bins onto the first station on the line (and this was necessary only because the company had not been able to get the housing delivered in a tray); loading the component parts, such as lenses, into the magazines supplying the assembly stations; and packing the completed assemblies at the end of the line. In concept, this was an elegant design for automatic function and minimal worker intervention. It was to be operated on "just-in-time" principles, where no buffer stock would be maintained.

Safety was an important concern in this company, and the machines were designed to ensure complete protection for all workers. Plexiglass enclosures covered the entire line. Hinged doors were provided for access to the line, and each door was equipped with a safety interlock that shut down the work station as soon as the door was opened.

Despite its design for nearly complete automation and lockout of operators, from the first day of its operation to 21 months later when we visited, operation of the line was possible only with constant worker intervention. Two supervisory workers were constantly busy during their shift attending to the line. The production statistics showed that, on average, during the 7 hours of possible run time during a shift, all stations were operational only 3 hours— about 40 percent of the planned utilization.

The plastic housings were continually jamming between assembly stations, lenses were not fully seated when inserted, and numerous other problems required workers constantly to reach in with their hands or picks (two foot long metal rods with hooks at the end) to unjam or adjust the plastic assemblies. In order to reach in, most of the safety covers had to be opened and the interlocks defeated through the use of wire "cheaters" that depressed the shutoff buttons while the door was open. The operators had obtained the cheaters along with the picks from the maintenance technicians. In this way, the operators could fix the minor problems that constantly occurred without stopping the line. They also kept buffer stock of partially assembled housings at each station to allow them to hand feed housings to the next station and thereby keep the line running when an individual work station was down. Extra workers were required at the end of the line to adjust manually the housings that were out of alignment or not assembled properly.

In short, the operators were able to keep the line operating only by constant attention and intervention, quite unlike the planned design. Using the prescribed just-in-time principles and safety procedures would have resulted in a fraction of the output they currently maintained. As it was, engineering staff were backlogged with repairs and adjustments. There was a constant battle to balance production requirements for keeping the system in operation, use just-in-time procedures, and maintain safety procedures that kept operators out of the range of moving machinery.

A simple design change in the safety guards would have eased this "battle": The company could have provided "cutouts" in the safety covers and installed picks with small shields to allow the operators to unjam the line without stopping it and to provide sufficient safety protection. Indeed, within the first year of operation, the operators had prevailed upon the engineers to cut a large hole in the safety door of the most troublesome assembly module to provide them access without stopping the line. The hole was made only reluctantly and was considered a temporary expedient until the module could be "fixed." When an engineer was asked about this type of modification, he called it a "kluge" design, and added that their effort would be better spent on the source of the problem—even though the problem had eluded solution thus far. The issue was also dismissed by several of the engineers as a typical failing of human nature rather than a design problem: "Don't you cut off the third prong on an electrical cord at home when the outlet only has two prongs?" asked one engineer. "You can't engineer systems to be entirely foolproof."

To fix the problems, the company was spending an additional sum equal to 50 percent of the original cost of the line to redesign the line and install new equipment (including removal of several robots and replacing them with hard automation pick-and-place machines). Senior managers said that the original design requiring only minimal operator intervention was sound in principle: Workers should only be loaders and unloaders to the system, while the engineers would continue to adjust, fix, redesign, and replace all the parts of the line until it operated "correctly." One engineer estimated that, by the time they were done, between 85 to 95 percent of the line would be replaced and the company would be two-thirds through the life cycle of the product it was producing.

In contrast, another area of the plant had just purchased a "fully automatic" assembly system from Sony Corporation. This machine would take nearly a dozen different parts, "palletize" them in trays, pick up the parts, and insert them into a plastic assembly. The machine, when delivered, was completely open and had no safety guards. The company told Sony they could not accept delivery of the machine because it did not conform to their safety policies and did not meet OSHA standards. It asked Sony to fit the machine with safety doors and interlocks to keep operators from reaching into the line without shutting off the system. The engineers at Sony were surprised at the request and reluctant to make the modifications. How, they asked, could they expect to run this fully automatic system if operators did not have constant access to the machine to adjust parts and the process?

While their lack of safety awareness is not to be applauded, Sony engineers saw people as an integral part of automated production. The optics assembly line design, by contrast, attempted to stretch the technology well beyond any demonstrated technical capability solely to eliminate operator involvement in production. Further automation was the only option considered by the engineers to remedy poor assembly operation; operator suggestions for other ways to improve effectiveness were neither solicited nor welcomed by the engineers.

Aerospace Machining Shop

The second case is an aerospace company's machining shop that produced critical parts for aircraft engines. It illustrates the benefits of active worker involvement in the design process.

This shop underwent a redesign to integrate an entire machining process that had involved 33 discrete machines scattered throughout the plant. The new process had 6 cells consisting of a total of 21 machine tools connected by automated handling and linked to a mainframe computer for program downloading.

Operators were actively involved in the process of designing the new system. When the design team, which included machine operators, completed a conceptual design, they made a story board with the proposed layout of the cells and displayed it on easels on the shop floor near the machinists. During this phase, a number of improvements were suggested by the machinists. For example, one machinist noted that the cutoff saw, which operated on an intermittent basis, was designed as an independent work station requiring a full-time operator. He suggested that the team move the saw next to the radial drill he was going to operate. Since his work had long cycle times, he could run the cutoff saw during the drilling cycle and the plant would need one fewer operator.

Another change was made when the machinists saw that a threading operation occurred midway through the machining steps. Since the threads were critical and they knew it would be difficult to protect the threads through subsequent machining operations, the machinists suggested moving the threading operation to the end of the machining cycle.

One operator, who was dissatisfied with the time it took to tighten parts in fixtures, suggested that hydraulic fixtures would be faster and safer. This change dramatically decreased set-up time and nearly eliminated the risk of parts being pulled out of the fixture during machining. Numerous other quality, efficiency, and safety changes were made as a result of this prior review by the machinists and operators.

In general, worker involvement in the new process was unexpectedly high. Machinists participated on a rotating basis on the design team and in the selection of new equipment, and shopfloor personnel developed their own review and recommendations to management for vendor selection. The machinists' interest in selecting the most appropriate equipment inspired many of them to travel on their own time and at their own expense to trade shows to examine and evaluate different equipment options.

The new cell design modified operator interest in and interactions around skill development. In the old processes, operators tended to "protect" their machine- or process-specific skills. In one instance there was only one operator who knew how to operate a particular machine because he refused to teach others. When he died unexpectedly, there was a significant period of downtime and inefficiency until a new worker learned to master the process. In contrast, in the new machining cells, workers had a view of the entire process and were in close proximity to other workers and processes. This led workers to want to learn new skills and to cross-train one another at their own initiative. The atmosphere encouraged operators to learn more about their processes. The greater complexity of the new technology led a number of workers to take computer and math classes at the local junior college, again at their own initiative. These operators began to solve problems by "trigging it out," as they referred to their use of trigonometry, and this motivated other operators to enroll in school.

The plant also had an active postimplementation suggestion system. The vice president of machining assigned every suggestion to the appropriate office for evaluation and required a completed evaluation or status report within 30 days. This emphasis on evaluating worker suggestions led engineers to follow up by talking with the person making the suggestion rather than just reviewing the written suggestion. In many cases, the engineering staff discovered after talking to the machinists and operators that suggestions that had not seemed feasible in writing were, in fact, quite feasible and valuable. Written suggestions were often poorly communicated because of the difficulty of accurately describing the idea in writing and because many of the operators had poor writing skills. The suggestion acceptance rate increased dramatically as a result of direct followup, and some workers actually doubled their annual income through suggestions. (Workers were paid $25 to $5,000 based on the cost savings achieved from their suggestions.)

Although management encouraged worker initiative and skill acquisition overall, it opposed any modification by machinists of part programs. The programming department had full responsibility for programming and modifications. Supervisors and managers had an explicit policy prohibiting program changes by machinists. They reported that the machines were designed in ways that made it impossible for machinists to change programs. Yet in interviews and observations, we discovered that the machinists had learned on their own a special procedure that enabled them to change programs. Although somewhat cumbersome and temporary since they could not store the changes longer than the duration of their shift, this procedure was faster than waiting for changes from the programming staff. They also claimed that these program modifications led to significant improvements in efficiency and quality.

In another area of this plant, management had installed operator-programmable machines that allowed shopfloor modification of part programs (which were initially downloaded from a central computer). A group of operators had convinced their supervisors and the engineers that they were capable of modifying programs effectively, and that it would be much more efficient for them to do so than to restrict modifications to programmers. An operator-written program or modification was usually completed within one day, whereas the same program or modification would take up to five days when handled by the programming department (because of a backlog of requests and because of the number of trials during the modification process). Operators also commented that when programming was done at the machine, whether by a programmer or operator, it was completed with fewer "bugs" because the actual tool path and machine operation were in view while programming took place. As a result, management in this area was able to reduce the higher-paid programming staff by 50 percent over five years. It is likely, although not certain, that an operator-programmable approach would eventually be adopted throughout the plant as upper-level management prevails upon the managers and supervisors who still resist such changes.

Aircraft Electrical Plant

Although increases in skill requirements are common with advances in technology, equipment is not always designed or implemented with the intention of fully utilizing operator skill. This was evident in our study of a machining shop in the aircraft electrical components division of a large diversified manufacturer.

The company decided in 1984 to replace its antiquated machining equipment with automated machining centers, and assembled a team to design the new process and select equipment vendors. The first machining centers were installed in 1987. Our site visit took place in 1989, 2 years after the centers began operation.

In contrast to the previous company, the design efforts were undertaken with minimal machinist participation. Only quarterly meetings were held with the machinists and union for purposes of "communicating" current automation plans. The design team felt that machinists and operators would not have much to contribute to the effort since the technology was too advanced.

The machining centers were designed to have all part programs created in the programming department and then distributed through a host computer. An important motivation for this design was the goal of maintaining tighter control of the machining operations by "returning this control to the engineers." This was combined with a central tooling preset station that calibrated tool setups for specific jobs, thus limiting the substitutions or adjustments the operator could make to a job at the work station. Overall, the stated design principles focused on automating as many aspects of operation as possible to minimize operator intervention.

The system achieved significant improvements in quality and productivity. Run time doubled from the previous system; process cycle time and number of operations were reduced by 50 percent. However, there were also significant problems, some of which appeared to result from the gap between the shopfloor requirements of operations and the system's design. For example, troubleshooting proved to be surprisingly difficult because the software people were not aware of the particular coding requirements of machines. The planned direct distribution of programs by the host computer was not functioning successfully and operators had to load the programs locally (programs were loaded onto tapes that were sent to operators to mount on their machines). Improving the quality of production was an important criterion in the design of the system, and sophisticated measuring instruments were purchased, but their location required cumbersome movements of parts to the measurement tools and stations.

Several of the engineers regretted not involving operators on the design team and said in retrospect that reassigning a few seasoned machinists to work full time with the design team would have helped. One engineer commented that they relied too much on automation, and that instead of always trying to replace people with technology, they should recognize that "people have pretty good computers in their heads." Operators said they welcomed the technological advances but were dissatisfied with and offended by management's approach of attempting to use computer systems to replace their skill and by a design process that excluded them. The operators and machinists felt they could have made significant contributions to the design process had they been given the opportunity.

The new technology required increases in skills, despite the plant's efforts to use automation to obviate the need for skilled machinists. The complexity of written instructions and operation of the shopfloor computers required greater reading skills and substantial additional training. Displays provided process information, but some were in machine code, which the operators nevertheless learned to interpret. Recruitment policies, amended for this area, included two-year technical college degrees as a preferred hiring criterion.

The supervisors found that the added complexity of the operations required a different type of management. Previously, the supervisors managed machinists' and operators' work by direct order. After two difficult years following the installation, some of the supervisors had begun to change their roles to encourage operator initiative and "ownership" of the process. Other supervisors still maintained their traditional roles, did not encourage worker suggestions for improvement, and would not hold meetings with their operators and machinists.

Steel Plant

The fourth case is a small steel plant that produced special order alloy steel. In contrast to the previous case, this one illustrates a design for decentralized decision making highly dependent upon operator skill and judgment.

In 1978, the steel division of a large manufacturing company began a ten-year plan for updating its steel-making technology. Engineering and construction of a $500 million state-of-the-art plant was started in 1982 and completed in 1985. The process of designing this plant did not involve the operators, but nevertheless the design itself aimed for extensive skill-based operation.

The steel operation was an electric arc furnace that used scrap steel to produce billets, blooms, and ingots according to customer requirements. It could produce 700 different steel alloys. The process involved melting scrap and adding additives to produce the specified steel alloy. The scrap loading and melting systems were computer based, and included systems that selected rail cars of scrap for each batch of steel and analyzed the contents of each rail car to calculate the cost and technical feasibility of a selected mixture of scrap to make a particular batch of steel.

The system also provided estimates of the cost and feasibility of any changes the operator might propose. During the melting operation the computer system provided the operator information on furnace condition, electrical usage, and communications with the metallurgical assay laboratory. The operator had to melt the scrap to a specified state, sample the furnace contents for the metallurgical assay, and move the molten steel to the ladle for alloy mixing. The computer calculated a least-cost mix of alloy additives that gave the molten steel the desired metallurgical qualities. The operator could use the mix planned by the computer or have the system give the cost and quality of other mixtures he or she proposed.

The design of the system was based on an explicit principle of operator control of the process. The system was designed to provide operators with the information and technology necessary to make nearly all production decisions without supervision. It provided operators with a display showing the status of all the heats. At each operation, it provided a computer-calculated "recommended" procedure and an analysis of any operator-proposed changes. There were also manual overrides for all equipment in the process. The system had on-line diagnostic capabilities for operator analysis of equipment problems. It also provided operators the production schedule for the next several days' production. Overall, there was a computer network that gave all levels of production information to operators as well as managers. Operators were even given business information such as materials and operating costs.

The design of the system was based on the principle that the function of the computer was not to make all decisions automatically nor to reduce the operator to a process monitor. Rather, the system was designed to provide the operator with the information and capabilities to determine and execute the optimal process. In most steps of the process, the system calculated the optimal processing parameters based on an algorithm, and the operator had full authority to accept or reject the recommendation, ask for alternatives, or override the system completely based on his or her knowledge of steel making. In essence, the system was designed as a decision support tool for the operator.

The system performance exceeded expectations. The first melt of the system resulted in a saleable product, which was unusual for the first run of a steel plant. The steel exceeded industry standards for dimensional tolerances, surface finish, and purity levels. There was no provision for rework of the product, but only three of the first 125 batches had to be scrapped, and none of the subsequent 3000 batches had to be scrapped. The system was designed to make 12 batches a day, but two and a half years after it began operation, it was able to do 14 batches a day. Labor per ingot-ton was less than 30 percent of the industry average, and energy usage was about a quarter of comparable plants. The division found that by giving workers access to information, a flow of process improvement ideas was created.

CONCLUSION

The textbook review, survey results, and case studies illustrate traditional design principles and a set of emerging practices that have implications for developing skill-based design principles. To develop more effective technology designs, which I argue requires a skill-based approach, it is important to change the implicit assumptions underlying engineers' view of the role of workers.

The prevailing design approaches are based on a mechanistic view of humans. The recent (modest) interest in ergonomics and safety bring the physiological requirements of human activity to the attention of equipment designers, but have not altered the fundamental principles by which engineers conceptualize their goals and objectives. Our case studies show some embryonic changes but also the tenacity of traditional design approaches.

The lockout and skill-based approaches share the goals of efficiency, quality, and safety, but pursue different design strategies to achieve those goals. The traditional approach centralizes analysis, decision making, and process adjustment; it automates wherever possible. The alternative approach pushes decision-making and process adjustment responsibilities down to the worker.

Our survey did not provide systematic evidence on the relative effectiveness of the two approaches, but the interviewees reported that the lockout strategy was successful in only 11 percent of the firms surveyed. The case studies provide at least anecdotal evidence of the superiority of the skill-based design approach.

The steel plant is perhaps the most eloquent example, but the other cases provide indirect evidence of the value of a skill-based design strategy. In the first case, the optics assembly line, there was a genuine concern for the physical well being of the workers, but the design ignored workers' potential contribution to production. This approach was maintained even in the face of demonstrated failures of their automation strategy. The choices presented to the workers as a result of the equipment design led them to compromise safety in order to bolster efficiency. The workers' suggestions to modify the equipment so as to allow them to run the assembly line more effectively were rejected by the engineering staff, who steadfastly held onto their design principles even at exorbitant cost.

The second and third cases of machining illustrate how new technology can require higher levels of skill despite design intentions. The intrinsic properties of the technology, coupled with the nature of production requirements, resulted in greater worker intervention and involvement than planned. It is interesting to note that worker initiative promoted the efficiency of machining operations, even where it was formally prohibited. This is in marked contrast to the traditional machine shop, where workers often restrict their output. The motivating factors appeared to be the opportunity to exercise their skill in programming and the satisfaction of creating an efficient and sometimes elegant program. Machinists also believed they would benefit by increasing the competitiveness of the company.

Stepping back from our survey and cases, it seems apparent that the production environment has changed and that increasingly these changes are being recognized by managers and workers. Design policies have not yet changed to the same degree, but we can nevertheless trace in outline the key points of contrast between the traditional technology-based model and the emergent skill-based model of design (see Table 4.3).

Several related factors suggest that new policies will become increasingly prevalent in the coming era. First, competitive pressures have increased with the internationalization of production and markets. This makes workers' involvement in quality and efficiency improvements more important than in the past. Second, levels of capital investment and productivity have reduced the direct labor component to less than 10 percent of product costs in most industries, so further reductions of direct employment levels or wage rates are less competitively significant than improving machine utilization and product quality. Finally, production systems are being designed as integrated systems, and interactions among system components and operations are thus increasingly complex. While this integration reduces the local autonomy and flexibility, it also increases the consequences of any failures and thus increases the value of workers' problem-solving skills.

The combination of these factors will intensify the pressure to reconsider

Table 4.3. Contrasting Two Design Approaches

Technology-based design	Skill-based design
Productivity is the primary goal.	Productivity and quality are equally important goals.
Productivity is achieved through direct labor reduction.	Productivity and quality are achieved through process improvement, not necessarily direct labor reduction.
Labor is a "risk," a source of error. System performance should be independent of direct labor involvement.	Technology has inherent limitations and risks. Worker intervention to correct machine errors is planned.
Automation requires human intervention limited to monitoring.	Direct labor is utilized for machine supervision and production analysis.
Process improvement is performed exclusively by engineering; information is distributed on a "need-to-know" basis only.	Process improvement requires the skills and knowledge of both engineers and workers. Improvement requires broad access to information at all levels.
Output is standardized through centralization of process settings and modification.	Output is standardized by a short feedback/adjustment loop, which requires decision making at lowest possible level.
The value added by labor is exclusively through task performance (usually physical activity).	Labor adds value by task and process analysis and improvement as well as by task performance.

the role of humans in production and in system design. The standards for competitively effective production are rising, and can only be met if production responsibility is driven down to the shopfloor, to those who can affect the process at the point of production. This will, of necessity, lead to a profound change in design strategies.

Acknowledgments

This paper is based upon research supported by the Ethics and Values Studies section of the National Science Foundation, under Grant No. BBS-8619534, and the Engineering Division of the National Science Foundation, under Grant No. DDM-8604472. The research on the first grant was conducted in collaboration with Stephen Rosenthal and the second with Robert Lund, Albert Bishop, and Ann Newman. Research assistance was provided by Abhijeet Ghatak, Katie Riley, and Amy Silverstein. Paul Adler was most helpful with detailed comments on this paper.

REFERENCES

Adler, Paul (1986). New technologies, new skills. *California Management Review,* Fall.

Alluisi, Earl A. (1987). Human factors technologies—past promises, future issues, in L.S. Mark, J.S. Worm, R.L. Huston (eds.) *Ergonomics and Human Factors: Recent Research*, New York: Springer–Verlag.

Bjorn-Andersen, Niels, and Bo Hedberg (1977). *Designing Information Systems in an Organizational Perspective.* Amsterdam: North–Holland Publishing Company.

Blackler, Frank, and Colin Brown (1986). Alternative models to guide the design and introduction of the new information technologies into work organizations. *J. Occupational Psychol.*, January, 287–313.

Blanchard, Benjamin, and Wolter Fabrycky (1981). *Systems Engineering and Analysis,* Englewood Cliffs, N.J.: Prentice–Hall.

Brodner, Peter (1986). Skill based manufacturing vs. "unmanned factory"—which is superior?" *Int. J. Ind. Ergonomics* 1, 2, Dec., 145–153.

Cherns, Albert (1987). Principles of socio-technical design revisited. *Human Relations* **40**(3), 153–162.

Coulter, Jeffery (1979). *The Social Construction of Mind.* London: Macmillan.

Coulter, Jeffery (1983). *Rethinking Cognitive Learning.* London: Macmillan.

Dreyfus, Hubert (1979). *What Computers Can't Do.* New York: Harper and Row.

Ehn, Pelle (1989). *Work-Oriented Design of Computer Artifacts.* Hillsdale, N.J.: Lawrence Erlbaum.

Ellis, David O., and Fred J. Ludwig (1962). *Systems Philosophy.* Englewood Cliffs, N.J.: Prentice–Hall.

Gibson, John E. (1968). *Introduction to Engineering Design.* New York: Holt, Rinehart and Winston.

Hedberg, Bo, and Enid Mumford (1975). The design of computer systems: Man's vision of man as an integral part of the system design process, in Enid Mumford and Harold Sackman (eds.). *Human Choice and Computers,* New York: American Elsevier Publishing Company.

Hindhede, Uffe (1983). *Machine Design Fundamentals—A Practical Approach.* New York: John Wiley & Sons.

Hirschhorn, Larry (1984). *Beyond Mechanization.* Cambridge, Mass.: MIT Press.

Jaikumar, Ramchandran (1986). Postindustrial manufacturing. *Harvard Business Review,* November–December, 69–76.

Kusterer, Ken (1978). *Know-How on the Job,* Boulder, Co.: Westview Press.

Lund, Robert, Albert Bishop, Harold Salzman, and Ann Newman (1990). Human/machine design in manufacturing. Final Report to NSF, Engineering Division.

Majchrzak, Ann (1988). *The Human Side of Factory Automation.* San Francisco: Jossey-Bass.

Markus, Lynne M., and Jeffery Pfeffer (1983). Power and the design and implementation of accounting and control systems. *Accounting, Organizations and Society* **8**, 205–18.

Mumford, Enid (1987). Sociotechnical system design—evolving theory and practice, in G. Bjerknes, P. Ehn and M. Kyng (eds.). *Computers and Democracy—A Scandinavian Challenge.* Aldershot, UK: Avery.

Noble, David F. (1977). *America by Design.* New York: Alfred Knopf.

Noble, David F. (1984). *Forces of Production: A Social History of Industrial Automation.* New York: Oxford University Press.

Perrow, Charles (1983). The organizational context of human factors engineering. *Administrative Science Quarterly,* December, 521–541.

Rosenthal, Stephen, and Harold Salzman (1989). Values in the design of new technology: The case of software. Report to the National Science Foundation, Ethics and Values Studies Section, August.

Rouse, William B., and William J. Cody (1987). On the design of man–machine systems: Principles, practices, and prospects. *IFAC World Congress*, München.

Salzman, Harold (1989). Computer-aided design: limitations in automating design and drafting. *IEEE Transactions on Engineering Management*, November **36,** 4.

Skinner, Wickham (1986). The productivity paradox. *Harvard Business Review*, July–August, 55–59.

Vidosic, Joseph P. (1969). *Elements of Design Engineering.* New York: The Ronald Press.

Walton, Richard, and Gerald Susman (1987). People policies for new machines. *Harvard Business Review*, March–April, 98–106.

Zuboff, Shoshana (1988). *In the Age of the Smart Machine.* New York: Basic Books.

CHAPTER 5

Scandinavian Design: On Participation and Skill

PELLE EHN

In Scandinavia we have for two decades been concerned with participation and skill in the design and use of computer-based systems. Collaboration between researchers and trade unions on this theme, starting with the pioneering work of Kristen Nygaard and the Norwegian Metal Workers' Union, and including leading projects like DEMOS and UTOPIA, has been based on a strong commitment to the idea of industrial democracy. This kind of politically significant, interdisciplinary, and action-oriented research on resources and control in the processes of design and use has contributed to what is often viewed abroad as a distinctively Scandinavian approach to systems design.

This Scandinavian approach might be called a work-oriented design approach. Democratic participation and skill enhancement, and not only productivity and product quality, are themselves considered objective of design. [Based on the two research projects, DEMOS and UTOPIA, I have elaborated this approach in detail in *Work-Oriented Design of Computer Artifacts* (1989). This paper is based on that work.]

Two important features of participatory design shape its trajectory as a design strategy. The political one is obvious. Participatory design raises questions of democracy, power, and control in the workplace. In this sense it is a deeply controversial issue, especially from a management point of view. The other major feature is technical—its promise that the participation of skilled users in the design process can contribute importantly to successful design and high-quality products. Some experiences, perhaps most developed in Scandinavia, support this prediction and contribute to the growing interest in participatory design in the United States and other countries; by contrast, "expert" design strategies have too often turned out to be failures in terms of the usability of the resulting systems. These two features together suggest that there should be a strong link between the skill and product quality aspect of user participation and the democracy and control aspect, or else participatory design will be a deeply controversial issue from the point of view of the employees and trade unions.

The trade-union-oriented democracy aspect of skill and participation in design is discussed in the first part of the chapter. I start with an introduction to the concept of industrial democracy and an overview of the Scandinavian setting. After this background, research projects forming the Scandinavian work-oriented design approach are presented and discussed.

In the second part, I focus on the role of skill and participation in design as a practical activity. This focus has grown out of a dissatisfaction with traditional theories and methods for systems design. Not only has traditional design been oriented towards deskilling workers, but this traditional approach has been encouraged by a theoretical assumption, namely, that skill can be exhaustively characterized by a purely formal description. The political critique of the design process discussed in the first part leads to a theoretical critique of the scientific rationality of methods for systems description and systems development. In the second part, a philosophical foundation for a skill-based participatory design approach is outlined based on the language-game philosophy of Ludwig Wittgenstein. Taken together, these critiques shape the Scandinavian work-oriented design approach, an approach based on an emancipatory perspective and encompassing both the inner everyday life of skill-based participatory design and the societal and cultural conditions regulating this activity.

DESIGNING FOR DEMOCRACY AT WORK

The democratic ideal is a beautiful human invention: Every human should have the right to participate equally in decisions concerning his or her life. In practice this freedom has always been limited. The first democrats, the ancient Greeks, constrained participation to free men, excluding women and a class of slaves. The modern democratic state in capitalistic societies has, in theory and in many practical aspects, removed these constraints. Representative democracy is a formal arrangement for securing decisions in the interest of the majority, and often manages to assure freedom for minority groups.

In many sectors of life, however, democratic rights remain merely formal, without real content for those concerned. In this paper, I am concerned with democracy behind the factory gates and office doors—democracy at work.

Fundamentally, democracy at work or industrial democracy concerns freedom, another value-laden concept. It concerns *freedom from* the constraints imposed by the market economy and the power of capital. And it also concerns *freedom to* practically formulate and carry out particular projects that further democratize work. Attempts to democratize at work address:

1. The power of capital owners to control how resources are used, such as economic goals, structural changes in the company, investments in new technology, choice of business idea, and product range;
2. Owners' organizational and technological power to decide how the production process in general is organized and how technology is designed and used;
3. Their power over the workers to decide how work is to be organized, planned, and controlled;
4. Their power to limit an individual's autonomy at work, including the individual's choice of tools and pace of work (Dahlström, 1983).

The research projects on work-oriented design that I will discuss in this paper concerned industrial democracy in all these aspects. They aimed both at a better understanding of freedom from managerial control and at freedom to develop and implement strategies for democratization at work. In particular, the studies looked at the design of computer-based systems in the context of democratization of work in Scandinavia.

The Scandinavian Setting

Scandinavian countries have for quite some time been well known for their distinctive industrial relations. The following features are particularly noteworthy:

1. A highly educated and relatively homogeneous workforce;
2. A high level of unionization;
3. Strong national trade union federations;
4. Centralized negotiation systems;
5. Large social democratic parties with strong links to the the national trade union federations of blue (and some white) collar workers, parties which for long periods of time have led the governments;
6. Relations between trade unions and employers that are, to a large extent, regulated by laws and central agreements;
7. A positive attitude to new technology from the trade union federations, at least since World War II and despite some opposition at the local level, based on the assumption that job loss due to the introduction of new technology would be compensated by active labor market government policies.

These features have contributed to the relative stability of Scandinavian labor relations and the relatively high degree of workplace democratization:

> Democracy [in the United States] stops at the office door and the factory gate. Western Europe is extending democracy into working life. Democratization of

> work has gone further in Scandinavia than elsewhere in Europe. Job redesign projects, codetermination arrangements, health and safety legislation, employee representatives on corporate boards. (Einhorn and Logue, 1982)

These historical factors help explain the emergence of the participatory trade-union-based work-oriented approach to design of computer artifacts. But just as important is the other side of the coin: The Scandinavian countries are still market economies, and an integral part of international capitalism. Workers and their unions therefore confront basically the same forces of rationalization of work and technology as those in other market economies.

Laws on Democratization of Work

The 1970s was the decade when democracy at work truly appeared on the agenda for industrial policy. In that decade, an intensive debate took place in trade unions, and a number of new labor laws were enacted (Fry, 1986).

In Norway, employees obtained the right to elect one-third of the members of the so-called "company assembly." In 1975, the first collective agreement on the development and introduction of computer-based systems was concluded, giving the trade unions the right to appoint so-called data shop stewards. In 1977, the Norwegian Work Environment Act gave workers extensive rights to stop production that was dangerous to their health. New codetermination procedures for work environment issues were established, and a system of sanctions was defined for employers who did not fulfil the new work environment requirements.

The Swedish "work democracy package" in the 1970s revised existing legislation and introduced several new acts. The work democracy package included the act concerning Labor Representatives on Company Boards, the Companies Act concerning disclosure of financial information, the act concerning the Status of Shop Stewards, and the Work Environment Act.

Finally, and most important, the Joint Regulation Act (MBL) concerning workers and trade unions' right to codetermination in production issues such as design and the use of new technology and work organization was enacted in January 1977. It was this law that the late Prime Minister Olof Palme described as the greatest reform in Swedish society since the introduction of the universal right to vote. In practice this act's impact has turned out to be far less dramatic, and as a result there was considerable disappointment among many union members who had received the impression that the act was the decisive step towards democracy at work.

Nevertheless, MBL did create new conditions for the design and use of computer-based systems and other production equipment. Article 11 stipulates that the employer has to negotiate with the local union before making "major changes" in production. Article 12 give the union the right to initiate negotiations on any production issue. Articles 18 and 19 stipulate the right of unions to have access to documents to which management refers in negotiation, and to receive information continually on production issues, their employer's financial situation, and personnel policy.

These were important changes encouraging democratic control over the introduction and use of new technology, but they were limited. The Act gave the employer the exclusive right to make decisions when trade unions and management could not reach an agreement in negotiations. Furthermore, the "major changes" in production to which the Act referred are open to interpretation, as is the obligation to inform, which may or may not include early plans, say, to introduce a computer-based system.

Finally, Article 32 should be mentioned. This article concerns the right for trade unions to negotiate agreements on "the management and assignment of working duties, and the conduct of the operation at large." The number of this article was chosen to parallel Article 32 in the Swedish Employers' Confederation (SAF) Statutes, which requires its members to retain the right of decision when entering collective agreements. The Act stipulates that if a collective codetermination agreement (MBA) is reached, the union has "priority of interpretation" over disputed issues covered by the agreement until the dispute is settled in negotiations. This gives the trade unions the opportunity to postpone decisions. However, the main idea behind Article 32 was that central agreements should be negotiated, and that local agreements should be developed on the basis of these agreements.

In 1978, the first central collective agreement on codetermination was reached in the public sector. Not until 1982 was an agreement reached in private industry. By that time the forms of codetermination had become more concrete, but the trade unions' democratization offensive had to a significant extent faded out. What started as a trade union response to local demands for democratization in the late 1960s, often expressed as wildcat strikes concerning the work environment and the introduction of new technology, had assumed a form sanctioned by parliament, national trade union federations, and national employers' federations.

The wildcat strike by the workers' collective of iron miners at the Ikab mines in the north of Sweden was the starting point for these democratization reforms that concerned not only the democratization of the work place, but also internal trade union democracy. The work-oriented design approach emerged in the midst of the practical implementation of these reforms.

The Trade Unions as Vehicles for Industrial Democracy

In Scandinavia, trade unions have served as the vehicles for industrial democracy by advancing the interests of the workers' collective.

The workers' collective is a concept developed by the Norwegian sociologist Sverre Lysgaard (1961) to designate the informal defense organization of workers in the workplace. The workers' collective is manifested as shared norms concerning how workers should behave in relation to management and the rationality of technical–economic organization. The norms shape workers' responses to management's efforts to intensify work, to tighten control of the labor process, and to rationalize the use of new technology. As hired labor, the workers are also part of the technical–economic organization of the workplace, but the workers' collective reflects workers' response to their subordinated position in this technical–economic organization.

According to Lysgaard, the degree of strength in the workers' collective comes from the "we-feeling" created by shared experiences. The basis for this we-feeling is physical proximity at the workplace, which makes interaction possible; similarity in working conditions, which makes the workers identify with each other; and a similar problem situation that they interpret in a similar way. The norms of the workers' collective define what it means to be a "good work mate" as well as what it means to be a "traitor." The workers' collective is a "buffer" between the individual worker and management's interests in shaping the technical–economic organization of the workplace.

However, the workers' collective has two major weaknesses when compared with institutionalized forms of industrial democracy. First, the workers' collective can only informally defend the individual worker. It is not an acknowledged formal organization, meaning that it has no formal organizational power for achieving structural changes in the workplace. Second, as a defensive organization responding to management initiative, it lacks the organizational ability to formulate and carry through an offensive strategy for changes in the direction of industrial democracy.

The trade union movement is a formal organization through which workers' interests can be developed and implemented. This by no means implies that trade unions always represent the interests of the workers' collective. Trade unions have a hierarchical structure, and the gap between shop-floor experiences and central decisions can be huge. Furthermore, the trade union movement is far from homogeneous. Different groups of workers have different interests. There are differences in interests and power between skilled and unskilled workers, between men and women, between workers organized in different trade unions, etc. In the design and introduction of new technology, these differences can manifest themselves as jurisdictional disputes and conflicts concerning skill development, work organization, and the right to operate the new technology. The problem of solidarity is a central one in the trade union movement's struggle for industrial democracy.

Nevertheless, trade unions have served the interest of the workers' collective in two ways that are important for the present argument: They have been an essential instrument for workers in wage negotiations, and they have been a key instrument for furthering democracy in society as a whole.

Unions and Design

The design and use of new technology requires new trade union activities. Traditionally, trade unions have focused on what Åke Sandberg (forthcoming) calls *distribution* issues such as wages, working hours, and general terms of employment. Such issues are characterized by:

1. Relatively well-developed union objectives;
2. Clearly formulated demands, often quantified;
3. Demands based on the workers' own practical experience; and
4. Clearly delimited, short negotiation cycles.

In contrast, the design and use of computers are, in Sandberg's terminology, *production* issues. They are characterized by:

1. Only vaguely formulated union objectives;
2. Demands that are difficult to quantify;
3. Practical on-the-job experiences that must be supplemented by more theoretical, technical/scientific knowledge;
4. Design processes that stretch over long periods of time; and
5. Negotiation situations that are difficult to define clearly.

As Sandberg points out, the design of new models for work seem to require the consideration of more deep-seated and qualitative aspects than can easily be fitted into the traditional trade union strategy or the traditional management–labor negotiation process.

What are the key elements of a union technology strategy? Obviously, one element is decentralization of decision making and participation in the design process, which can give workers more influence and better access to important information. However, the position we took in DEMOS, UTOPIA, and the other projects that constituted the work-oriented design approach was that decentralization of decision making and a participative approach to the design process are not sufficient.

Our position is based on a recognition of the different interests of management and workers concerning industrial democracy. We rejected the harmony view of organizations, according to which conflicts in an organization are seen as stemming from misunderstandings and can resolved by good analysis. We also rejected an understanding of design as a rational decision making process based on common goals. Instead, our research was based on a conflict view of industrial organizations in our society. In the interest of emancipation, we deliberately made the choice of siding with workers and their organizations, supporting the development of their resources for a change towards democracy at work (Sandberg, 1979; Ehn and Sandberg, 1979). We found it necessary to identify with the we-feeling of the workers' collective rather than with the overall we-feeling that "modern management" attempts to create in order to elicit greater effort from the work force. Although trade unions had a structure that was problematic for functioning as vehicles for designing for democracy at work, they were also the only social force that in practice could be a carrier of that ideal.

From Sociotechnical Solutions to Work-Oriented Design

It is difficult to overstate the influence of the sociotechnical approach on user participation and industrial democracy initiatives in Scandinavia in the early 1970s (Kubicek, 1983). Hence, it may appear paradoxical that some Scandinavian researchers and trade unions developed the work-oriented approach to democratization of design and use of computer-based systems in opposition to the sociotechnical tradition rather than within that tradition. I will try to explain why, and outline the main points of this alternative, "collective resource" approach.

Although initially implemented in Norway, the widespread use of the sociotechnical approach in Scandinavian industry took place in Sweden. Thoralf Qvale, in one of the evaluations of the sociotechnical approach to democratization in Norway, gives the following explanation:

> Apart from the researchers, there are very few persons trying to convey experience from one company to another. In Sweden "job satisfaction" and "productivity" have been the slogans, and a network of employers/production engineers have taken care of the diffusion. In Norway, the slogans were "industrial democracy" and "participation," and the union networks were expected to play a central part. As explained, ideological support has come from the top of LO (the Norwegian national trade union federation), but the practical involvement from the individual unions' officials has systematically been lacking. (Qvale, 1976)

In the late 1960s in Sweden, rapid technological and structural change was considered a problem by both the trade unions and employers. The unions were concerned about deskilling, lack of influence, health, and safety. Employers experienced personnel problems in recruitment, turnover, and absenteeism, and production problems in efficiency, planning, and quality. Both parties came to see the Tayloristic organization of production—its narrowly specialized jobs and separation of conception and execution—as the source of these problems. The sociotechnical experiments in Norway seemed a promising way forward.

Similar experiments were initiated by the central unions and employer organizations jointly in both private and public sectors in Sweden. Increased job satisfaction and higher productivity were considered equally important goals in these tests. Several of the experiments that started in the late 1960s came up with interesting ideas on work organization and democratic participation, but practical implementation was a different story, as explained by Åke Sandberg:

> However, the second phase of deciding upon an actual program of change made manifest differences of interest: management was primarily seeking solutions to personnel problems and possibilities for better control of the wages, whereas unions viewed the experiments as part of a strategy for democratization and union influence at various levels.   (Sandberg, 1982)

Most of the Swedish sociotechnical experiments were controlled by local management and coordinated by the Technical Department of the Swedish Employers' Confederation (SAF). The employers were obviously satisfied with the sociotechnical approach but not with the joint experiments. The LO (the Swedish national trade union federation) was also skeptical of joint work, as expressed in a program document:

> This method of working proved difficult to implement. Later, when the conflict of views between the two sides with regard to industrial democracy development became more manifest, the problems grew greater. Within the private sector, SAF drew its own conclusions from this fact and set up its own development projects with the aid of its Technical Department. In its development projects, SAF stressed the individual in a form which complicated collective solutions and the possibilities available to the trade union movement.   (Swedish Federation of Trade Unions, 1977).

In 1975, SAF launched a new sociotechnical strategy. The Technical Department of SAF coordinated the "new factory" project, which aimed at creating more stable production systems based on the principle of coordinated independence of small subsystems (Arguren and Edgren, 1979). This principle was not new—it came from basic sociotechnical theory—but this project used a different strategy. On the one hand, it went further than earlier projects—it did not accept production technology as given, but as something that should be designed to allow the control of semiautonomous groups rather than individuals. On the other hand, changes were restricted to the shopfloor production level, and the vertical division of labor was not altered at all. Management's overall control was therefore strengthened. Democratic participation was not one of the aims of these experiments (Kronlund, 1978). The internationally known production technology at the Volvo Kalmar plant is as good an example as any of these new experiments. Participation for democracy was not an aim of the design (Ehn and Sandberg, 1979).

As we understand it, democratization of design and the use of computer-based systems in the Scandinavian setting had to be based on strong local union involvement. In practice, the sociotechnical approach had failed to support such democratization. The first action program on industrial democracy and computers from LO, issued in 1975, outlined the situation and union strategy:

> The workers and the trade unions are not satisfied with managers and their experts who say they develop systems for planning and control which take human beings into consideration by paying attention to needs for self-realization and the social impact of technical systems, etc. On the contrary, the unions must work for a situation that makes it possible for workers to develop their own organizational and knowledge resources. This creates the capability to scrutinize and influence, via negotiations, the various aspects of corporate planning and control, and, by extension, to develop worker-controlled systems. Thus, the present situation in organizations makes increasing demands upon the commitment and knowledge of the workers. The crucial point is whether these demands become absorbed in an employers' strategy for decentralization and so-called autonomous groups, or whether they will be developed within a workers' strategy for democratization, transcending the level of the work organization. (Swedish Federation of Trade Unions, 1975).

This critique of the sociotechnical approach should not be seen as a complete rejection of all aspects of the sociotechnical approach. Many of the sociotechnical tools are extremely useful in analyzing work organization and production technology, and the job requirements and group autonomy criteria are, when taken seriously, important criteria for democracy at work. The problem is that these requirements have often disappeared in the practical application of the approach. This flaw reflects questionable assumptions of harmony between social forces and a lack of sensitivity to the pervasive influence of the asymmetrical distribution of power. The critique is therefore not directed at sociotechnical design methods but at its theory and practice in the context of the democratization of work. We should also note that over the past decade the sociotechnical approach has evolved in a much more participatory and less manipulative direction (Gustavsen, 1985; Hedberg, 1980), making it more of an instrument for democratic design.

In the early 1970s, however, the sociotechnical approach seemed inadequate for democratizing the design and use of computer-based systems in the workplace. We had to look for an alternative based on a historical, social, and political understanding of the Scandinavian situation—an alternative that allowed the trade unions to play a major role. These were basic criteria in the emerging work-oriented approach to the design of computers.

The NJMF Project

In 1970, the Norwegian Iron and Metal Workers Union (NJMF) decided to initiate research of its own. When the NJMF project was first set up, the design was quite traditional. It involved a steering committee, a project group, and associated local unions at four different work places. The associated local unions were to act as reference groups. The project group consisted of two researchers and two staff members from the national union, and, according to the research plan, the researchers were to carry out a number of investigations in close cooperation with the two other members of the project group. Those investigations included:

1. A study of two or three computer-based planning and control systems;
2. A survey of the goals of the union in areas such as working conditions and control of organizations;
3. Formulation of demands on computer-based systems based on the survey;
4. An evaluation of the need for knowledge within NJMF in the areas of planning, control, and data processing, and possibly development of teaching material.

However, as the project progressed, it turned out to be impossible for the union people involved to apply the project's findings to the daily work at the factories, the local unions, and the national unions. The original project design had to a large extent been copied from a traditional research project approach used by managers and management consultants in a context where the goals were clear and the means for applying the project results had been discussed for decades. For the unions, there had been no extensive discussions on planning, control, and computer-based systems, and there were no established or clear goals for their involvement.

A completely new research strategy had to be developed. In the new strategy, the most important change was the new role to be played by the local unions. Instead of supporting the researchers, the researchers would support them. The local unions would choose the topics for study from important problems at the workplace, and they would receive assistance from external consultants as well as consultants and other resources provided by the company. At each of the four workplaces, a number of investigative groups consisting of union members was formed to:

1. Accumulate knowledge about planning, control, and data processing;
2. Investigate selected problems in these areas, that were considered of special importance by the local unions; and
3. Take actions directed at management to change the use of new technology.

The groups always began with discussions of practical workplace problems, problems with which every worker was familiar. Attempts to analyze and to solve these problems led to the search for new knowledge and the start of an educational process. The groups met regularly, for two to three hours at least twice a week, and between the meetings, the members did a lot of "homework," such as preparing proposals, discussing ideas with fellow workers, and participating in different kinds of educational activities.

One investigation group made evaluations of some of the computer-based planning and control systems in the company, including an on-line production information system under development. The other investigation groups evaluated experiences of participation in the planning of a new plant, made proposals for reorganizing one of the main assembly lines, and drafted a company policy action program for the local union.

One of the most tangible, and certainly the most widely studied and publicized outcome, of the NJMF project was the earlier-mentioned data agreements. These agreements primarily regulate the design and introduction of computer-based systems, especially the availability of information. The first agreement, a local one, was signed at the beginning of 1974. It was followed in April 1975 by a central agreement between the Norwegian Trade Union Federation and the Norwegian Confederation of Employers. A large number of local agreements soon followed, as did the election of numerous so-called data shop stewards, a new kind of shop steward introduced in the central agreement.

Among other things, the central agreement stated:

> Through the shop stewards, the management must keep the employees orientated about matters that lie within the area of the agreement in such a way that the shop stewards can put forward their points of view as early as possible and before the management puts its decisions into effect. The orientation must be given in a well-arranged form and in a language that can be understood by nonspecialists. It is a condition that the representatives of the employees have the opportunity to make themselves acquainted with general questions concerning the influence of computer-based systems on matters that are of importance to the employees. The representatives must have access to all documentation about software and hardware within the area of the agreement.   (Norwegian Employers Federation and Norwegian Federation of Trade Unions, 1975)

The NJMF project inspired several new research projects throughout Scandinavia and the development of a research tradition of cooperation between researchers and workers and their trade unions. This tradition is known as the *collective resource approach,* or the Scandinavian approach to work-oriented design.

The DEMOS Project

In Sweden, the DEMOS project on "trade unions, industrial democracy, and computers" started in 1975, and lasted four years. The Swedish Trade Union Confederation (LO) supported the project, with its "data council" acting as an advisory group. The project was carried out by an interdisciplinary research team (with competence in computer science, sociology, economics, and engineering) in cooperation with workers and their trade unions at four different enterprises—a daily newspaper, a locomotive repair shop, a metal factory, and a department store.

This cooperative effort tried to identify possibilities for the unions to influence the design and use of computer-based systems at the local level in the companies. It emphasized what the unions could do to safeguard and promote their members' interests in meaningful work when the technology, the work organization, and the supervision of work are altered. As a complement to these local activities, the project also sought to examine obstacles and limits confronting this democratization process.

The design work at a locomotive engine repair shop in Örebro serves as an example of the local approach in the DEMOS project. In 1974, the State Employees' Union was informed by the State Railway's central administration that a computer-based planning system, ISA-KLAR, would be introduced in its work shops in, among other places, Örebro. The main responsibility of the repair shop in Örebro was engine maintenance.

Management wanted to use ISA-KLAR to adapt the general maintenance system to local circumstances, and, in the process, to test ISA-KLAR. The union had won an elimination of piecework at the repair shop, and management hoped ISA-KLAR would help it redesign the workplace and develop automatic work orders and instructions to direct employees.

To implement ISA-KLAR, management formed project groups that included at least one trade union representative each. These groups interviewed workers in the workplace on how they carried out their jobs. The workers' tasks were then analyzed into smaller steps and the information coupled with an MTM database compiled from several big companies. ISA-KLAR used the combined information to specify detailed work steps, including their timing and sequence, and the tools to be used. The level of detail was very fine. The computer generated work sequences such as: "(1) get tools A and B, (2) go to carriage, (3) crawl into position, (4) remove cotter pin, (5) remove washer and bolt, (6) repeat steps 3 through 5 for other bolts, (7) remove bolts, etc."

After two years' work with ISA-KLAR, the union turned to DEMOS to resolve dissatisfaction with its lack of influence and information on the project. In March 1976, the union established an investigative group of its own with 14 participants. At first, the local union asked for researchers from DEMOS to serve only as "data experts" to check the timings of the various tasks that were to be incorporated into the computer-based system for measuring performance. In subsequent discussions, the union researchers agreed that the key implication of ISA-KLAR—that work on the shopfloor could be deskilled—was a far more significant issue for investigation than the timing of steps in the performance of various tasks.

They shifted the investigation's focus to the whole question of production planning. There was further agreement that the union should conduct its own investigation, using the DEMOS researchers, separate from that of the management project groups. The DEMOS researchers would provide technical expertise in an analysis of the computer-based system and a structure for the union study. The union's basic investigation was completed in June 1977. Followup by the local union committee and researchers consumed another year.

The group's findings were summarized and transformed by the union into demands for local agreements of codetermination and rationalization. As a first step, the group issued a report describing the current work situation, pointing out what was good and what was bad. This description was then used as a basis for further studies regarding planning, control, and computer use, as well as for collective agreements within the Joint Regulation Act (MBL). It should be emphasized that the investigation was initiated before the introduction of MBL.

The report stressed that the changeover from piecework to a system of fixed monthly wages was extremely important, not only in terms of group solidarity among the workers and job satisfaction, but also in terms of the quality of production. Lack of planning and an uneven rate of work on the engines had created major problems, and the fact that neither the tools nor the spare parts were always available had been a great source of irritation at all workshops. Too much time was taken up searching for tools and spare parts. The poorly maintained work facilities had caused a number of problems in the work environment, such as draughts and working positions that were damaging workers' health. Uncertainty over the consequences of ISA-KLAR did not make the working conditions any better, and there was great dissatisfaction about the lack of information workers were receiving.

The investigation was completed by studies of various topical issues important to the trade union. These studies gave rise to a special group on planning, control, and computer use. This group compared the principles of Taylorism to the current work situation at the workshops and reviewed basic facts on computers, design, and planning methods in order to broaden worker discussions and to elicit views from as many members as possible.

One demand of the union—presented in various management project groups—was that problems with the planning, material administration, and work organization be solved before any discussion of computer-based time measurement. However, it became obvious that the union's chances of influencing the design of production planning by participating in the project groups were more or less illusory. Under the cover of technical discussions, management and its consultants continued to develop ISA-KLAR. The basic question of how planning in the shops would be conducted in the future never appeared on the agenda.

In response to management's investigation, and based on its own analysis of ISA-KLAR, the union's investigation group concluded that the system had to be stopped until an agreement on codetermination could be reached that would regulate its design and use. The local union demanded, and got, central union support for this position.

Management officially accepted the position of the union and appointed planning groups to "construct and test a planning model" for two different items in the production process (components on bogies and work on certain types of engines). Each of the planning groups consisted of two repair workers, a supervisor, and a production technician.

The investigation group of the union collaborated with the two planning groups. It appointed workers from its own investigation on ISA-KLAR as union participants and supported them. In practice the repair workers themselves did the design work. A technical specialist was asked to look over the proposals, and only minor adjustments were made.

Although the planning groups had very little time at their disposal, they managed to present concrete propositions on changes in work organization as well as other conditions. Their basic proposition was that repair workers should be granted flexibility in their work—predemolition, demolition, test of cracks, welding, installation, mounting of wheel axles, and final installation. Flexibility meant that all workers would participate in the entire work cycle, from demolition to final installation, and that all workers should all be able to handle all the tasks. The main emphases were on skill, training, and job rotation. Special emphasis was placed on the work teams' right to plan their own work. This was considered necessary not only as a move towards democratic work organization but also as a measure facilitating production.

The repair workers claimed that their proposition had demonstrated that they could have a well-functioning workplace without ISA-KLAR. The local union felt that their approach could serve as a model for other workplaces as well. Their experiences were reflected in May 1978 in a number of demands that served as a basis for local agreements on rationalization and codetermination on the design and use of computer artifacts. The demands were adjusted to MBL and to a central collective agreement on codetermination. Among the demands were:

1. That long-term planning be conducted by management for (among other things) technical development, training, and staff policy;
2. That repair and maintenance work be carried out within the company;
3. That rationalization not reduce the requirements for skilled repair personnel; and
4. That rationalization not result in work measurement of individuals or groups or in incentive payments of any kind.

With special regard to the design process, the union demanded

1. That directives for a project be negotiable before the project starts;
2. That design methods be approved by the union;
3. That investigations in the design work not only include technical and economic considerations, but also changes in employment, work environment, work organization, and possibilities for cooperation, codetermination, and development in the daily work;
4. That the union be provided the necessary resources for conducting a parallel independent investigation;
5. That the cost for these resources be calculated as part of the investment in the rationalization;
6. That participation by trade union representatives and users be a natural aspect of the design work, and that it be planned to allow this; and
7. That participants receive what the union regards as the necessary training to participate in the design work.

What has been the long-term impact of the DEMOS investigation work at the repair shop in Örebro? We ourselves did not conduct such evaluations, but a report (Brulin, 1988) from an ongoing democratization project at the State Railroad sums up developments during the decade since DEMOS in the following way:

> The trade union work in Örebro from DEMOS onward has given a trade union perspective that perhaps is best formulated in the title of the DEMOS report: We are opposed to Detailed Control. The collective agreement on design and use of computer-based systems created conditions for a dialogue with management. The repair shop in Örebro got a new managing director with a view on efficient organization that, to a great extent, overlaps the trade union perspective. In summary, as we understand it, what happened and is happening in Örebro can be explained by the above-mentioned three motivating forces: a trade union perspective, use of the collective agreement on design and use of computer-based systems, and a real dialogue with management.

The UTOPIA Project

Although growing, the extent and impact of research on designing for democratization in NJMF, DEMOS and similar projects did not meet initial expectations. It seemed that one could only influence the introduction of technology, training, and the organization of work to a certain degree. From a union perspective, important aspects for workers such as the opportunities to develop skills and to increase influence on work organization were limited. Societal constraints, especially those of power and resources, had been underestimated. In addition, the existing technology presented significant limits to finding desirable alternative local solutions.

To broaden the scope of available technology, we decided to try to supplement the existing elements of the work-oriented approach with union-based efforts to design new technology. The main idea of the first projects, to support democratization of the design process, was complemented by the idea of designing tools and environments for skilled work and good-quality products and services. To try out these ideas, the UTOPIA project was started in in 1981 as a cooperation between the Nordic Graphic Workers' Union and researchers in Sweden and Denmark with experience from the first generation of work-oriented design projects. It was a research project on the trade-union-based design of, and training in, computer technology and work organization. The research focused on page makeup and image processing in the newspaper industries. In the Scandinavian languages, UTOPIA is an acronym for Training, Technology, and Products from a Quality of Work Perspective.

Besides working directly in the project group, the Scandinavian graphic workers' unions followed and supported the project through a reference group consisting of representatives from Sweden, Denmark, Finland, and Norway, appointed by the Nordic Graphic Workers' Union (NGU). At various stages, the project involved the computer supplier Liber/Tips and the newspaper Aftonbladet in Stockholm.

In the UTOPIA project, we developed a design approach that we called the tool perspective (Ehn and Kyng, 1984; see also Bødker, forthcoming, and Kammersgaard, 1985). The tool perspective was deeply influenced by the way the design of tools takes place within traditional crafts. The idea is that new computer-based tools should be designed as an extension of the traditional practical understanding of tools and materials used within a given craft or profession. Design must therefore be carried out by the common efforts of skilled, experienced users and design professionals. Users possess the needed practical understanding but lack insight into new technical possibilities. The designer must understand the specific labor process that uses a tool. Computer-based tools present special challenges because they are technically complex but, if designed well, can be simple and powerful for the skilled worker.

In the UTOPIA project, we tried such a process of mutual learning. Graphics workers learned about the technical possibilities and constraints of computer technology, while we as designers learned about their craft or profession. Initially, the group worked to build a mutual understanding of the specific labor processes of the profession, of the design situation, and of the technical possibilities and limitations. Apart from discussions, visits to workplaces employing different generations of technology and visits to research laboratories and vendors proved to be important early activities.

However, as designers we ran into severe difficulties when we tried to communicate with the graphic workers using traditional approaches such as data or information flows. The situation drastically improved when we shifted towards a design-by-doing approach. With the use of mockups and other prototyping design artifacts, the skilled workers could actively participate in the design process and express their craft skills by actually doing page makeup. (The theoretical foundation of the tool perspective and these design methods will be discussed in the second part of this chapter.)

The UTOPIA project was in many ways a success story. An appreciative article in *Technology Review* concluded:

> So the impact of UTOPIA is continuing to expand, and the idea that workers and their unions have an important role in the design of new technology is reaching a wider and wider audience. Today Scandinavia. Tomorrow, perhaps, the rest of the world. (Howard, 1985)

However, as in all success stories, UTOPIA had its share of failures as well. The failures were due to the limited resources in Scandinavian countries rather than to limitations of the model itself. The system, TIPS, was tried at several newspaper test sites, but before final development as a market product, the vendor ran short of capital and was forced to sell the rights to the system to another company interested mainly in image processing. These experiences indicate that a shortage of both technological competence and financial resources within small Scandinavian countries may keep them from successfully competing in the international technological race.

The UTOPIA project clearly showed that the latest technology may be designed and put into use to improve, not decrease, the skills of graphics workers. Whether the Scandinavian newspaper owners will exploit the possibilities for a constructive discussion on technology, organization, and training depends to a great extent upon whether the graphics workers and journalists succeed in overcoming their professional clash of interests and develop a common strategy.

The historical study conducted by the project provides some insight into this. New technology creates "demarcation disputes" between professional groups as well as between trade unions. The UTOPIA project demonstrated that solutions can, however, be found. For newspapers, there are technical and organizational alternatives that do not harm any professional group and that ensure product quality and reasonable efficiency. Nevertheless, the lack of trade union cooperation—rather than the technology, the newspaper owners, or the equipment vendors—may become the decisive factor frustrating the dream of UTOPIA.

The design process in the UTOPIA project was really utopian. The preconditions for such a design process are not present in corporate business as we know it today. Resources for skilled workers, trade union staff, and computer and social scientists to work together over a long period of time designing tools in the interest of the end users do not generally exist as yet, not even in Scandinavia. UTOPIA was not only a challenge to design, but also to a more democratic working life.

Other Projects

The NJMF, DEMOS, and UTOPIA projects are by no means the only projects of the participatory work-oriented design approach, nor is the approach restricted to the design and use of computer-based systems. Some other projects within or related to this Scandinavian tradition are:

1. The DUE project on "democracy, education, and computer-based systems" was a sister project to DEMOS carried out in Denmark (Kyng and Matthiassen, 1982).
2. The Dairy Project, which was conducted by architects but used methods and perspectives similar to the DEMOS and DUE projects (Steen and Ullmark, 1982).
3. The PAAS project, which in addition to contributing to a theoretical understanding of changes of skills when computer artifacts are used also contributed to methods for trade union design work (Göranzon, 1984).
4. The Bank Project, which was conducted by researchers originally from the sociotechnical tradition, although they worked closely with trade unions and with methods and perspectives very similar to the work-oriented design projects (Hedberg and Mehlmann, 1983).
5. The TIK-TAK project, in which local trade unions in the public sector developed union resources in relation to "office automation" (Foged et al., 1987).
6. The Carpentry Shop project, which worked with methods and a design perspective similar to the UTOPIA project but within a "low-tech" area (Sjögren, 1979–83).
7. The Florence project, focusing on the work situation of nurses, which was another second-generation work-oriented project designing computer-based environments for skill and quality production (Bjerknes and Bratteteig, 1987).

These are by no means the only work-oriented design projects. Today the approach is no longer limited to Scandinavia. Despite a very different trade union structure, there are several projects using similar perspectives and methods in Britain (Williams, 1987).

Some Lessons on Design and Democratization

Some of the *general lessons* learned from DEMOS, UTOPIA, and other work-oriented design projects include:

1. A participatory approach to the design process is not sufficient in the context of democratization at work.

2. In democratization of design and use of computer-based systems in Scandinavia, trade unions—especially on a local level—must play an active role.

Some specific lessons about the *participation of local trade unions* in the design of computer-based systems include:

1. A clear distinction based on negotiations between union and management roles in the design process is not in opposition to, but a prerequisite for cooperation and the democratization of decision making in the work organization.
2. The design and use of computer-based systems requires new trade union activities.
3. The most important prerequisite for trade union participation in the design process is a parallel and independent process of accumulation of knowledge on the part of the union.
4. Local unions need external resources and support in their design activities.
5. A local trade union strategy has to be based on solidarity between the different groups of workers involved—a solidarity that goes beyond the traditional division of labor in the labor process and the traditional jurisdictions between the unions involved.

Some specific lessons on *national trade union support for democratization* of the design and use of computer-based systems include:

1. Today's computer-based systems often restrict the ability of trade unions to reach local objectives, especially with respect to skill but also with respect to work organization.
2. However, it is possible to design computer-based technology based on criteria such as skill and democracy at work.
3. National trade unions must influence the process of research and development of new technology to change the supply of technological and organizational solutions.
4. Equally important is a trade union strategy to influence the demand for these technological and organizational alternatives.
5. National trade unions must provide training with a trade union perspective on the design and use of computer artifacts, and influence the supply of professional training for skilled work.
6. A strategy like the new Scandinavian model for research and technological development—focusing on a new form of cooperation among governments, trade unions, and high tech industry in the production of new technology that supports good working conditions and good use quality prod-

ucts and services—is a promising approach to support more democratic design and use of computer-based systems.

TOWARDS A PHILOSOPHICAL FOUNDATION FOR SKILL-BASED PARTICIPATORY DESIGN

This paper does not argue for a reinvention of the wheel. The instrumental power of systems thinking for purposive rational action is beyond doubt. Many of the computer applications that function well today could not have been designed without rational methods. Instead, I suggest a reinterpretation of design methods to take us beyond the deeply embedded Cartesian mind–body dualism and beyond the limits of formalization towards an understanding that supports more creative ways of thinking and doing design as participatory work (involving the skills of both users and designers).

Efforts to pursue such a rethinking of the design of computer-based systems and to develop a new practice of design are now emerging within computer science. One important example is a new orientation in software engineering proposed by Christiane Floyd (1987). It is based on a dissatisfaction with "anomalies" in the product-oriented view of software engineering that treats computer programs as formal mathematical objects derived by formalized procedures from an abstract specification. Floyd argues that the product-oriented view leaves the relationship between programs and the living human world entirely unexplored, providing no way to check the relevance of the specification or to accommodate learning and communication.

As a remedy to these anomalies, Floyd sees a new process-oriented paradigm in software engineering with a focus on human learning and communication in both the use and development of the software. She views the products of this process as tools or working environments for people and not as pieces code or an abstract software system. Hence, the quality of the product depends on its relevance, suitability, or adequacy in practical use. Quality cannot be reduced to features of the product such as reliability and efficiency. From this perspective, prototyping can be seen as an alternative or complement to traditional, more formalized, and detached descriptions.

Another important example of new tendencies in the design of computer-based systems is the development of a new philosophical foundation in the tradition of hermeneutics and phenomenology proposed by Hubert and Stuart Dreyfus (1986) and Terry Winograd and Fernando Flores (1986). This philosophical endeavor focuses on the differences between human activity and computer performance. In doing so, it departs from other traditions by focusing on what people *do* with computers, how in cooperation with one another they use computers, and what they might do better with computers. In this approach, the origin of design is in involved practical use and understanding, not detached reflection, and design is seen as an interaction between understanding and creation. This research aims not to create just another design method but to create a new foundation for a science of design.

In the following, I will propose that this new understanding can be buttressed by an awareness of language games and the ordinary language philosophy of Ludwig Wittgenstein. My focus is on the shift in design from *language as description* towards *language as action*.

Rethinking Systems Descriptions

A few years ago I was struck by something I had not noticed before. While thinking about how perspectives make us select certain aspects of reality as important in a description, I realized I had completely overlooked my own presumption that descriptions in one way or another are mirror images of a given reality. My earlier reasoning had been that because there are different interests in the world, we should always question the objectivity of design choices that claimed to flow from design as a process of rational decision making. Hence, I had argued that we needed to create descriptions from different perspectives in order to form a truer picture. I did not, however, question the Cartesian epistemology and ontology of an inner world of experiences (mind) and an outer world of objects (external reality). Nor did I question the assumption that language was our way of mirroring this outer world of real objects. By focusing on which objects and which relations should be represented in a systems description, I took for granted the Cartesian mind–body dualism that Wittgenstein had so convincingly rejected in *Philosophical Investigations* (1953). Hence, although my purpose was the opposite, my perspective blinded me to the subjectivity of craft, artistry, passion, love, and care in the system descriptions.

Our experiences with the UTOPIA project caused me to re-examine my philosophical assumptions. Working with the end users of the design, the graphics workers, some design methods failed while others succeeded. Requirement specifications and systems descriptions based on information from interviews were not very successful. Improvements came when we made joint visits to interesting plants, trade shows, and vendors and had discussions with other users; when we dedicated considerably more time to learning from each other, designers from graphics workers and graphics workers from designers; when we started to use design-by-doing methods and descriptions such as mockups and work organization games; and when we started to understand and use traditional tools as a design ideal for computer-based tools.

The turnaround can be understood in the light of two Wittgenstinian lessons. The first is not to underestimate the importance of skill in design. As Peter Winch (1958) has put it, "A cook is not a man who first has a vision of a pie and then tries to make it. He is a man skilled in cookery, and both his projects and his achievements spring from that skill." The second is not to mistake the role of description methods in design: Wittgenstein argues convincingly that what a picture describes is determined by its use.

In the following I will illustrate how our "new" UTOPIAN design methods may be understood from a Wittgenstinian position, that is, why design-by-doing and a skill-based participatory design process works. More generally, I will argue that design tools such as models, prototypes, mockups, descriptions, and representations act as reminders and paradigm cases for our contemplation of future computer-based systems and their use. Such design tools are effective because they recall earlier experiences to mind. It is in this sense that we should understand them as *representations*. I will begin with a few words on practice, the alternative to the "picture theory of reality."

Practice Is Reality

Practice as the social construction of reality is a strong candidate for replacing the picture theory of reality. In short, practice is our everyday practical activity. It is the human form of life. It precedes subject–object relations. Through practice, we produce the world, both the world of objects and our knowledge about this world. Practice is both action and reflection. But practice is also a social activity; it is produced in cooperation with others. To share practice is also to share an understanding of the world with others. However, this production of the world and our understanding of it takes place in an already existing world. The world is also the product of former practice. Hence, as part of practice, knowledge has to be understood socially—as producing or reproducing social processes and structures as well as being the product of them (Kosik, 1967; Berger and Luckman, 1966).

Against this background, we can understand the design of computer applications as a concerned social- and historical-conditioned activity in which tools and their use are envisioned. This is an activity and form of knowledge that is both planned and creative.

Once struck by the "naive" Cartesian presumptions of a picture theory, what can be gained in design by shifting focus from the correctness of descriptions to intervention into practice? What does it imply to take the position that what a picture describes is determined by its use? Most importantly, it sensitizes us to the crucial role of skill and participation in design, and to the opportunity in practical design to transcend some of the limits of formalization through the use of more action-oriented design artifacts.

Language as Action

Think of the classical example of a carpenter and his or her hammering activity. In the professional language of carpenters, there are not only hammers and nails. If the carpenter were making a chair, other tools used would include a draw-knife, a brace, a trying plane, a hollow plane, a round plane, a bow-saw, a marking gauge, and chisels (Seymour, 1984). The materials that he works with are elm planks for the seats, ash for the arms, and oak for the legs. He is involved in saddling, making spindles, and steaming.

Are we as designers of new tools for chairmaking helped by this labeling of tools, materials, and activities? In a Wittgenstinian approach the answer would be: only if we understand the practice in which these names make sense. To label our experiences is to act deliberately. To label deliberately, we have to be trained to do so. Hence, the activity of labeling has to be learned. Language is not private but social. The labels we create are part of a practice that constitutes social meaning. We cannot learn without learning something specific. To understand and to be able to use is one and the same (Wittgenstein, 1953). Understanding the professional language of chairmaking, and any other language-game (to use Wittgenstein's term), is to be able to master practical rules we did not create ourselves. The rules are techniques and conventions for chairmaking that are an inseparable part of a given practice.

To master the professional language of chairmaking means to be able to act in an effective way together with other people who know chairmaking. To "know" does not mean explicitly knowing the rules you have learned, but rather recognizing when something is done in a correct or incorrect way. To have a concept is to have learned to follow rules as part of a given practice. Speech acts are, as a unity of language and action, part of practice. They are not descriptions but actions among others in a given practice.

Below I will elaborate on language-games, focusing on the design process, descriptions in design, design artifacts, and knowledge in the design of computer applications.

Language-Games

To use language is to participate in language-games. In discussing how we in practice follow (and sometimes break) rules as a social activity, Wittgenstein asks us to think of games, how they are made up and played. We often think of games in terms of a playful, pleasurable engagement. I think this aspect should not be denied, but a more important aspect for our purpose here is that games are mainly interested activities, as are most of the common language-games we play in our ordinary language.

Language-games, like the games we play as children, are social activities. To be able to play these games, we have to learn to follow rules, rules that are socially created but far from always explicit. The rule-following behavior of being able to play together with others is more important to a game than the specific explicit rules. Playing is interaction and cooperation. To follow the rules in practice means to be able to act in a way that others in the game can understand. These rules are embedded in a given practice from which they cannot be distinguished. To know them is to be able to "embody" them, to be able to apply them to an open class of cases.

We understand what counts as a game not because we have an explicit definition but because we are already familiar with other games. There is a kind of family resemblance between games. Similarly, professional language-games can be learned and understood because of their family resemblance to other language-games that we know how to play.

Language-games are performed both as speech acts and as other activities, as meaningful practice within societal and cultural institutional frameworks. To be able to participate in the practice of a specific language-game, one has to share the form of life within which that practice is possible. This form of life includes our natural history as well as the social institutions and traditions into which we are born. This condition precedes agreed social conventions and rational reasoning. Language as a means of communication requires agreement not only in definitions, but also in judgments. Hence, intersubjective consensus is more fundamentally a question of shared background and language than of stated opinions (Wittgenstein, 1953).

This definition seems to make us prisoners of language and tradition, which is not really the case. Being socially created, the rules of language games, like those of other games, can also be socially altered. There are, according to Wittgenstein, even games in which we make up and alter the rules as we go along. Think of systems design and use as language games. The very idea of the interventionistic design language-game is to change the rules of the language-game of use in a proper way.

The idea of language-games entails an emphasis on how we linguistically discover and construct our world. However, language is understood as our use of it, as our social, historic, and intersubjective application of linguistic artifacts. As I see it, the language-game perspective therefore does not preclude consideration of how we also come to understand the world by use of other tools.

Tools and objects play a fundamental role in many language-games. A hammer is in itself a sign of what one can do with it in a certain language-games. And so is a computer application. These signs remind one of what can be done with them. In this light, an important aspect in the design of computer applications is that its signs remind the users of what they can do with the application in the language-games of use (Brock, 1986). The success of "what-you-see-is-what-you-get" and "direct manipulation" user interfaces does not have to do with how they mirror reality in a more natural way, but with how they provide better reminders of the users' earlier experiences (Bødker, forthcoming). This is also, as will be discussed in the following, the case with the tools that we use in the design process.

Knowledge and Design Artifacts

As designers we are involved in reforming practice, in our case typically computer-based systems and the way people use them. Hence, the language-games of design change the rules for other language-games, in particular those of the application's use. What are the conditions for this interplay and change to operate effectively?

A common assumption behind most design approaches seems to be that the users must be able to give complete and explicit descriptions of their demands. Hence, the emphasis is on methods to support this elucidation by means of requirement specifications or system descriptions (Jackson, 1983; Yourdon, 1982).

In a Wittgensteinian approach, the focus is not on the "correctness" of systems descriptions in design, on how well they mirror the desires in the mind of the users, or on how correctly they describe existing and future systems and their use. Systems descriptions are design artifacts. In a Wittgensteinian approach, the crucial question is how we use them, that is, what role they play in the design process.

The rejection of an emphasis on the "correctness" of descriptions is especially important. In this, we are advised by the author of perhaps the strongest arguments for a picture theory and the Cartesian approach to design—the young Wittgenstein in *Tractatus Logico-Philosophicus* (1923). The reason for this rejection is the fundamental role of practical knowledge and creative rule following in language-games.

Nevertheless, we know that systems descriptions are useful in the the language-game of design. The new orientation suggested in a Wittgenstinian approach is that we see such descriptions as a special kind of artifact that we use as "typical examples" or "paradigm cases." They are not models in the sense of Cartesian mirror images of reality (Nordenstam, 1984). In the language-game of design, we use these tools as reminders for our reflection on future computer applications and their use. By using such design artifacts, we bring earlier experiences to mind, and they bend our way of thinking of the past and the future. I think that this is why we should understand them as *rep*-resentations (Kaasbøll, forthcoming). And this is how they inform our practice. If they are good design artifacts, they will support good moves within a specific design language-game.

The meaning of a design artifact is its use in a design language-game, not how it "mirrors reality." Its ability to support such use depends on the kinds of experience it evokes, its family resemblance to tools that the participants use in their everyday work activity. Therein lies a clue to why the breakthrough in the UTOPIA project was related to the use of prototypes and mockups. Since the design artifacts took the form of reminders or paradigm cases, they did not merely attempt to mirror a given or future practice linguistically.

They could be experienced through the practical use of a prototype or mockup. This experience could be further reflected upon in the language-game of design, either in ordinary language or in an artificial one.

A good example from the UTOPIA project is an empty cardboard box with "desktop laser printer" written on the top. There is no functionality in this mockup. Still, it works very well in the design game of envisioning the future work of makeup staff. It reminded the participating typographers of the old "proof machine" they used to work with in lead technology. At the same time, it suggested that with the help of new technology, the old proof machine could be reinvented and enhanced.

This design language-game was played in 1982. At that time, desktop laser printers only existed in advanced research laboratories, and certainly typographers had never heard of them. To them, the idea of a cheap laser printer was "unreal."

It was our responsibility as professional designers to be aware of such future possibilities and to suggest them to the users. It was also our role to suggest this technical and organizational solution in such a way that the users could experience and envision what it would mean in their practical work, before the investment of too much time, money, and development work. Hence, the design game with the mockup laser printer. The mockup made sense to all participants—users and designers (Ehn and Kyng, 1991).

This focus on nonlinguistic design artifacts is not a rejection of the importance of linguistic ones. Understood as triggers for our imagination rather than as mirror images of reality, they may well be our most wonderful human inventions. Linguistic design artifacts are very effective when they challenge us to tell stories that make sense to all participants.

Practical Understanding and Propositional Knowledge

There are many actions in a language-game, not least in the use of prototypes and mockups, that cannot be explicitly described in a formal language. What is it that the users know, that is, what have they learned that they can express in action, but not state explicitly in language? Wittgenstein (1953) asks us to "compare knowing and saying: how many feet high Mont Blanc is—how the word 'game' is used—how a clarinet sounds. If you are surprised that one can know something and not be able to say it, you are perhaps thinking of a case like the first. Certainly not of one of the third."

In the UTOPIA project, we were designing new computer applications to be used in typographical page makeup. The typographers could tell us the names of the different tools and materials that they use such as knife, page ground, body text, galley, logo, halftone, frame, and spread. They could also tell when, and perhaps in which order, they use specific tools and materials to place an article. For example, they could say, "First you pick up the body text with the knife and place it at the bottom of the designated area on the page ground. Then you adjust it to the galley line. When the body text fits you get the headline, if there is not a picture," and so forth. What I, as designer, get to know from such an account is equivalent to knowing the height of Mont Blanc. What I get to know is very different from the practical understanding of really making up pages, just as knowing the height of Mont Blanc gives me very little of understanding the practical experience of climbing the mountain.

Knowledge of the first kind has been called *propositional knowledge.* It is what you have "when you know that something is the case and when you also can describe what you know in so many words" (Nordenstam, 1985). Propositional knowledge is not necessarily more reflective than practical understanding. It might just be something that I have been told, but of which I have neither practical experience nor theoretical understanding.

The second case, corresponding to knowing how the word *game* is used, was more complicated for our typographers. How could they, for example, tell us the skill they possess in knowing how to handle the knife when making up the page in pasteup technology? This is their practical experience from the language-games of typographic design. To show it, they have to do it.

And how should they relate what counts as good layout, the complex interplay of presence and absence, light and dark, symmetry and asymmetry, uniformity and variety? Could they do it in any other way than by giving examples of good and bad layouts, examples that they have learned by participating in the games of typographical design? As in the case of knowing how a clarinet sounds, this is typically sensuous knowing by familiarity with earlier cases of how something is, sounds, smells, and so on.

Practical understanding—in the sense of practical experience from doing something and having sensuous experiences from earlier cases—defies formal description. If it were transformed into propositional knowledge, it would become something totally different.

It is hard to see how we as designers of computer systems for page makeup could manage to come up with useful designs without understanding how the knife is used or what counts as good layout. For this reason we had to have access to more than what can be stated as explicit propositional knowledge. We could only achieve this understanding by participating to some extent in the language-games of use of the typographical tools. Hence, participation applies not only to users participating in the language-game of design, but perhaps more importantly to designers participating in use. Some consequences of this position for organizing design language-games will be discussed in the following.

Rule Following and Tradition

Now, I turn to the paradox of rule-following behavior. As mentioned, many rules that we follow in practice can scarcely be distinguished from the behavior in which we perform them. We do not know that we have followed a rule until we have done it. The most important rules we follow in skillful performance defy formalization, but we still understand them.

As Michael Polanyi (1973), the philosopher of tacit knowledge, has put it: "It is pathetic to watch the endless efforts—equipped with microscopy and chemistry, with mathematics and electronics—to reproduce a single violin of the kind the half-literate Stradevarius turned out as a matter of routine more than 200 years ago." This is the traditional aspect of human rule-following behavior. Polanyi points out that what may be our most widely recognized, explicit, rule-based system—the practice of Common Law—also uses earlier examples as paradigm cases. Says Polanyi, "[Common Law] recognizes the principle of all traditionalism that practical wisdom is more truly embodied in action than expressed in the rules of action." According to Polanyi this is also true for science, no matter how rationalistic and explicit it claims to be: "While the articulate contents of science are successfully taught all over the world in hundreds of new universities, the unspecifiable art of scientific research has not yet penetrated to many of these." The art of scientific research defies complete formalization; it must be learned partly by examples from a master whose behavior the student trusts.

Involving skilled users in the design of new computer application when their old tools and working habits are redesigned is an excellent illustration of Polanyi's thesis. If activities that have been under such pressure for formalization as Law and Science are so dependent on practical experience and paradigm cases, why should we expect other social institutions that have been under less pressure of formalization to be less based on practical experience, paradigm cases, and tacit knowledge?

Rule Following and Transcendence

If design is rule-following behavior, is it also creative transcendence of traditional behavior. Again, this is what is typical of skillful human behavior, and is exactly what defies precise formalization. Through mastery of the rules comes the freedom to extend them. This creativity is based on the open-textured character of rule-following behavior. To begin with, we learn to follow a rule as a kind of dressage, but in the end we do it as creative activity (Dreyfus and Dreyfus, 1986). Mastery of the rules puts us in a position to invent new ways of proceeding. As the Wittgenstein commentator Alan Janik has put it: "There is always and ineliminably the possibility that we can follow the rule in a wholly unforeseen way. This could not happen if we had to have an explicit rule to go on from the start . . . the possibility of radical innovation is, however, the logical limit of description. This is what tacit knowledge is all about" (Janik, 1988). This is why we need a strong focus on skill both in design and in the use of computer systems. We focus on existing skills, not at to inhibit creative transcendence, but as a necessary condition for it.

But what is the role of "new" external ideas and experiences in design? How are tradition and transcendence united in a Wittgensteinian approach? It could, I believe, mean utilizing something like Berthold Brecht's theatrical "alienation" effect (*Verfremdungseffekt*) to highlight transcendental untried possibilities in everyday practice by presenting a well-known practice in a new light: "the aspects of things that are most important to us are hidden because of their simplicity and familiarity" (Wittgenstein, 1953). However, as Peter Winch (1958, p. 119) put it, in a Wittgenstinian approach: "the only legitimate use of such a *Verfremdungseffekt* is to draw attention to the familiar and obvious, not to show that it is dispensable from our understanding."

Design artifacts, linguistic or not, may in a Wittgenstinian approach certainly be used to break down traditional understanding, but they must make sense in the users' ordinary language-games. If the design tools are effective, it is because they help users and designers to see new aspects of an already well-known practice, not because they convey such new ideas. It is I think fair to say that this focus on traditional skill in interplay with design skill may be a hindrance to really revolutionary designs. The development of radically new designs might require leveraging *other* skills and involving *other* potential users. Few designs, however, are really revolutionary, and for normal everyday design situations, the participation of traditionally skilled users is critical to the quality of the resulting product.

The tension between tradition and transcendence is fundamental to design. There can be a focus on tradition or transcendence in the systems being created. Should a word processor be designed as an extension of the traditional typewriter or as something totally new? Another dimension is professional competence: Should one design for the "old" skills of typographers or should new knowledge replace those skills in future use? Or again, with the division of labor and cooperation: Should the new design support the traditional organization in a composing room or suggest new ways of cooperation between typographers and journalists? There is also the tension between tradition and transcendence in the goods or services to be produced using the new system: Should the design support the traditional graphical production or completely new services, such as desktop publishing?

Tradition and transcendence, that is the dialectical foundation of design.

Design by Doing: New "Rules of the Game"

What do we as designers have to do to qualify as participants in the language-games of the users? What do users have to learn to qualify as participants in the language-game of design? And what means can we develop in design to facilitate these learning processes?

If designers and users share the same form of life, it should be possible to overcome the gap between the different language-games. It should, at least in principle, be possible to develop the practice of design to the point where there is enough family resemblance between a specific language-game of the users and the language-games in which the designers of the computer application are intervening. A mediation should be possible.

But what are the conditions required to establish this mediation? For Wittgenstein, it would make no sense to ask this question outside a given form of life: "If a lion could talk, we could not understand him" (1953). In the arguments below, I have assumed that the conditions for a common form of life are possible to create, that the lions and sheep of industrial life, as discussed in the first part of this chapter, can live together. This is more a normative standpoint of how design ought to be, a democratic hope rather than a reflection on current political conditions.

To develop the competence required to participate in a language-game requires a lot of learning within that practice. But, in the beginning, all one can understand is what one has already understood in another language-game. If we understand anything at all, it is because of the family resemblance between the two language-games.

What kind of design tools could support this interplay between language-games? I think that what we in the UTOPIA project called design-by-doing methods—prototyping, mockups, and scenarios—are good candidates. Even joint visits to workplaces, especially ones similar to the ones being designed for, served as a kind of design tool through which designers and users bridged their language-games.

The language-games played in design-by-doing can be viewed both from the point of view of the users and of the designers. This kind of design becomes a language-game in which the users learn about possibilities and constraints of new computer tools that may become part of their ordinary language-games. The designers become the teachers that teach the users how to participate in this particular language-game of design. However, to set up these kind of language-games, the designers have to learn from the users.

However, paradoxical as it sounds, users and designers do not have to understand each other fully in playing language-games of design-by-doing together. Participation in a language-game of design and the use of design artifacts can make constructive but different sense to users and designers. Wittgenstein (1953) notes that "when children play at trains their game is connected with their knowledge of trains. It would nevertheless be possible for the children of a tribe unacquainted with trains to learn this game from others, and to play it without knowing that it was copied from anything. One might say that the game did not make the same sense as to us." As long as the language-game of design is not a nonsense activity to any participant but a shared activity for better understanding and good design, mutual understanding may be desired but not really required.

User Participation and Skill

The users can participate in the language-game of design because the application of the design artifacts gives their design activities a family resemblance with the language-games that they play in ordinary use situations. An example from the UTOPIA project is a typographer sitting at a mockup of a future workstation for page makeup, doing page makeup on the simulated future computer tool.

The family resemblance is only one aspect of the methods. Another aspect involves what can be expressed. In design-by-doing, the user is able to express both propositional knowledge and practical understanding. Not only could, for example, the typographer working at the mockup tell that the screen should be bigger to show a full page spread—something important in page makeup—he could also show what he meant by "cropping a picture" by actually doing it as he said it. It was thus possible for him to express his practical understanding, his sensuous knowledge by familiarity. He could, while working at the mockup, express the fact that when the system is designed one way he can get a good balanced page, but not when it is designed another way.

Designer Participation and Skill

For us as designers, it was possible to express both propositional knowledge and practical understanding about design and computer systems. Not only could we express propositional knowledge such as "design-by-doing design tools have many advantages as compared with traditional systems descriptions" or "bit-map displays bigger than 22 inches and with a resolution of more than 2000×2000 pixels are very expensive," but in the language-game of design-by-doing, we could also express practical understanding of technical constraints and possibilities by "implementing" them in the mockup, prototype, simulation, or experimental situation. Simulations of the user interface were also important in this language-game of design.

As designers, our practical understanding will mainly be expressed in the ability to construct specific language-games of design in such a way that the users can develop their understanding of future use by participating in design processes.

As mentioned above, there is a further important aspect of language-games: We make up the rules as we go along. A skilled designer should be able to assist in such transcendental rule-breaking activities. Perhaps, this is the artistic competence that a good designer needs.

To really learn the language-game of the use activity by fully participating in that language-game is, of course, an even more radical approach for the designer. Less radical but perhaps more practical would be for designers to concentrate design activity on just a few language-games of use, and for us to develop a practical understanding of useful specific language-games of design (Ehn and Kyng, 1987). Finally, there seems to be a new role for the designer as the one who sets the stage for a shared design language-game that makes sense to all participants.

Some Lessons on Design, Skill, and Participation

As in the first practice-oriented part of this paper on designing for democracy at work, I end this second philosophically oriented part on skill-based participatory design with some lessons for work-oriented design.

General lessons on work-oriented design include:

1. Understanding design as a process of creating new language-games that have family resemblance with the language-games of both users and designers gives us an orientation for doing work-oriented design through skill-based participation—a way of doing design that may help us transcend some of the limits of formalization. Setting up these design language-games is a new role for the designer.
2. Traditional "systems descriptions" are not sufficient in a skill-based participatory design approach. Design artifacts should not be seen primarily as means for creating true "pictures of reality," but as means to help users and designers discuss and experience current situations and envision future ones.
3. "Design-by-doing" design approaches such as the use of mockups and other prototyping design artifacts make it possible for ordinary users to use their practical skill when participating in the design process.

Lessons on skill in the design of computer-based system include:

1. Participatory design is a learning process in which designers and users learn from each other.
2. Besides propositional knowledge, practical understanding is a type of skill that should be taken seriously in a design language-game since the most important rules we follow in skillful performance are embedded in practice and defy formalization.
3. Creativity depends on the open-textured character of rule-following behavior, hence a focus on traditional skill is not a drawback to creative transcendence but a necessary condition. Supporting the dialectics between tradition and transcendence is the heart of design.

Lessons on participation in design of computer-based systems include:

1. Really participatory design requires a shared form of life—a shared social and cultural background and a shared language. Hence, participatory design means not only users participating in design but also designers participating in use. The professional designer will try to share practice with the users.

2. To make real user participation possible, a design language-game must be set up in such a way that it has a family resemblance to language-games the users have participated in before. Hence, the creative designer should be concerned with the practice of the users in organizing the design process, and understand that every new design language-game is a unique situated design experience. There is, however paradoxical it may sound, no requirement that the design language-game make the same sense to users and designers. There is only requirement that the designer set the stage for a design language-game in which participation makes sense to all participants.

BEYOND THE BOREDOM OF DESIGN

Given the Scandinavian societal, historical, and cultural setting, the first part of this chapter focused on the democratic aspect of skill-based participatory design, especially the the important role of local trade unions and their strategies for user participation. In the second part, some ideas inspired by Ludwig Wittgenstein's philosophical investigations were applied to the everyday practice of skill-based participatory design. Practical understanding and family resemblance between language-games were presented as fundamental concepts for work-oriented design.

The concept of language-games is associated with playful activity, but what practical conditions are needed for such pleasurable engagement in design? Is the right to democratic participation enough?

In fact, the experiences from the work-oriented design projects indicates that most users find design work boring, sometimes to the point where they stop participating. This problem is not unique to the Scandinavian work-oriented design tradition. It has, for example, been addressed by Russell Ackoff (1974), who concluded that participation in design can be only successful if it meets three conditions: (1) it makes a difference for the participants, (2) implementation of the results is likely, and (3) it is fun.

The first two points concern the political side of participation in design. Users must have a guarantee that their design efforts are taken seriously. The last point concerns the design process. No matter how much influence participation may give, it has to transcend the boredom of traditional design meetings to really make design meaningful and full of involved action. The design work should be playful. In our own later projects, we have tried to take this challenge seriously and have integrated the use of future workshops, metaphorical design, role playing and organizational games into work-oriented design (Ehn and Sjögren, 1991).

Hence, the last lesson from Scandinavian design is that formal democratic and participatory procedures for designing computer-based systems for democracy at work are not sufficient. Our design language-games must also be organized in a way that makes it possible for ordinary users not only to utilize their practical skill in the design work, but also to have fun while doing so.

REFERENCES

Ackoff, R. L. (1974). *Redesigning the Future.* New York: John Wiley.

Aguren, S., and J. Edgren (1979). *Annorlunda fabriker—Mot en ny produktionsteknisk teori.* Stockholm: The Swedish Employers Confederation.

Berger, P. L., and T. Luckmann (1966). *The Social Construction of Reality—A Treatise in the Sociology of Knowledge.* New York: Doubleday & Company.

Bjerknes, G., and T. Bratteteig (1987). Florence in wonderland—systems development with nurses, in G. Bjerknes, P. Ehn and M. Kyng (eds.). *Computers and Democracy—A Scandinavian Challenge.* Aldershot, U.K.: Avebury.

Bødker, S. (forthcoming). *Through the Interface—A Human Activity Approach to User Interface Design.* Hillsdale, N.J.: Lawrence Erlbaum.

Brock, S. (1986). Wittgenstein mellem fænomenologi og analytik, in S. Brock et al. (eds.). *Sprog, Moral & Livsform.* Århus, Denmark: Philosophia.

Brulin, G., et al. (1988). *På rätt spår.* Stockholm: Arbetsmiljöfonden.

Dahlström, E. (1983). *Bestämmande i arbetet—Några idékritiska funderingar kring arbetslivets demokratisering.* Gothenburg: Department of Sociology, University of Gothenburg.

Dreyfus, H. L., and S. D. Dreyfus (1986). *Mind over Machine—The Power of Human Intuition and Expertise in the Era of the Computer.* Glasgow: Basil Blackwell.

Ehn, P. (1989, second edition). *Work-Oriented Design of Computer Artifacts.* Hillsdale, N.J.: Lawrence Erlbaum.

Ehn, P., and M. Kyng (1984). A tool perspective on design of interactive computer support for skilled workers, in M. Sääksjärri (ed.). *Proceedings of the Seventh Scandinavian Research Seminar on Systemeering.* Helsinki.

Ehn, P., and M. Kyng (1987). The collective resource approach to systems design, in Bjerknes et al. (eds.). *Computers and Democracy—A Scandinavian Challenge.* Aldershot, U.K.: Avebury.

Ehn, P., and M. Kyng (1991). Cardboard computers—mocking-it-up or hands-on the future, in J. Greenbaum and M. Kyng (eds.). *Design at Work.* Hillsdale, N.J.: Lawrence Erlbaum.

Ehn, P., and Å. Sandberg (1979). *Företagsstyrning och löntagarmakt—planering, datorer, organisation och fackligt utredningsarbete.* Stockholm: Prisma.

Ehn, P., and D. Sjögren (1991). From systems descriptions to scripts for action, in J. Greenbaum and M. Kyng (eds.). *Design at Work.* Hillsdale, N.J.: Lawrence Erlbaum.

Ehn, P., et al. (1985). *Datorstödd Ombrytning.* Stockholm: Swedish Center for Working Life.

Einhorn, E., and J. Logue (eds.) (1982). *Democracy at the Shop Floor—An American Look at Employee Influence in Scandinavia Today.* Kent, Ohio: Kent Popular Press.

Floyd, C. (1987). Outline of a paradigm change in software engineering, in G. Bjerknes et al. (eds.). *Computers and Democracy—A Scandinavian Challenge.* Aldershot, U.K.: Avebury.

Foged, J., et al. (1987). *Håndbog om klubarbejde, edb-projekter og nye arbejdsformer.* Ärhus: HK kommunal.

Fry, J.(ed.) (1986). *Towards a Democratic Rationality—Making the Case for Swedish Labor.* Gower: Aldershot.

Göranzon, B. (1984). *Datautvecklingens Filosofi.* Malmö: Carlsson & Jönsson.

Gustavsen, B. (1985). Workplace reform and democratic dialogue. *Economic and Industrial Democracy* 6, 4, Nov, 461–479.

Hedberg, B. (1980). Using computerized information systems to design better organizations, in N. Bjørn-Andersen (ed.). *The Human Side of Information Processing.* Amsterdam: North-Holland.

Hedberg, B., and M. Mehlmann (1983). *Datorer i bank.* Stockholm: Swedish Center for Working Life.

Howard, R. (1985). UTOPIA—Where workers craft new technology. *Technology Review* **88,** April, 43–49.

Jackson, M. (1983). *System Development.* Englewood Cliffs, N.J.: Prentice–Hall.

Janik, A. (1988). *Style, Politics and the Future of Philosophy.* London: Kluwer Academic Publishers.

Kaasbøll, J. (forthcoming). *A Theoretical and Empirical Study of the Use of Language and Computers.* Dissertation, Department of Informatics, University of Oslo.

Kammersgaard, J. (1985). On models and their role in the use of computers, in *Papers Presented at Working Conference on Development and Use of Computer Based Systems and Tools.* Aarhus University, Denmark, Aug. 19–23.

Kosik, Karel. (1967). *Die Dialektik des Konkreten.* Frankfurt: Suhrkampf.

Kronlund, Jan. (1978). *Produktionslivets förnyelse—teknik, organisation, människa, miljö.* Conference in Uppsala, The Swedish Work Environment Fund.

Kubicek, H. (1983). User participation in system design, in Briefs et al. (eds.). *Systems Design for, with, and by the Users.* Amsterdam: North-Holland.

Kyng, M., and L. Mathiassen (1982). Systems development and trade union activities, in N. Bjørn-Andersen (ed.). *Information Society, for Richer, for Poorer.* Amsterdam: North-Holland.

Lysgaard, S. (1961). *Arbeiderkollektivet.* Stavanger: Universitetsforlaget.

Mumford, E. (1987). Sociotechnical system design—evolving theory and practice, in Bjerknes et al. (eds.). *Computers and Democracy—A Scandinavian Challenge.* Aldershot, U.K.: Avebury.

Nordenstam, T. (1984). Två oförenliga traditioner, in B. Göranzon (ed.). *Datautvecklingens Filosofi.* Malmö: Carlsson & Jönsson.

Nordenstam, T. (1985). *Technocratic and Humanistic Conceptions of Development.* Stockholm: Swedish Center for Working Life.

Norwegian Employers Federation and Norwegian Federation of Trade Unions (1975). *General Agreement on Computer-Based Systems.* Stockholm.

Polanyi, M. (1973). *Personal Knowledge.* London: Routledge and Kegan Paul.

Qvale, T. (1976). A Norwegian strategy for democratization of industry. *Human Relations* **5,** 468.

Sandberg, Å. (1976). *The Limits to Democratic Planning—Knowledge, Power, and Methods in the Struggle for the Future.* Dissertation, Stockholm: Liber.

Sandberg, Å. (1979). (ed.). *Utredning och föröndring i förvaltningen.* Stockholm: Liber förlag.

Sandberg, Å. (1982). *From Satisfaction to Democratization—On Sociology and Working Life Changes in Sweden.* Stockholm: Swedish Center for Working Life.

Sandberg, Å. (forthcoming). *Technological Change and Co-determination in Sweden—Background and Analysis of Trade Union and Managerial Strategies.* Philadelphia: Temple University Press.

Seymour, J. (1984). *The Forgotten Arts—A Practical Guide to Traditional Skills.* London: Dorling Kindersley.

Sjögren, D. (ed.) (1979–83). *Nyhetsblad från Snickeriprojektet.* Stockholm: Swedish Center for Working Life.

Steen, J., and P. Ullmark (1982). *De anställdas Mejeri.* Stockholm: Royal Institute of Technology.

Swedish Federation of Trade Unions (1975). *Handlingsprogram för företagsdemokrati och data.* Stockholm.

Swedish Federation of Trade Unions (1977). *Codetermination on the Foundation of Solidarity.* Stockholm: Prisma.

Williams, R. (1987). Democratising systems development—technological and organisational constraints an opportunities, in G. Bjerknes et al. (eds.). *Computers and Democracy—A Scandinavian Challenge.* Aldershot, U.K.: Avebury.

Winch, P. (1958). *The Idea of a Social Science and Its Relation to Philosophy.* London: Routledge & Kegan Paul.

Winograd, T., and F. Flores (1986). *Understanding Computers and Cognition—A New Foundation for Design.* Norwood, N.J.: Ablex.

Wittgenstein, L. (1923). *Tractatus Logico-Philosophicus.* London: Kegan Paul.

Wittgenstein, L. (1953). *Philosophical Investigations.* Oxford: Basil Blackwell & Mott.

Yourdon, E. (1982). *Managing the System Life Cycle.* New York: Yourdon Press.

CHAPTER 6

Work at the Interface: Advanced Manufacturing Technology and Job Design

J. MARTIN CORBETT

The currently dominant view among researchers interested in advanced manufacturing technology (AMT) and job design is that an organization's choice of job design options—whether skill based or management-control oriented—is socially determined and independent of any technological constraint. Technology is seen as effectively neutral. From the perspective of such research, skill-based production system design is achieved through judicial redesign of organizational variables such as supervisory style, training, role, responsibilities, and/or decentralization of decision making. This view, which one may term *technological indeterminism,* is summed up by Buchanan (1983), who declares that technological imperatives are weak while organizational choice is strong.

The aims of this chapter are twofold. The key theoretical aim is to explore the extent to which the development of skill-based production systems may be constrained by the production technology being utilized within a manufacturing organization. Within the social science research literature examining the relationship between AMT and job design, this is a fundamental, yet largely unanswered, question. A second, related aim is more practical: to examine the ways in which social scientists, users, and others can (re)shape the design and implementation of AMT in order to reduce or remove such constraints. This examination is aided by the inclusion of a number of case examples.

I will argue that, although organizational variables are undoubtedly important in the development of skill-based production systems, the neglect of technological variables and the reluctance to open the "black box" of technology may seriously undermine the validity of organization-centered research programs in the longer term. Developments in the theory and practice of "human-centered technology" will be used to support this line of argument.

The chapter is in five parts. In the first part, the case against technological indeterminism is examined. This is followed by a brief argument to support the case for a "soft" technological determinism that views the relationship between technology and job design as one in which the design of hardware and software technology may constrain key aspects of job design choice. In the third part, the background to two international project case studies is given. These projects focus on the design and development of AMT systems in which the aforementioned constants on job design are minimized and in which the role of users is optimized through the appropriate design of hardware and software technology.

In the fourth part, the technical design process is examined in more depth. The concept of "technically embedded constraint" is employed as a basis for this examination. A number of multidisciplinary design methods, utilized by participants within the projects outlined in part three, are described and evaluated in this section of the paper. These methods explicitly aim to overcome the constraints inherent in conventionally designed advanced manufacturing technology. The fifth part draws further on the case studies to identify five key criteria for effective human-centered design. The chapter concludes with a discussion on the possible future trends in AMT design and use.

THE CASE AGAINST TECHNOLOGICAL INDETERMINISM

With few exceptions, the empirical evidence supporting the case for technological indeterminism in job design has amassed through case study analyses. Research in a variety of organizations typically shows that similar manufacturing technologies are used in different ways and associated with different job designs (for example, Wilkinson, 1983; Sorge et al., 1983; Buffo et al., 1988; Burnes, 1988; Kelley, 1988; Francis and Grootings, 1989). In interpreting these findings, researchers have examined the mediating role of organization size, culture, industrial relations, management style, and other nontechnical variables.

However, this case study approach to AMT and job design research has five inherent weaknesses. First, the research lacks a developmental focus. By far, the majority of the research focuses on one of the basic building blocks of advanced manufacturing systems, namely, stand-alone computer-numerically-controlled (CNC) machine tools. What is missing is the wider systemic context within which the CNC machines under scrutiny are operating. While it may be true that significant organizational choice exists concerning the design of operating tasks with stand-alone CNC machines, does this hold true for flexible manufacturing systems (FMS) and computer-integrated manufacturing (CIM) systems that integrate the functions and pace of CNC machines? Given the rate of technological developments in manufacturing processes, it may be more prudent to set case study findings in a more developmental context. Indeed, Littler (1983) cautions that case study research is unavoidably time bound and is

> sampling organizations at a particular historical point, one in which the form of the technology has not yet been closed off by a series of decisions and technical developments which in combination constitute sunk costs.   (p. 144)

A second weakness of the indeterminism approach stems from its theoretical one-sidedness. Much of this research aims to undermine both the simplistic technological determinism of earlier studies such as Blauner (1964) or Woodward (1965) and the equally simplistic social determinism of Braverman (1974), who argued that technology is designed and implemented with an explicit managerial objective of deskilling the labor process. While the new "strategic choice" perspective offered by writers such as Child (1987) and Buchanan (1983) rightly criticizes these earlier approaches for their somewhat undialectical analysis of technology and skill, they still tend to overplay the rationality of management decision making (Armstrong, 1989). This leads them to understate the crucial role played by technical rationality in general (and by systems analysts and technical experts in particular) within the technical design process (Corbett and Scarbrough, forthcoming). As a result, the notion that technological change may have unanticipated consequences within an organization is also given little consideration.

It is interesting to note that the idea of "constraining" technology is implicit in many writings in the job design field, but it is one that has yet to be fully articulated or researched. For example, the psychologists Hackman and Oldham (1980), the founders of the highly influential job characteristics model of job design, have argued that

> if work is to be meaningfully redesigned in an organization either (1) the technology must be of the type that provides at least moderate employee discretion or (2) the technology itself must be changed to be compatible with the characteristics of enriched work.   (p. 122)

Similar qualifying statements can be found in many case study reports, but these are rarely, if ever, followed through. It should be noted also that while sociotechnical systems theory is relatively explicit with regard to the possibility of technical constraint on job design (for example, the principle of "joint optimization"), in the practice of job redesign any such constraints are taken as given. In his overview of over 130 job redesign experiments based on sociotechnical systems theory, Taylor (1977a, b) found that technological characteristics of work were redesigned in less than 10 percent of cases.

A third weakness of the case study approach stems from confusion over definitions of technology. The use of terms such as *organizational technology* contribute to a certain amount of confusion over what actually is being studied. At the more micro level, it would be useful to know what types of controllers, material, and parts transfer devices and part scheduling programs are being used by organizations undergoing case analysis. This information is absent from almost all case studies, which makes it difficult to generalize across research findings.

A fourth weakness of the case study approach is the ambiguous nature of the dependent variable under study in the vast majority of cases. Attewell (1987) points out that Braverman develops his notion of deskilling by contrasting two ideal types, a "craft worker" and a "detail worker." On the one hand, the former requires a broad range of abstract theoretical knowledge via formal training that, in combination with manual dexterity, is used to plan and execute a variety of tasks under the craft workers' own direction. Detail work, on the other hand, can be learned quickly and requires no planning or theoretical knowledge. Such work is routinized and closely supervised.

The ambiguity here is that this formulation of skill combines several dimensions to define skilled versus degraded work and these dimensions are themselves interrelated in a complex manner. For example, specialization does not necessarily imply a lack of skill (Littler, 1982) and neither does routinization (Kusterer, 1978). Furthermore, computerization tends to go hand in hand with abstract knowledge demands on the part of the user (Zuboff, 1988; and see discussion to follow). With such ambiguity in the definition of skill, it is small wonder that case study findings are ambiguous.

A final weakness of the case study research to date is that it treats technology as a black box. In most cases, there is no examination of the social choices that influence and shape the design of production technology. Although there is a growing literature focusing on the ways in which technology is socially constructed (for example, MacKenzie and Wajcman, 1985; Bijker et al., 1987), this approach has rarely found its way into the research on job design. There is little or no discussion of the ways in which technological design choices may pre-empt or constrain organizational choices concerning job design. Although not in the manufacturing area, one notable exception here is the research carried out by Rose et al. (1986) examining the ways in which different telephone exchange technology designs directly affect operating jobs design.

In highlighting these weaknesses of the case study research by AMT and job design researchers, I am not arguing against the case study method itself. Indeed, the case studies cited above have been useful in showing that simplistic technological or social determinist positions are untenable. Yet few researchers on AMT have argued for such simplistic positions except either as rough-cut generalizations (Woodward, 1965) or as thought-provoking polemic (Braverman, 1974). Hence, these case studies call into question a position which is not actually held by serious researchers in the first place. Perhaps a more interesting research agenda would be to investigate why perceptions of technological determinism are so prevalent among designers, managers and users despite the case study evidence (see Corbett and Scarbrough, forthcoming).

THE CASE FOR A "SOFT" TECHNOLOGICAL DETERMINISM

Having criticized the case for technological indeterminism in the relation between AMT and job design, it is necessary to examine briefly the nature of the technological imperatives associated with advanced manufacturing systems. In other words, how, and to what extent, can the design of advanced manufacturing technology constrain an organization's job design options?

First, although software is very flexible in theory, in practice it is very difficult to (re)design in order to adapt it to a given work organization or job design strategy. The complexity of modern software programs and the successful marketing of standardized software packages and "turnkey" systems contribute to this inflexibility. As a result, the organization typically adapts its job design and local management and planning structures to the software and not vice versa. Thus, the organization's choice of software technology may have considerable repercussions for job design unless steps are taken at the design stage to avoid a premature closure of job design options.

Retaining flexibility has become more difficult because the systemic nature of these turnkey system developments has meant that systems analysts are taking an increasingly active role in AMT design. Research suggests that both the analytical style of systems analysts and the design methodologies they use are incompatible with the design of skill-based or human-centered job designs (DeMarco, 1979; Markus, 1984). Systems professionals tend to make assumptions about employee needs and practices that are often inaccurate but are nevertheless reflected in designs that encourage job designs in which jobs are well defined and structured, with carefully set targets and close supervision. "Hard systems thinking" dominates systems development (Willcocks and Mason, 1987). This type of thinking assumes a clear-cut system that has obvious objectives and views organizations as consensual, centrally coordinated and regulated, predictable, reducible to clearly defined rules, and quantifiable.

A second aspect of AMT as a constraining technology stems from the fact that many contemporary developments in AMT (particularly software) explicitly aim to integrate the design, manufacture, and planning components of the production process (Corbett et al., 1991). Hence, as Brandt et al. (1978) point out, AMT is often a "technology of organization and control." In a similar vein, Sydow (1987) argues that the potential of associated software (for example, Manufacturing Automation Protocol, Materials Requirements Planning) to dovetail technology and organization rationally decreases the scope of organizational choice as it makes the organization more autonomous of qualified employees, who had the function of the rational dovetailing of technology and organization in the past. Hence, there is less of an economic need to design work situations offering a high quality of working life for many where only a few remain in vital jobs.   (p. 69)

A third constraining factor relates to the relative irreversibility of technological implementation. While the jobs design associated with stand-alone CNC machines can often be changed after installation, this is much less true of the implementation of centrally controlled, highly automated, and integrated FMS, CAD/CAM (computer-aided design and manufacturing), and CIM systems. With such systems, human action and knowledge are replaced, in part, by computer control and computer-based decision support technology, and "the resulting lack of qualification makes it almost impossible to withdraw this technology from the organization and to return to former organization structures, even if the installation of the technology turned out to be inefficient" (Sydow, 1987, p. 70).

A final constraining factor relates to the abstract nature of the operating job designs associated with AMT. Observers agree that the operators' jobs in AMT settings tend to be computer mediated and hence of a more formalized and abstract nature (Zuboff, 1988). This is a key insight of human factors research on human–machine interaction in the AMT domain and of great interest to cognitive, social, and work psychologists, but apparently of little concern to the sociologists who dominate the case study research field. Yet it is an issue that is fundamental to the human-centered perspective. It is discussed at greater length in the following.

Taken together, these four factors suggest that the technical design specification of AMT may play an important role in shaping job design. Once organizational decision makers have chosen a particular technological system, they have also made important, albeit implicit, decisions concerning the design of jobs relating to the operation of that system. In this view, design and implementation are not regarded as separate fields of empirical enquiry. As Rose et al. (1986) argue, there is a strong case for examining the way technology and social variables interact at the design stage as well as at the stages of workplace implementation and use.

The thesis that AMT can overly constrain the range of realizable job design options reverses the customary wisdom that organizational and job design has the potential to frustrate the full performance capabilities of AMT. The latter is often the argument used to support the move towards skill-based manufacturing. Clearly, however, these two causal arrows are not mutually exclusive. Yet few commentators have taken the middle ground since the heady days, in the 1950s and 1960s, of sociotechnical systems theory and the concept of "joint optimization."

But we should not elide the fact that our analysis leads to a "soft technological determinism." The term *soft* is used here to distinguish this line of argument from the more simplistic and all-embracing "hard" determinist position. A soft determinism differs from hard determinism in two important respects. First, it is not my intention to argue that all aspects of job design are determined by technology; the extent and scope of this determination will depend upon the particular technology under scrutiny. Second, the hard determinist position sees technology as possessing an autonomous "inner logic" that is entirely divorced from the social, cultural, economic, and political context of its development, diffusion, and use. Determinism in its softer form rejects such an assertion. Indeed, the human-centered design tradition, while critical of the way in which Western science and technology has been shaped and developed to the present day, anticipates a more desirable development path shaped by new social arrangements (see Cooley, 1987).

OVERCOMING TECHNICALLY EMBEDDED CONSTRAINTS ON JOB DESIGN: BACKGROUND TO CASE STUDIES

In the following sections of this chapter, the concept of technically embedded constraint is used as a basis for analyzing the relationship between AMT and job design in theory and practice. Examples of parallel design methods within two design projects supported by the Commission of European Communities are used throughout. Both projects explicitly aim to develop parallel design methods to reshape traditional AMT design practice. If the predominance of technology-centered hard systems thinking has created an increasingly determinist relationship between AMT design and user job design, the use of human-centered parallel design methods may be seen as an attempt to reshape the technical design process with a view towards increasing the scope and flexibility of job design options.

The ESPRIT Program

The ESPRIT program arose from an initiative by the Commission of European Communities (CEC), which approached the twelve largest European information technology (IT) businesses in 1983 to help put together a research program that would help reverse the decline in the European IT industry. The ESPRIT program had three main objectives:

1. To contribute towards providing European IT industry with the basic technologies it needs to meet the competitive requirements of the 1990s;
2. To promote European industrial cooperation in IT; and
3. To contribute to the development of internationally accepted standards (Commission of European Communities, 1987)

The ESPRIT research program began in 1984 and received a five-year budget of 1500 million European Currency Units (ECU). (At the time, 1 ECU was worth approximately $US 1.00.) Of this, half comes from the CEC and half from the participating organizations (universities, research institutes, and industrial partners). Thirteen percent of this budget was allocated to research and development in the CIM area.

Of the 227 projects financed by ESPRIT, only two made any explicit provision for the incorporation of social and organizational aspects into the technical design process. These two projects form the basis for the more detailed consideration of the human-centered perspective in the next section.

ESPRIT Project 534

This project focused on the development of a Flexible Automated Assembly Cell and included a human factors study. It began in 1985 and, although scheduled for five years, was terminated after only two years for a variety of political, corporate, and economic reasons. Its objective was to design and develop a prototype automated flexible assembly cell for the manufacture of mechanical assemblies of up to 0.5 cubic meter in size and 30 kilos in weight. The project also included a study of the related human and organizational factors relating to the technical design process with a view to developing a set of generalizable human and organizational design criteria for CIM applications. An overview of this study can be found in Corbett et al. (1987).

ESPRIT Project 1217

This three-year project began in 1986. Its objective was to develop a prototype CIM system comprising integrated computer-aided design, manufacturing, and planning packages in which the role of the user is optimized. The main theme of the project was to demonstrate that a CIM system that allows for the full use and development of human skills and abilities can be more effective, more robust, and more economical than its more conventional technology-centered counterpart. Eight industrial and academic partners were involved, based in the UK, West Germany, and Denmark. Engineering and social science specialists were equally represented. A more detailed description of the project may be found in Cooley (1987) and Corbett et al. (1991).

LESSONS LEARNED

Hard systems thinking predominates in the field of technological design (Willcocks and Mason, 1987; Hampden-Turner, 1970; Noble, 1984; Cooley, 1987). Hard systems thinking involves the imposition of a clear-cut problem definition on a relatively unstable organizational reality and a "fuzzy" system. It also means the adoption of linear, top-down design procedures that handicap design in a very complex organizational reality. The overriding concern in a hard design approach is technical design; little attention is accorded either the organizational context in which the system is to operate or the social implications of the system. The technology-centered approach leaves the engineering and computer professionals to decide the extent to which user participation is useful and permissible.

As part of this hard technology-centered approach to systems design, the designer will make (often implicit) assumptions about the way the technical system will be operated by manufacturing personnel. In hard, technology-led systems thinking, where technical considerations are paramount and a high level of automatic computer control is emphasized, the role of the user can only be readily understood and modeled when operating tasks are predictable and well defined. As a result of these assumptions about human nature and specifications for job design, decision makers within user organizations tend towards a narrow view of human potential and worth. While choice exists at all stages of AMT design, the failure of social scientists and/or users to participate in the making of these choices until the implementation stage can lead to a substantial restriction on the degree of choice over the allocation of personnel responsibilities.

However, there is a growing realization among a number of researchers and commentators that this technology-led approach to technological change needs to be replaced by a parallel design process in which technological and organizational factors are considered together from the onset of design. A number of potential benefits accrue from a parallel approach (see Clegg and Corbett, 1987).

For example, including system users in the design process may improve the resulting design because it better meets the users' specific needs and because the users have job-specific knowledge about the production process that should inform the design (Mumford and Henshall, 1979). Kusterer (1978) observes that even so-called "unskilled" production workers often possess knowledge and skills that are crucial to the effective operation—and, by extension, the effective design—of an AMT system. If the human–computer interface were difficult to comprehend, if operator jobs were poorly designed, if their training were inadequate, or if the support they are given by programmers and engineers were ineffective, then any system would be unable to perform to its potential.

One of the goals of the ESPRIT projects was therefore to illustrate the benefits of a parallel approach and they explicitly focused on the development of parallel design methods. In both projects, social scientists and engineers rejected a sequential approach to AMT system design and worked together on the design of advanced manufacturing technology that provides a minimum constraint on job design prior to its implementation and use. However, such a shift in approach to the design of AMT is not unproblematic.

Difficulties in the Development of Parallel Design Methods

Conventional engineering systems design practice takes little or no account of the social dimension of AMT design and application. Where human factors or ergonomic specialists have been involved in design, the human is typically identified in a very narrow, mechanistic way either as an information processor or perceptual–motor system component. Yet even when employing such a narrow, essentially quantifiable, definition of the human being, human factor engineers and ergonomists have experienced considerable difficulty in getting their views incorporated into technical design specifications. Why is this?

David Meister (1987) argues that the relationship between ergonomists and engineering designers can be characterized thus:

1. Most designers are at best neutral, at worse actively hostile to ergonomists. They do not read ergonomics literature, and they accord ergonomics a low priority in the design process.
2. Their attitudes towards ergonomics are bolstered by a series of beliefs and assumptions that are largely erroneous or simplistic.
3. Ergonomists know little about the designer's task. The designer has difficulty communicating his or her rationale for design decisions to the ergonomist.
4. Many ergonomists assume a reactive posture because they assume there must first be a design before it can be examined for its ergonomic aspects.
5. Because of designers' negative attitudes towards ergonomics, ergonomists spend a great deal of time and effort persuading the designer to assume a more positive viewpoint, with little success.

While Meister assigns most of the blame to the engineering designer, Clegg (1987) has compiled a complementary series of statements written from the viewpoint of the systems designer:

1. Ergonomics expertise is highly fragmented, which makes it difficult for designers to find (let alone utilize) the relevant ergonomics state of the art.
2. Ergonomists often have a poor understanding of engineering problems.
3. Ergonomists have failed to provide usable sets of tools, criteria, or procedures for designers.
4. Ergonomists have not been effective at educating and persuading designers in their views and methods.
5. Ergonomists have failed to demonstrate that ergonomics is worth the effort, partly because of the points above, but also financially.

Taken together, the views of Meister and Clegg are suggestive of the hurdles to be surmounted in the development of parallel AMT design methods.

The most popular parallel design method employed by design teams comprising engineers and ergonomists is based on the evaluation of design alternatives through the use of explicit ergonomic design criteria. Indeed, the social scientists working within ESPRIT Project 534 focused most of their energy and time in this direction during the first year of that project.

However, problems arising from the use of design criteria soon became apparent (Corbett, 1987b). Such problems include:

1. Ambiguities in interpretation that arise in the face of particular technical problems. Even Smith and Aucella's (1983) 580 design criteria were frequently found to be too general.
2. Difficulty in using design criteria in the generation of design options. Although design criteria may aid the moulding of a designer's approach to design problem solving, they are most often used retrospectively to evaluate solutions derived from purely technical considerations.
3. The many dimensions of engineering design, which is not simply a matter of applying design criteria, whether technical, economic, or ergonomic. The design process has additional subjective, aesthetic, and tacit dimensions, particularly at the generative stage. As a result, "good" design criteria do not guarantee "good" design.

An important lesson learned from Project 534 was therefore that parallel design should not be based solely on the use of design criteria. Additional methods must be employed that engage more directly the creative problem-solving design task in order to open up AMT design.

It became clear that participation in parallel design practice should not be limited to engineers, ergonomists, and social scientists. A tradition of user participation has emerged (most noticeably in Scandinavia) that would appear to offer considerable benefits to the development of parallel design methodologies (see Chapter 5 by Pelle Ehn, this volume).

Yet user participation is not unproblematic in the context of AMT systems design. Participative design practice (see Eason, 1982) has a number of inherent weaknesses. These include:

1. The "tyranny of the immediate." When prospective users are placed in front of new software or hardware, they find themselves in a very awkward position. In the experience of the ESPRIT project participants, the users will typically restrict their comments to superficial aspects of the design, usually based on a comparison with the technology they use in the workplace. Often the users are impressed by the novelty of the artifact, offer positive feedback, and limit their criticisms to relatively insignificant details

such as screen layout. The situation is often akin to being placed in the driving seat of a new automobile in a showroom and being asked to offer detailed feedback on the design of the automobile. Without a number of test drives, this feedback will concentrate only on the most superficial aspects.

2. Users will often lack the necessary technical expertise to respond constructively and insightfully to design options or prototypes.

3. User participation is often restricted to an evaluation of one or more design options, rather than the generation of alternative design options. Hence, there remains a danger that the design process will remain technically driven.

4. Partly because of the points listed, the social scientists and, more importantly, the engineers hold significantly more expert power than the user in the prototyping environment. Hence there is a tendency for user participation to take the form of consultation.

5. Sometimes it is difficult to find appropriate users. For example, within ESPRIT project 1217, the development of a prototype shopfloor monitoring and control software package ran into trouble when prospective users could not be found. The package was designed for use by metal workers, but the only people who could be found who were familiar with such systems had little or no practical knowledge of the shopfloor environment, being either line managers or production planning office staff.

Despite these difficulties, the direct engagement of social scientists and users in the design process was seen as a key element in the development of effective parallel design methods in the two projects.

LESSONS LEARNED: DESIGN CRITERIA

Job designs associated with AMT derive from five interrelated areas of decision making (see Corbett, 1987a). These are:

1. The allocation of functions between humans and machines;
2. The configuration or architecture of the system;
3. The control characteristics of the human–machine interface;
4. The informational characteristics of the human–machine interface; and
5. The allocation of responsibilities among users (operating and support personnel).

Researchers who follow the technological indeterminist line focus their attention on the social variables that impinge on only the last of these. However, it will be argued here that the preceding four areas of decision making within a technical system design process have as great (or greater) potential for opening up or constraining job design choices. Although these points will be discussed separately, in practice they should be analyzed together as subsets of an overall systems specification. A discussion of each of these decision criteria in turn reveals the dynamic of technically embedded constraint and the superiority of a human-centered approach.

Allocation of Functions

The allocation of functions in the design of AMT systems is concerned with determining the functions to be performed by the different components (human, software, hardware) within the system. Chapanis (1965) describes this phase as one of the first and most important problems in human–machine systems design and one that influences all later design thinking about the system.

The method most commonly used to allocate functions derives from the work of Fitts (1951). This method involves the systematic analysis of system functions to assess the relative strengths and weaknesses of human and machines in the performance of those functions. Allocations are made accordingly.

Yet the nature of human–machine comparability crucially depends on the criteria and measures being used. Typically, designers describe human functions in mathematical terms comparable to the terms used in describing mechanical functions. This leads to a paradox whereby any time one can reduce a human function to a mathematical formula one can generally build a machine that can do it more efficiently than a human:

> In other words, to the extent that man becomes comparable to a machine we do not really need him any more since he can be replaced by a machine. (Jordan, 1963, p. 162).

Hence the designer automates as many functions as possible, leaving the human to perform those functions that remain.

The implications of this for job design are clear: By designing human–machine systems for the human to do least, engineers remove much of the skill and knowledge from the job and transfer them into machines. Hence, although allocation choices do not entirely determine job design—there remains a choice over the way that the residual human tasks are combined and distributed among personnel—they can constrain job design options even in this first phase of the design process. Indeed, some have argued that a logic of job simplification is inherent within this technically led decision making process (see Cooley, 1987; Clegg et al., 1989).

Social scientists and engineers working within Project 534 explicitly rejected the Fitt's list approach to allocating functions between human and machine. They focused on the complementarity, rather than comparability, of humans and machines. Such an idea was by no means new (see Jordan, 1963), but this perspective had not given rise to any method for allocating functions in a systematic way. Consequently, the researchers spent a great deal of time developing a new method that would overcome the fundamentally technology-centered nature of the Fitt's list approach.

The new method was successfully employed by the interdisciplinary design team and resulted in some functional allocations that differed markedly from those that had previously been envisaged through the use of the Fitts list approach. The reasons for this difference stem from the inclusion of the following considerations in the decision making process. First, unlike the Fitts list approach, the new method incorporated situational considerations and criteria (financial, economic, organizational, and psychological) into the allocation process. Second, it recognized that functional allocation is not always non-zero-sum. There are many tasks that neither machines nor humans can do well, and others that both can perform equally well. Third, the new method stressed the iterative and contextual nature of design. Fourth, the new method allowed some allocation choices to be deferred in order to enable users to decide whether humans or machines carry out certain functions depending on production circumstances and uncertainties. This design allows a dynamic allocation of function.

The overall structure of this method for allocating function is shown diagrammatically in Figure 6.1 and is discussed in more detail in the following. In this description, examples from Project 534 are used to illustrate the procedure, and the reader is directed to Clegg et al. (1989) for further elaboration.

In Phase 1, the objectives of the system are specified.

In Phase 2, a more detailed operational statement of what the system is required to undertake is drawn up. In addition to a technical requirements specification (which forms part of the conventional hard systems design), a detailed scenario of how the resulting system will operate in an organizational context is drawn up. This scenario specifies job and organizational design objectives and offers the designers a fairly detailed picture of how the system would operate on a day-to-day basis. In this case, the scenario emphasized the role of multiskilled, flexible operators who have the skills to solve most of the everyday problems that occur in the system. These operators are organized in semiautonomous workgroups and undertake many of the traditional supervisory responsibilities themselves (see Clegg et al., 1989, for elaboration, and Corbett et al., 1991, for a similar example of scenario building within ESPRIT Project 1217).

Phase 3 involves the development of a functional specification and the identification of the functions and subfunctions of the system. It was at this stage that the interdisciplinary design team (engineers and social scientists) chose a system comprising a circular configuration with workstations branch-

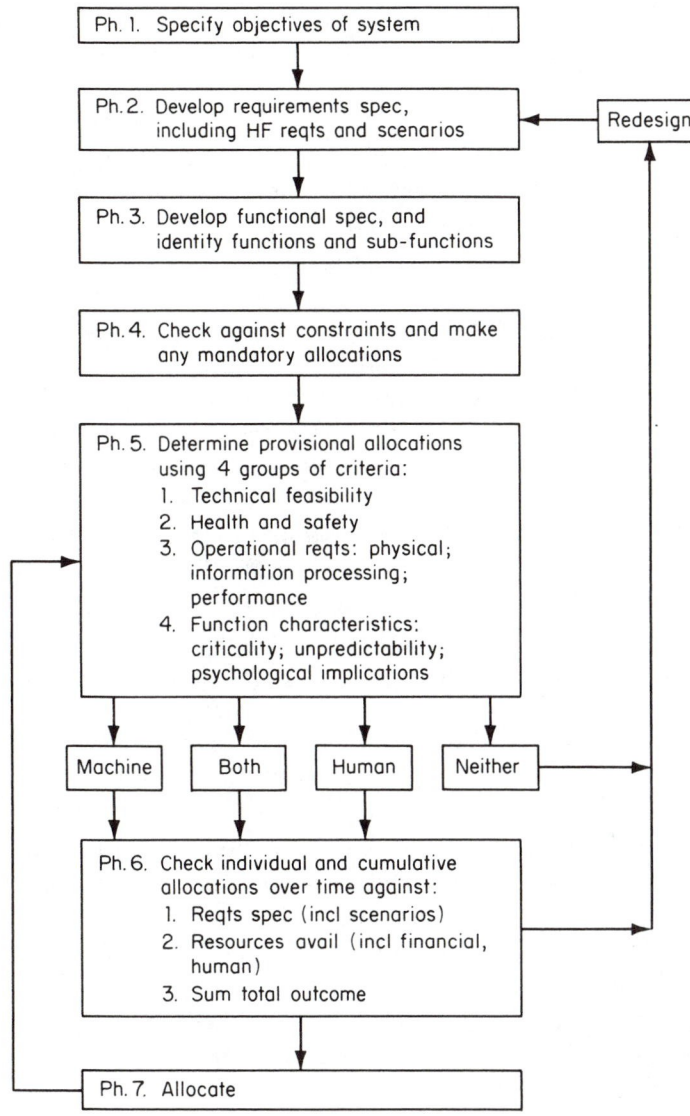

Figure 6.1. A method for allocating functions (from Clegg et al., 1988).

ing off for specialist activities such as parts presentation, manual assembly, and final assembly. The identification of major and subfunctions proved relatively straightforward for the engineering designers, although Clegg et al. (1989) note that:

> In this project it is fair to say that this phase remained technology driven, in part because of the ambitions of ESPRIT, which are concerned primarily with technological innovation and development. In more usual design environments we

would argue there should be fewer technological "givens," and there would be more debate about the appropriate extent of automation.   (p. 185)

In Phase 4, functions are checked against any constraints, and initial mandatory allocations are made. A constraint may be legal or set by the initial objectives of the project. For example, in Project 534, one key technical objective was to develop a robot equipped with an optical vision system to recognize parts. Certain mandatory allocations to machines directly derived from this technical constraint.

At the onset of Phase 5, a majority of functions will be unallocated, and, through an assessment of complementarity of humans and machines, a provisional allocation of function is made to human, machine, or both. In Project 534, four sets of criteria were used to assess the complementary abilities of humans and machines to carry out specific functions to the required level of performance (see Fig. 6.1). The first two sets—feasibility and health and safety—are self-explanatory. The third set of criteria relates to operational characteristics and concern three issues: the physical requirements of the function, such as weights carried; the cognitive, perceptual, and information-processing requirements of the function, such as data analyzed; and the performance requirements of the functions, such as required operating speeds and levels of precision.

The fourth set of criteria concerns the characteristics of specific functions in the context of the overall system operation. The criteria include a consideration of the criticality of the functions to the effective operation of the system, for example, whether the failure of the function would jeopardize the performance of the whole system; the unpredictability associated with the function, for example, when or how frequently a particular function will be required; and the psychological implications (both positive and negative) of the function for the people working within the system, particularly concerning their needs for control.

An example helps clarify the issues in this phase. Prior to using these criteria as a decision aid, the design engineers had decided that all workstation scheduling within the system would be carried out by the computer. With regard to scheduling at the manual workstation, the first few steps of the decision aid suggest that this would be a sensible decision, especially as an incorrect decision might have potentially disastrous repercussions. However, the decision aid highlighted the fact that human flexibility could be invaluable in dealing with unpredictable events and situations beyond the scope of the computer, such as variances in the availability of necessary equipment for a particular assembly operation. In addition, this function clearly has very obvious psychological implications for personal control. As a result of working through the decision aid, the project design team concluded that the computer should determine which tasks must be carried out at the workstation within a given period, and the operators should then be able to schedule these tasks in whichever order they wish, with computer support to allow them to check that their decisions do not cause problems elsewhere.

In Phase 6, the allocations are checked against the requirements specification (Phase 2) to ensure that both technical and social/organizational requirements are met.

In Phase 7, the function allocation is made, and the designer returns to Phase 5 to consider all remaining functions. The sequence is highly iterative, working through major functions first and becoming more specific and detailed over time. At this stage, it is important to recall the scenario developed in Phase 2, since it provides a general description of how the system should be organized and of the roles of different AMT system users. A financial appraisal is also conducted at this stage.

This method for allocating functions between humans and machines proved time consuming but effective in Project 534. Many of the problems associated with the use of design criteria discussed earlier were overcome by the specificity and structured nature of this method. However, it was found that the conventional financial appraisal of systems design options carried out in Phase 7 produced a noticeable degree of bias toward the "harder," more technically sophisticated options. While our functional allocation method was successful in generating human-centered design options, it was less successful when financial considerations were brought to bear. In part, this seemed to arise from the financial importance of reducing direct labor costs. While the engineers in the project fully endorsed the emphasis on high skill levels and job enrichment in the Phase 3 scenario, from the viewpoint of machine utilization, flexibility, and product quality, the conventional accounting cost–benefit models employed in Phase 7 did not translate such technical advantages into financial benefits. As a result of this failure to incorporate nonfinancial criteria into a cost–benefit analysis, the design options biased towards skilled humans were often rejected as too costly.

Luckily, there are encouraging signs that U.K. management accountants are beginning to accept that changes in their methods are needed to match the changes in AMT, particularly with regard to nonfinancial criteria and overhead allocation (Bromwich and Bhimani, 1990).

Systems Architecture

With the development of integrated AMT systems, the specification and design of systems architecture has taken on an increasingly significant role within the technical design process. The architecture of a system refers to the information and control system within which machine tools and other system components (including humans) are configured, organized, coordinated, and controlled. In the design of a stand-alone CNC machine tool with provision for manual data input, systems architecture is largely a matter of organizational design and choice. However, in the design of a highly integrated FMS or CIM system, the technology has organizational choice already embedded within it (Williams, 1988).

The automobile assembly line offers a classic example of how a technical systems architecture can directly affect job design. By configuring the production process in such a manner, the scheduling, timing, and pacing of operating tasks are technically embedded. No allowance for individual differences among operators in these matters can be made without a radical redesign of the systems architecture because of the tightly coupled nature of the system. Indeed, Volvo had to undertake just such a redesign in order to carry out successfully their well-publicized job redesign exercises at Kalmar and, more recently, at Uddevalla.

The example of the car assembly line is particularly apt when discussing AMT systems architecture. The tightly coupled nature of the assembly line is now being reproduced in small batch producing metal working industries and elsewhere through the use of sophisticated hardware and software packages that explicitly aim to decrease throughput time and inventory. Similarly, developments in computer-aided design, solid modeling, direct numerical control (DNC), and error detection and recovery software and hardware technology enable highly sophisticated production systems to be placed under centralized computer control, thereby limiting operator discretion and control. Again, we see that constraints on job design may be embedded within technology.

For the participants in ESPRIT Project 1217, it became increasingly clear as the project reached the end of its first year that new methods were needed to enable the parallel design of the technical and organizational/job design elements at the systems level. As documented in Corbett et al. (1991), the project engineers were eager to complete a technical systems specification as quickly as possible, while their social science colleagues felt that such an approach would preclude the effective incorporation of key social considerations. The subsequent development of the "shaping workshop" was to prove an effective and innovative parallel design method.

The human-centered CIM system developed in Project 1217 was based on the concept of production islands developed by Peter Brodner in his influential book, *Fabrik 2000* (1985). Brodner extends the principles of group technology to the entire organization of a factory. He advocates a four-stage developmental process to achieve effective and efficient production island implementation and operation. In Stage 1, products and parts with similar manufacturing requirements are grouped together. In Stage 2, the technology and equipment needed for the manufacture of complete products or part families are grouped together in the same physical location on the shopfloor. In Stage 3, semiautonomous work groups, comprising multiskilled workers, are set up and allocated to each of these manufacturing facilities. In Stage 4, the design, planning, and controlling tasks necessary for the complete production of products or part families are integrated within these groups. All necessary human, technical, and material resources are concentrated within these islands to enable workers to produce components and complete products insofar as possible from raw materials. These production islands are interlinked by basic components of CIM architecture (common database, data highway, and data exchange interfaces), although the personnel within the islands are responsible for almost all aspects of scheduling, programming, and production planning.

The island concept is based on the idea of redesigning key organizational factors in and around the production process. However, it soon became clear to project participants that at stage 4 such a design may be incompatible with conventionally designed top-down scheduling, planning, and materials transfer software and hardware. Hence the social scientists' worries concerning the speed of the engineers' work during the first year of the project. As a result, a "shaping workshop" was organized in an effort to examine both the shortcomings of conventional system protocols and topographies, and to draw up a systems architecture specification compatible with a concept of the decentralized production island.

In the first year of the project, the social scientists had developed a detailed scenario outlining how a CIM system based on the idea of production islands would operate on a day-to-day basis. As with the scenario developed in Project 534, it was intended that such a scenario would enable the engineers to visualize the types of operating and support tasks and roles they were designing. In this case, the scenario was developed by social scientists in collaboration with engineers and potential users in West Germany, Denmark, and the United Kingdom.

The shaping workshop was organized around an iterative, although highly structured, dialogue between social scientists and engineers working within the project and two outside experts (including Peter Brodner). In the course of the workshop, the technical implications and preconditions presented by the production island factory scenario were analyzed. In the subsequent dialogue, the engineers presented technical descriptions of a human-centered CIM architecture. These were then analyzed by the social scientists with regard to their social implications, presuppositions, and effects. Additional considerations of work organization, skills and CIM building blocks (CAD, CAM, and computer-aided planning, or CAP) were incorporated into the dialogue in an attempt to develop a detailed reference model for human-centered CIM as well as an aid to the gradual transformation of social descriptions into technical specifications and vice versa.

The results of the workshop focused on the importance of viewing human-centered CIM systems as loosely coupled, decentralized systems, not necessarily of a highly automated kind, integrated by means of common data-bases and data exchange capability that are far less sophisticated than those envisaged by most CIM proponents (see, for example, Yeomans et al., 1985), who stress the need for centralized, automatic real-time monitoring and control.

The effectiveness of the workshop was hampered by the lack of any detailed technical description of a human-centered CIM architecture concerning such issues as levels of control, data highway, and database interface design, and intensity of subsystem coupling. Consequently, the second dialogue (the input to which was to be supplied by the engineers) turned into a wide-ranging discussion of the form and content of a possible reference model for CIM. This technical description was developed a few months later by an interdisciplinary project team based on the preliminary results of the workshop. Workshop participants agreed that a detailed technical description of a CIM system (whether human centered or not) is only practicable when developed in direct collaboration with the user company. This view also appears to be supported by consulting engineers engaged in technically led CIM systems development (Chalmet, 1987).

One important lesson learned from the workshop is that human-centered CIM crucially depends on the simultaneous and detailed consideration of organizational, educational, and technical factors within a structured design process. Ongoing dialogue between engineers, social scientists, and end-users is a key attribute of this process. Failure to engage in such a dialogue can lead to a systems design with unacceptable levels of technically embedded constraints, as evidenced by the experience of the U.K. group.

The U.K. group focused its attention on the design and implementation of a human-centered CAM cell comprising two CNC lathes, a grinding machine, and automatic parts transfer capability, supported by shopfloor parts programming and scheduling software. Discussions on systems architecture—specifically on the interface between the scheduling system within the cell and the factory-wide production planning system—were not carried out with the user company until a late stage in the design process. This oversight was to have serious repercussions for the project.

The U.K. user company installed a highly sophisticated (and very expensive) proprietary production planning and shopfloor monitoring system at the behest of its Head Office immediately prior to the implementation of the CAM cell. Unfortunately, this was a top-down, management controlled, real-time shopfloor monitoring and control (SMC) system designed to enable automatic rescheduling of parts machining and transfer. Its hierarchical hard design made no technical provision for any shopfloor input other than signalling the end of a batch run. The integrated nature of its architecture was such that the ripple effect of any localized schedule editing would be felt right through the production process and could be catastrophic. Essentially, its technical design was such that the SMC system was unworkable without centralization of parts programming and production planning.

Clearly, such an architecture was incompatible with the production island scenario and a compromise solution had to be reached by which the SMC software treated the production island as a virtual machine. In other words, the software only processed data concerning the inputs and outputs to the island, effectively decoupling the machines within the island from the real-time monitoring and control capability that lay at the heart of the SMC system. While this solution did allow a degree of shopfloor autonomy, it also meant that the production process within the island was invisible to systems management, was relatively unpredictable, and therefore undermined the efficiency, integrity and cost-effectiveness of the overall SMC system. It was only a matter of weeks before the company decided that the relatively inexpensive and unsophisticated cell scheduling software should be discarded to allow centralized control to be established.

This experience clearly demonstrates the capability of systems architecture to act as a constraint on job design and the importance of developing parallel design methods such as the shaping workshop. While many companies do not shirk from writing off investments sunk into the training and skills of direct labor in times of financial hardship (redundancies resulting from company "rationalization"), they are far more reticent to write off costs sunk into AMT. When they do undertake the latter, companies rarely publicize such actions for fear of shaking shareholders' confidence.

Control Characteristics of the Human-Machine Interface

Autonomy and control are key elements in job design and redesign and are fundamental to the concept of human skill. The development of the digital computer and the microprocessor has led to greater distance between human operator and machine. The operator of a CNC machine tool, for example, shares control of machine functions with a CNC controller via an interface (typically a visual display terminal). Clearly the design of the interface control hardware and software will have a direct impact on the nature and extent of operators' autonomy and control at the individual level of analysis.

Control may be viewed as a process in which workers articulate their own meaning through action. For instance, a CNC interface that requires data input from an operator in simple numerical format in response to preprogrammed, fixed sequence software prompts effectively reduces operator control in the sense that the meaning of the operator's actions is imposed by the structure of the software. Such an interface is of a qualitatively different nature from a controller that allows graphical entry of data and the creation of user-definable macros. Controllers that are not designed to enable operator data input of any kind (as with early NC controllers) have the highest level of technically embedded constraint in this design area.

The human-centered approach to interface design raises two key questions. First, does the interface allow the imposition of the user's definition of the manufacturing process or does the designer of the interface software do the prescribing? And second, does the interface allow the users to express intent directly or must they express meaning through machine code or programs defined by computer experts who may have little or no understanding of the thought processes involved in machining?

Within Project 1217, the Danish CAD research team was particularly successful in developing a CAD workstation that enabled the user to retain full control of the work process. They developed the specification for, and a working prototype of, an electronic sketch pad. This sketch pad retained the three main functions of the drawing in design work, namely, to help in the visualization of design ideas, to act as a means of communicating the design intention to manufacturing and other personnel, and to serve as a memory bank for what has been done. In addition, the sketch pad (which uses a wireless pencil) allows design sketches to be produced in a form amenable to electronic data storage in two or two-and-a-half dimensions. These data can then be transmitted as an exact geometrical shape to the CAD workstation for analysis.

The sketch pad thus represents a form of direct object manipulation that gives the user full control and full skill retention. Hence, the level of technically embedded constraint associated with this design is minimal. The term *direct object manipulation* was coined by Ben Shneiderman (1982) and highlights two important aspects of user control, namely, the reduction of semantic and articulatory distance (Hutchins, 1986).

Distance refers to the relationship between one's thoughts and the physical requirements of the system in use. A short semantic distance involves two important factors that the Danish CAD team posed in two questions: Is it possible to express one's intentions through the medium or tools in use? and Can the objects of interest be expressed in a straightforward manner, or are there complicated technical maneuvers to complete before one's meanings and intentions can be expressed? They argued that:

> In the case of the Electronic Sketch Pad, semantic directness is apparent. Designers who are familiar with the practice of a traditional sketch pad experience no difficulty in using it. When comparing it with a [conventional] CAD system, the two designers involved in its prototyping said that they felt as if they were "getting some of their freedom back." The important factor is the freedom to coordinate mental and manual activity in the same action. Therefore matters of interest can be expressed in a straightforward and individual fashion instead of

the standardized and indirect operations of the CAD system. (Laessoe et al., 1989: 76–7)

The second aspect of distance, articulatory distance, concerns the form of user expression—the relationship between the meanings of expressions and their physical form. Mike Cooley (1987) argues that, up to the 1940s in Europe, the drafting staff (and particularly the drawings they produced) was the center of the design activity. They would design a component, draw it, stress it out, and specify the material for it. Over the intervening years, each of these tasks has become isolated into fragmented functions that, with the advent of hard CAD systems, have been taken over by computer technology:

> With this equipment, the draughtsman no longer needs to produce a drawing and so the subtle interplay of interpretation and modification as the commodity was being designed and related to the skilled manual worker on the shopfloor is being ruptured. (Cooley, 1987: p. 17)

In a similar vein, the Danish research team argued that such technology, when used in the early stages of the design process, has a tendency to promote isolation, to induce passivity, and to alienate the designer from the world of machines, equipment, and their operational needs:

> Although CAD systems improved the speed and ease of modifying and plotting a drawing and increased the possibilities for combining two drawings and/or rescaling a drawing, it proved to be an inadequate tool in the more creative phases of design. Moreover, compared with the possibilities of an overall view at the drawing board, the screen was experienced like a microscope. Many designers felt that they were peering through a keyhole when working with the CAD system. (Laessoe et al., 1989: pp. 24–5)

Through the reinstatement of the drawing at the heart of the design activity, the Danish team believe that the articulatory distance between the skilled designer and his or her design tools is far closer than that achieved at present by conventional CAD systems. User control is also maximized insofar as the electronic sketch pad no more dictates the way it should be used than does a pencil.

It is important to note here that the idea of the electronic sketch pad was generated through discussions within the user groups working alongside the research team. A number of "future workshops" were held in which potential users were encouraged to discuss their problems and dissatisfactions with current CAD technology and to fantasize about how they would like to see the work of designers and the technology they use developing in the future.

In the ESPRIT case, users were encouraged to generate their own designs without being limited by the budgetary and technological constraints that inevitably shaped the thinking of the CAD research team. While clearly running the risk of either generating no solutions whatsoever or generating technically or economically unfeasible solutions, the technique of the future workshop helped overcome some of the problems mentioned earlier.

Informational Characteristics of the Human–Machine Interface

Operators can never be in full control of a machine or system unless they understand what it is actually doing and receive the appropriate feedback. The invisibility of many software functions means that operators must rely heavily on information that is transmitted or generated by computer in order to structure their work behavior. Software that only presents machine-specific information in the event of system malfunction, for example, will not permit operators to see the consequences of their actions for overall system performance, thereby restricting human control.

The interaction between operator and machine is, in effect, a mediated dialogue between user and designer in which the technical systems designer predefines the immediate work context and domain through the type and scope of information given to the user. Because of this, the designer has the means to constrain or enhance operator control and skill development in isolation from any organizational choice of job design. One has only to recall Milgram's dictum: "Control the manner in which a man interprets the world, and you have gone a long way toward controlling his behavior" (Milgram, 1974, p. 145).

Research by Markus (1984) revealed that conventional systems design practice treats information as a technical rather than a social variable. The emphasis is upon data flows and data management rather than face-to-face information and interpersonal information exchange. Yet, as Leithauser (1986) argues, there exists an informal "hidden situation" in every organization, largely unrecognized by external systems experts, that is fundamental to the successful functioning of an organization. Certainly a powerful weapon in the armory of an aggrieved trade union is the tactic of "working to rule." The power of this tactic stems from the fact that, in the absence of informal vertical and lateral communication, most complex organizations would cease to function effectively within a matter of days or even hours.

Current practice in AMT system design emphasizes formalized information and preplanned communication. The significance of nonformalized information and communication is often neglected by computer professionals, owing to the difficulties of making it visible and formalizable. As a result, many systems designed by computer professionals are intended to facilitate the activity of an individual working alone, thereby leaving out the essential collective dimension of work.

This trend may have a significant effect on the quality of working life of AMT system users. Since the days of the famous Hawthorne studies in the 1920s, research on organizational behavior has highlighted the important rule played by formal and informal work group membership in the maintenance and growth of job commitment and job satisfaction.

Furthermore, the predominant emphasis on formalized information and data in AMT systems design and use can create a number of problems for users. For example, research by Zuboff (1988) reveals that the complexity and level of abstraction associated with hard AMT system designs can produce something of a crisis of confidence among operating personnel. She quotes a paper mill operator who argued that:

> We have so much data from the computer, I find that hard drives out soft. Operators are tempted not to tour the plant. They just sit at the computer and watch for alarms. One weekend I found a tank overflowing in digesting. I went to the operator and told him, and he said, "It can't be, the computer says my level is fine." I am afraid of what happens if we trust the computer too much. (Zuboff, 1988, p. 69)

The British CAM research group within Project 1217 was eager to incorporate the views and needs of end users in the design of the CNC lathe control interface within the CAM cell and to avoid the premature closure of design options in this design process. As a result, the design of the interface was undertaken in two phases. First, the "CNC framework" was developed. This "framework" consists of the basic technical core (interpreters, effectors, servomotor drivers) of a CNC controller, which requires the input of machine code in order to control a machine tool. The second phase involves the design and development of a "user surface" —the human–machine interface software and hardware—in collaboration with prospective users. This user surface is inherently flexible and can be designed to suit the users' customary or preferred methods of working and programming.

The advantage of this two-phase design method stems from the fact that, unlike conventional interface design practice, the framework of the CNC controller can be built without closing off design options prematurely in the early stages of design. The user surface (which can take on many different forms during the iterative design process) can then be placed on the framework. During the course of the project, the user surface was finally completed only after it had been used on the shopfloor on an experimental basis for a period of time. Essentially this design process enables the user, in collaboration with an engineer, to shape the informational characteristics of the human–machine interface. Hence, any technically embedded constraints are negotiated with the user and are not imposed by engineering design.

Although similar to the design method of prototyping, this method has a more experimental and evolutionary character. Indeed, the Danish research team placed similar emphasis on experimentation in the design process during the prototyping phase that followed the future workshops. Both the U.K. and Danish methods contain elements of learning by doing. However, unlike the mockups employed in the Danish UTOPIA project, both teams employed prototype technologies that could actually perform technical functions recognizably similar to those carried out by the users in their place of work (see chapter 5 by Pelle Ehn, this volume). This provides greater realism, the opportunity for users to manufacture parts similar or identical to those made at their place of work, and the opportunity for engineers within the research teams to engage directly in discussion with the users.

For example, technical constraints evident in the prototype could be confronted at an earlier stage of the design process than is possible when using mockups. In the UTOPIA project, the engineering designers were subcontracted to develop the technology based on a detailed technical specification, drawn up by users and social scientists as a result of their experimentations with mockups. These engineers had given little or no input to this specification, which gave rise not only to the rejection of certain economically or technically infeasible aspects of the design (such as an A0-sized visual display screen) but also to uncertainties of interpretation that had to be resolved without recourse to experimentation. The involvement of engineering designers at the experimental prototyping stage would have enabled such uncertainties either to have been avoided or to have been resolved through discussion with users.

Allocation of Responsibilities

The four areas of decision making discussed here have clear implications for what may be termed the balance of control between AMT and shopfloor users. Decisions concerning the allocation of responsibilities between users, if left until the implementation stage of a technically led design process, will have been largely pre-empted by these earlier technical decisions. As discused earlier, the dominance of hard systems thinking among AMT system designers means that job designs (and frequently job designs based on incorrect assumptions about working practices) will arise almost by default unless steps are taken to reshape the earlier stages of design. The ESPRIT projects sought to widen the scope available to the users to shape their own working behavior and practices.

Of course, some choices concerning allocation of personnel responsibilities will always remain at the implementation stage. Team organization is feasible even with flowline technologies such as the car assembly line, albeit in a rather awkward and inefficient form. Indeed, the research evidence suggests that even the most inflexible and technology-centered AMT systems can be made to work more effectively by skilled operators. Given this evidence, it can be argued that organizational decision makers should take the opportunity to foster the development and use of these skills through the design of *enabling* rather than *constraining* technologies. With the growing sophistication of hard systems technologies, technically embedded constraints on multiskilled group-based job design seem likely to increase over time unless steps are taken to open up the interior of AMT design to end users.

Summary

Table 6.1 contrasts the options available in the five key areas of design decision making in terms of their affinity to either a hard-technology-centered or a human-centered perspective. Two caveats should be noted. First, as we suggested above, these five areas are not typically, and should not be treated as, independent. Second, the examples in the table are somewhat overstated in order to polarize the differences between the two approaches. In reality, design choices are typically located on the continuum between those poles. For example, at the present time, it may be that few FMSs are truly technology centered in terms of the variables shown in Table 6.1 owing to the lack of robustness and/or high capital costs of computer software and automatic machinery. Although hard systems professionals aim explicitly for a high level

Table 6.1. A Comparison of Technology-Centered and Human-Centered AMT Systems Design

Design choice point	Technology-centered systems	Human-centered systems
Allocation of function	Operator carries out those functions that cannot be automated	Operator allocates functions depending upon particular circumstances during production
Systems architecture	Centralized control system. Production machines controlled at highest possible level (e.g., part programs generated at CAD level)	Decentralized control system; machines controlled at lowest possible level (e.g., part programs generated on shopfloor)
Control characteristics of human–machine interface	User actions paced and regulated by directives stored in machine	User discretion and control maximized; technology does not dictate work methods
Information characteristics of human–machine interface	Systems status data presented only to management; restricted access for shopfloor users	System status data available at all machines; facilitation of cross-functional communication
Allocation of responsibilities	Work controlled by functional specialists	Work controlled by multiskilled shopfloor users

of consistency across these design choices (Markus, 1984), in practice many systems do not demonstrate such consistency.

CONCLUSION

The case examples in this chapter demonstrate that parallel design methods that overcome technically embedded constraints on job design can be successfully developed in a multidisciplinary design project given sufficient scope for interdisciplinary dialogue and negotiation. Although such methods tend to slow down the design process, it seems likely that their longer-term viability and acceptability would outweigh the time penalty. The fact that as many as 75 percent of companies that implement advanced manufacturing technologies do not achieve anticipated performance from the technology because of unforeseen job design and machine interface problems (Majchzrak, 1988) suggests that there is a need for such parallel design methods.

The concept of skill-based production is crucial to the future of manufacturing. Yet much of the literature that articulates this concept focuses on the issue of organizational design while ignoring technological design. This chapter has argued that there is an element of soft technological determinism associated with recent developments in advanced manufacturing technology. Badly managed, this determination will close off important skill-based organizational and job design options. Hence it has been argued that social scientists and users must collaborate with the engineering designers of AMT to overcome these technically embedded constraints. A number of examples of such collaborative design methods have been described to inform a wider debate and encourage active engagement in this shaping process.

Of course, constraints on the more widespread diffusion of parallel design methods and their derived technological artifacts are numerous. It has been argued here that the predominance of hard systems thinking among AMT designers and their associated cost–benefit accounting models play a major part in this process. The attitudes and behavior of higher management in the manufacturing arena may also prove to be a difficult constraint to overcome. The diffusion of the new approaches could, however, be facilitated by education; one practical recommendation that flows from the ESPRIT work is that an understanding of the nature of the relationship between AMT design and job design should become an integral part of the education of engineers.

REFERENCES

Armstrong, P. (1989). Management, labor process and agency. *Work, Employment and Society* **3**, 307–22.

Attewell, P. (1987). The deskilling controversy. *Work and Occupations* **14**, 323–46.

Bijker, W. E., T.P. Hughes, and T. Pinch (eds) (1987). *The Social Construction of Technological Systems.* Cambridge, Mass.: MIT Press.

Blauner, R. (1964). *Alienation and Freedom: The Factory Worker and His Industry,* Chicago: Chicago University Press.

Brandt, G., B. Kundig, Z. Papadimitriou, and J. Thomae (1978). *Computer und Arbeitprozess.* Frankfurt: Campus Press.

Braverman, H. H. (1974). *Labor and Monopoly Capital.* New York: Monthly Review Press.

Brodner, P. (1985). *Fabric 2000. Alternative Entwicklungspfade in die Zukunft der Fabrik.* Berlin: Sigma-Verlag.

Bromwich, M., and A. Bhimani (1990). *Management Accounting: Evolution Not Revolution.* London: Chartered Institute of Management Accountants Publications.

Buchanan, D. A. (1983) Technological imperatives and strategic choice, in G. Winch (ed.). *Information Technology in Manufacturing Processes.* London: Rossendale.

Buffo, M., J. Fix-Sterz, R. Schneider, and J. Wengel (1988). Arbeitsschutzpekte der CNC-technik und des CAD-einsatzes, in G. Peters (ed.). *Arbeitschutz, Gesundheit und Neue Technologien.* Opladen: Westdeutscher Verlag.

Burnes, B. (1988). New technology and job design: the case of CNC. *New Technology, Work and Employment* **2,** 100–11.

Chalmet, L. G. (1987). Increasing your competitive advantage through CIM, in K. Rathmill and P. MacConaill (eds.). *Computer Integrated Manufacturing.* Bedford: IFS/Springer.

Chapanis, A. (1965). On the allocation of function between men and machines. *Occupational Psychology* **39,** 1–11.

Child, J. (1987). Organizational design for advanced manufacturing technology, in T. D. Wall, C. W. Clegg, and N. J. Kemp (eds.). *The Human Side of Advanced Manufacturing Technology.* Chicester: Wiley.

Clegg, C. W. (1987). Appropriate technology for manufacturing: Some management issues, in G. I. Johnson and J. R. Wilson (eds.). *Ergonomics Matters in Advanced Manufacturing Technology.* London: Butterworths.

Clegg, C. W., and J. M. Corbett (1987). Research and development into "humanizing" AMT, in T. D. Wall, C. W. Clegg, and N. J. Kemp (eds.). *The Human Side of Advanced Manufacturing Technology.* Chicester: Wiley.

Clegg, C. W., S. Ravden, J. M. Corbett, and G. I. Johnson (1989). Allocating functions in computer integrated manufacturing: A review and a new method. *Behaviour and Information Technology* **8,** 175–90.

Commission of European Communities (1987). *Draft ESPRIT Work Program.* Brussels: Commission of European Communities.

Cooley, M.J.E. (1987). *Architect or Bee? The Human Price of Technology.* London: Hogarth Press.

Corbett, J. M. (1987a). Computer aided manufacturing and the design of shopfloor jobs: Towards a new research perspective in occupational psychology, in M. Frese, E. Ulich, and W. Dzida (eds.). *Psychological Issues of Human–Computer Interaction in the Workplace.* Amsterdam: North-Holland.

Corbett, J. M. (1987b). Human work design criteria and the design process: the devil in the detail, in P. Brodner (ed.). *Skill-Based Automated Manufacturing.* Oxford: Pergamon Press.

Corbett, J. M., L. Rasmussen, and F. Rauner (1991). *Crossing the Border: The Social and Engineering Design of Computer Integrated Manufacturing Systems.* London: Springer-Verlag.

Corbett, J. M., S.J. Ravden, and C.W. Clegg (1987). The development and implementation of human and organizational criteria in CIM environments, in K. Rathmill and P. MacConaill (eds.). *Computer Integrated Manufacturing.* Bedford: IFS/Springer.

Corbett, J. M. and H. Scarbrough (forthcoming). *Technology and Organization: Power, Meaning and Design*. London: Routledge.

DeMarco, T. (1979). *Structured Systems Specification*. New York: Yourdon.

Eason, K. D. (1982). The process of introducing new technology. *Behaviour and Information Technology* **1**, 197–213.

Fitts, P. M. (ed.) (1951). *Human Engineering for an Effective Air Navigation and Traffic Control System*. Washington, D.C.: National Research Council.

Francis, A., and Grootings, P. (eds.) (1989). *New Technologies and Work: Capitalist and Socialist Perspectives*. London: Routledge.

Hackman, J. R., and G.R. Oldham (1980). *Work Redesign*. Reading, Mass.: Addison–Wesley.

Hampden-Turner, C. (1970). *Radical Man*. Cambridge, Mass.: Schenken.

Hutchins, E. L. (1986). Direct manipulation interfaces, in D. Norman and S. Draper (eds.). *User Centered System Design*. Hillsdale, N.J.: Lawrence Erlbaum.

Jordan, N. (1963). Allocation of functions between man and machines in automated systems. *J. Appl. Psychol.* **47**, 161–65.

Kelley, M. R. (1988). Beyond the deskilling debate. *Working Paper 88-49*. Pittsburgh, Penn.: School of Urban and Public Affairs, Carnegie Mellon University.

Kusterer, K. (1978). *Workplace Know-How: The Important Working Knowledge of "Unskilled" Workers*. Boulder, Co.: Westview.

Laessoe, J., L.B. Rasmussen, and P. Tottrup (1989). *The Electronic Sketch Pad: Prototype Observation and Organizational Context*. Lyngby: Denmark Technical University Press.

Leithauser, Th. (1986). Subjektivitat im produktionprocess, in B. Vollmerg, E. Senghaase-Knobloch and Th. Leithauser (eds.). *Betriebliche Lebenswelt*. Opladen: Campus Press.

Littler, C. (1982). *The Development of the Labor Process in Capitalist Societies*. London: Heinemann.

Littler, C. (1983). A history of "new" technology, in G. Winch (ed.). *Information Technology in Manufacturing Processes*. London: Rossendale.

MacKenzie D., and J. Wajcman (eds.) (1985). *The Social Shaping of Technology*. Milton Keynes: Open University Press.

Majchzrak, A. (1988). *The Human Side of Factory Automation*. San Francisco: Jossey–Bass.

Markus, M. L. (1984). *Systems in Organizations*. London: Pitman Press.

Meister, D. (1987). Systems design, development and testing, in G. Salvendy (ed.). *Handbook of Human Factors*. New York: Wiley.

Milgram, S. (1974). *Odedience to Authority*. London: Tavistock.

Mumford, E., and D. Henshall (1979). *A Participative Approach to Computer Systems Design*. London: Associated Business Press.

Noble, D. (1984). *Forces of Production*. New York: Alfred Knopf.

Rose, H., I. McLoughlin, R. King, and J. Clark (1986). Opening the black box: the relation between technology and work. *New Technology, Work and Employment* **1**, 18–26.

Shneiderman, B. (1982). The future of interactive systems and the emergence of direct manipulation. *Behaviour and Information Technology* **1**, 237–56.

Smith, S. L., and A.F. Aucella (1983). Design guidelines for the user interface to computer-based information systems. *Technical Report ESD-TR-83-122*, Hanscom, Mass.: U.S.A.F.

Sorge, A., G. Hartmann, M. Warner, and I. Nicholas (1983). *Microelectronics and Manpower in Manufacturing*. Aldershot: Gower.

Sydow, J. (1987). Office automation—an organizational perspective, in M. Frese, E. Ulich, and

W. Dzida (eds.). *Psychological Issues of Human–Computer Interaction in the Workplace.* Amsterdam: North-Holland.

Taylor, J. C. (1977a). Experiments in work system design: Economic and human results. Part 1. *Personnel Review* **6**(3), 21–34.

Taylor, J. C. (1977b). Experiments in work system design: Economic and human results. Part 2. *Personnel Review* **6**(4), 21–42.

Wilkinson, B. (1983). *The Shopfloor Politics of New Technology.* London: Heinemann.

Willcocks, L., and D. Mason (1987). *Computerizing Work: People, Systems Design and Workplace Relations.* London: Paradigm.

Williams, T. A. (1988). Beyond software ergonomics? Human control of automated systems, in W. Karwowski, H. R. Parsaei, and M. R. Wilhelm (eds.). *Ergonomics of Hybrid Automation 1.* Amsterdam: Elsevier.

Woodward, J. (1965). *Industrial Organization: Theory and Practice.* London: Oxford University Press.

Yeomans, R. W., A. Choudry, and P.J.W. Ten Hagen (1985). *Design Rules for a Computer Integrated Manufacturing System.* Amsterdam: North-Holland.

Zuboff, S. (1988). *In the Age of the Smart Machine—The Future of Work and Power.* New York: Basic Books.

CHAPTER 7

Enacting Design for the Workplace

JOHN SEELY BROWN AND PAUL DUGUID

Innovative design for the workplace runs up against inadequate understanding of both work and design practices. Ideas about work practices comprise an odd mixture of folklore and explicit, programmatic descriptions. Thus, paradoxically, a call for union members to "work to rule" can bring a workplace to a complete halt: no set of rules can describe or define what work really is. Conventional ideas about design practices are similarly limited. Indeed, Thackera (1988b) suggests that the whole concept of design is expanding so rapidly that an entirely new term is needed to encompass the range of issues designers now confront. Our purpose in this chapter is to bring some of the implicit character of work and design into the daylight, as a first step towards making design for the workplace more valid.

We explore thirteen topics that we believe are central to understanding design for the workplace. We suggest that conventional design approaches often mask powerful but unnoticed resources that, if tapped, can contribute significantly to successful design. For example, a focus on explicit instruction obscures many other ways in which designs actually rely on valuable implicit understanding. Similarly, a focus on individual users conceals the community of users that develops around successful work systems or processes and is crucial to their successful use.

To examine the important collateral resources that conventional design overlooks, we pair such concepts as individual–social, narrow–broad, center–periphery. This is not to establish rigid dichotomies and thus threaten to shift existing imbalances from one inadequate extreme to another, but to expand the region of the "thinkable" in relation to work and design practices. In an insightful discussion of the way such dichotomies may tighten a noose rather than release it, Bourdieu (1989) describes "paired oppositions" as little more than "colluding adversaries" that "tend to delimit the space of the thinkable by excluding the very intention to think beyond the divisions they institute" (p. 87). But the elements of most of our pairs (though not all, for a few remained stubborn) are presented here as mutually constitutive components of good design. One of each pair has been masked by the attention paid to the other, but both must be understood if design is to be moved beyond current impasses. In thus trying to broaden the focus of design, we hope to expand ideas of what design is and what roles it can play in an organization.

OVERVIEW

We have separated the thirteen pairs roughly into three groups: design and learning in the workplace, design and innovation, and design and tools. These groups are useful for providing an overview, but they are not integral to the development of each pair. Furthermore, like each pair and each member of each pair, no group is self-contained. Learning, innovation, and artifacts are central topics in all three.

Design and learning in the workplace. We group the first four pairs under the theme of design and learning in work. The introduction of new tools and new processes places a continual demand on the learning ability of those that work there.

Many of the misconceptions about conditions for working can be traced to misconceptions about conditions for learning. Burton, Brown, and Fischer (1984) suggest that working environments can be designed to amplify productive and simultaneous working and learning. The reliability of such design depends on a good understanding of learning. Some conventional assumptions about working and learning, by contrast, unintentionally and paradoxically lead to the design of work systems that inhibit the very learning that is needed for their successful introduction and use.

Design and innovation. Pairs five through eight are grouped under design and innovation. Here we discuss the ways in which design can support innovation and the innovational approach that Daft and Weick (1984) call "enacting."

Designers have an important but underestimated position in the interface between organizations and their environments. From that position, they are able to affect how an organization and its products are seen by its environment. Moreover, they are also able to affect how the environment is seen by the organization. Thus, designers can play a central role in helping organizations change themselves in response to changes in their environments. Design, seen in this way, becomes a key component of innovation. We are arguing, therefore, not only that designers must recognize how they can affect implementation, but also that innovative organizations must broaden their notion of how design can effect innovation.

Design and tools. Pairs nine through thirteen are grouped under the theme design and tools. Three key aspects of tools emerge in relation to learning and use:

1. Tools are cultural artifacts. Tools can only be understood in the context of the community that uses them. A well-used tool embodies aspects of the community's view of the world and of its own history. [See, for example, Hutchins' description (forthcoming) of the alidade used for navigation.] Learning to use a tool therefore involves learning the community's viewpoint—an essential ingredient of membership in the community.
2. Tools provide "affordances." Its embodiment of the community's world view makes a tool capable, in Gibson's terms (1979), of *affording* knowledge. That is, tools are a structured part of the community's environment that support sense-making. A hammer indicates by its shape how it is held and how it is used. Thus, within the context of a community, tools not only reflect a portion of that community's insight, they also support learning about that insight and processes related to it.
3. Tools need to be capable of becoming ready-to-hand. People outside a community of practitioners view tools quite differently from the way insiders view them. Design must reflect the insiders' view. For members of a community, their tool can disappear as a separable object of observation and simply become an integral part of their practice—a condition Heidegger (1962) describes as readiness-to-hand. Good design results in a tool that can achieve this state of readiness-to-hand within a community.

DESIGN AND LEARNING IN THE WORKPLACE

Instruction and Learning

Design for the workplace must involve design for learning. But the success of such design is repeatedly compromised by tension between the ways people actually learn in work and prevailing theories of pedagogy.

Unfortunately, from the perspective of pedagogy, the causes of these clashes are usually invisible. Thus tools can be unlearnable, but why they are unlearnable cannot be explained. As a result, some assume users cannot learn, others assume instructors cannot teach, but few implicate inadequate design. To understand the significance of design for learning in work, it is essential to investigate the causes and cures of what is a fundamental misalignment between learning and the conventional theories of learning on which designers rely.

Learning as Transfer. For over 200 years, models of learning have rarely been separable from notions of instruction and formal education. Learning has predominantly been viewed from the perspective of teaching. Explicit instruction (of the sort found in workplace training) and explicit instructions (of the sort found in manuals) still dominate attempts to foster learning about machines (Orr, 1990a). Instruction is, in these cases, conventionally thought of as the transmission of explicit knowledge from the head of someone who knows to the head of someone who does not know but who, it is assumed, can simply be told. In the absence of an instructor, some text, chart, table, or whatever is assumed capable of communicating between the two.

The transmission metaphor, however, has come under increasing attack. With respect to new tools, the strongest attack is made by the users who put their manuals in the trash. In belated recognition of their own limitations, manuals now often include an almost pathetic plea: "For Those Who Don't Read Manuals." Yet this only emphasizes the underlying resilience of pedagogical theory: When instruction fails, add more instructions. Some alternatives, such as the "Tour of the Macintosh"—a demonstration of how the Macintosh computer operates—take a more enlightened approach to learning and use.

Meanwhile, theoretical attacks on the notion of teaching as knowledge transfer are beginning to reach a critical mass. From widely diverse sources that include philosophers (e.g., Heidegger, 1962, 1971; Austin, 1962), linguists (e.g., Reddy, 1979), discourse theorists (e.g., Clark and Schaeffer, 1989; Sacks, Schegloff, and Jefferson, 1974), communications theorists (e.g., Williams, 1976a; Carey, 1989; Habermas, 1979), literary theorists (e.g., Sartre, 1978; Iser, 1974; Fish, 1971, 1980), learning theorists (e.g., Schön, 1984), and from designers themselves (e.g., Alexander, Ishikawa, and Silverstein, 1977; Alexander, 1988; Frampton, 1988; Thackera, 1988a) has come work that explicitly or implicitly regards learning less as the product of transmission than a process of *construction*.

Learning as Construction. The idea of learning and communication as construction seems to provide far more insight. Learners can usefully be thought of as constructing an understanding of their world, as making sense of what they do not know by whatever means are at hand. In constructing their understanding of a new tool, for instance, learners are not limited to the tool and its explicit instructions alone. Ambient social and physical circumstances and the histories of the people involved contribute significantly to their understanding. Like magpies building nests, learners grab whatever is at hand in the process of learning. This view of learning is thus similar to Levi-Strauss's concept of *bricolage*. In all, learning is a far more diffuse process than the mere acquisition of explicit facts about a restricted domain.

One of the most versatile accounts of this sort of construction is provided by Lave and Wenger's (1990) concept of legitimate peripheral participation (LPP).

LPP, it is important to emphasize, is an analytical tool for understanding learning; it is not a method of education. The learning examined may or may not involve teaching or instruction. Thus, Lave and Wenger's analysis allows us to escape problems that arise from examining learning from instruction's one-sided viewpoint.

Learning viewed from the learning side, Lave and Wenger argue, is a process of constructing an identity through joining (or developing) a "community-of-practice." Learning involves becoming an "insider." Learners do not receive abstract, "objective" knowledge; rather, they learn to function as a member of the community in which knowledge is situated—be it the community of nuclear physicists, cabinet makers, or street corner society.

Latour and Woolgar (1986) reveal the ways in which the transactions within a biology laboratory were, in many ways, simply uninterpretable by outsiders. For instance, although the grammar and the basic structure of the sentences in papers the biologists wrote were not dissimilar to the sort of prose written by the investigators, the papers and their uses were, in fact, "quite unfathomable" (p. 75). Becoming a biologist in that laboratory involved learning to read and write *as a member of the laboratory community* in ways that are only understood by that community.

Apprenticeship provides a helpfully transparent model of LPP understood this way. Apprentices become legitimate participants in the practices of a community and, through involvement in the authentic tasks of that community, assimilate the identity and the perspective of its members, changing themselves and the community in the process. All learners are acquiring not just explicit, formal "expert knowledge," but also the ability to behave as community members. Learning thus viewed draws attention away from abstract knowledge and cranial processes and focuses it on the praxis and communities in which knowledge takes on significance.

In the field of literary criticism, Fish (1971, 1980) argues toward an intriguingly compatible conclusion. The ability to recognize and understand a text, he claimed, requires the formation of or membership in "communities of interpretation" to frame and give meaning to what a text is and what it means. Building on Fish's analysis, but taking the concept of interpretation more broadly to include all forms of sense-making about objects, we suggest that learning about new devices is best understood (and best achieved) in the context of the community in which the devices are used and the community's particular interpretive conventions. Lave and Wenger, Latour and Woolgar, and Fish, among others, forcefully suggest that learning, understanding, and interpretation involve a great deal that is not explicit or explicable. This "great deal" is developed and framed in a crucially communal context.

Approaching learning this way widens the focus of design for the workplace from the tight, sharp-edged circle of an individual tool, an individual user, and conventional workplace training to the broad, fuzzy-edged area of the locale and the community and the activities of the tool user. Given the apparent tractability of transfer-through-explicit-training approaches, designers may be daunted by such a diffusion of focus. A broader focus, properly understood, however, does not so much erect intractable challenges (they exist anyway; our analysis merely brings them to light), as offer a broad array of physical and social affordances for realigning the actual processes of learning in work with the designers' models of learning for work.

Although Lave and Wenger caution against separating the concept of LPP into parts, we suggest that well-designed tools must provide:

1. *Legitimacy* of participation in the target community in which the tool is embedded;
2. *Peripherality,* which Lave and Wenger rephrase as access to the actual, authentic practices of the community; and
3. Fluidity of *participation.* That is, tools must enable and empower learners to increase the depth of their involvement in proportion to the development of their knowledgeable skill.

If, in contrast, tools and instruction serve to distinguish learners from workers, to isolate people from the target practice, or to hide the target community, then the target learning is inevitably undermined. This is not to say that learning does not take place. In isolating or contradictory conditions, interstitial communities form within the context of which learning is evident. This learning, however, is unlikely to be the learning expected by the canonical, target community (Orr, 1990a; Lave and Wenger, 1990; Eckert, 1989).

We do not claim that explicit instruction of individuals has no place in learning and thus in design. What we do claim is that pedagogical theory, with its reliance on explicit, individualized instruction, has distracted attention from the importance of implicit, social understanding and the community in which understanding is constructed. As long as instruction and design continue to disregard the social aspects of learning, the explicit–implicit relationship will remain a source of conflict rather than of synergy.

Explicit and Implicit

The problem of relying on explicit instruction alone to impart knowledge is revealed by the manufacturer of extremely complex machines, who, faced with correspondingly complex instructions, contemplated building a second set of instructions to tell users of the system how to read the first set. The manufacturer's concern reflects an intriguing intuition about the insufficiency of instructions and a hunch that, to be adequate, instructions do need some sort of interpretive framework. But the response—to add yet more instructions—puts designers on the giddy edge of an infinite regress. The manufacturer wisely abandoned the plan before regressing too far.

A user with instructions about instructions might feel trapped in one of those circles in which dictionaries involve readers when definitions are interdependent. The dictionary, of course, usually escapes such circles because users are grounded in language praxis. Their sense of how dictionaries work and their implicit understanding of the conditions of language use provide a means to break out of circular definitions. This sort of implicit grounding of the explicit is too easily overlooked in explicit instruction and gives rise to our second pair, explicit and implicit.

Again, we stress that we are not producing a binary choice here. The explicit is not self-sufficient, but neither is the implicit. The two are only productive in conjunction. In the sonorous prose of Kant, "Thoughts without content are empty; intuitions without concepts are blind" (1934/1787, p. 25). Implicit codes, developed through praxis by communities of practice, provide the framing assumptions that members use to construct an interpretation of explicit encounters. The codes act like a pair of invisible eyeglasses that allow people to bring the explicit into focus.

Even if their role were recognized, however, implicit codes could not simply be made the subject of yet more explicit teaching, just as instructions cannot simply be clarified by yet more instructions. Implicit codes are fundamentally distinct from explicit ones and resist attempts to make them explicit. This is why we use the term *implicit* rather than *tacit*. The latter term suggests that this part of understanding is merely hidden, and that once uncovered, can be made explicit. We claim, by contrast, that explication definitively changes the ontology of the implicit. You can either look at or look through a pair of glasses, but while you are doing one, you cannot do the other. It is because the implicit is ontologically distinct from the explicit that more explicit instruction will not suffice. Implicit understanding of a praxis is developed in praxis. As Lave and Wenger (1990) argue, this is quite distinct from talk about praxis. The codes for interpreting explicit knowledge and grounding it in praxis do not exist in the abstract. As a result, in the search for workplace learning, it is illusory to put faith in self-sufficient, independent, abstract explication.

Designs, like instruction, however much they are intended to remain independent and abstract, must fall prey to a situated interpretation. Ultimately, all artifacts have to be interpreted through some codes, which might encompass such relative but powerful intangibles as attitude, reputation, and intuition. Design must either try actively to engage in the construction and adoption of codes for interpretation or else passively accept the codes that users will themselves inevitably construct and engage. We do not claim that design can determine what codes are used. But it can, like all communications, attempt to cue relevant sets of codes and to dismiss others through its purposeful use of affordances (Brown, Duguid, and Nunberg, 1991).

Just as writers for a particular community can anticipate and deploy the background assumptions of typical readers to make a forceful point, so too can designers for a particular community use their understanding of implicit codes to help marshall a rewarding use of tools. Similarly, as writers who pay no heed to their readers' assumptions risk confusing or alienating them, so designers who ignore their target community's implicit understandings risk alienating it.

An understanding of how codes work is particularly important in times of radical innovation. Designers can more easily introduce new tools when they understand that old implicit codes, if not sympathetically accounted for, provide the most significant sources of resistance. The central problem for design in this area, then, involves discovering how to engage or develop the implicit so that the understanding of the explicit can be usefully constrained. As the next section suggests, the first step in this direction involves recognizing that the implicit, framing codes are generated not individually, but socially.

Individual and Social

Dominant design paradigms reflect pedagogical assumptions, not only in relying chiefly on the explicit, as we have just argued, but also in leaning heavily on the individual at the expense of the social. Much user-interface design is still highly individual and individuating, although it is used in the social milieu of work. Both pedagogy and design are still tightly bound to rationalist, symbol-manipulating, problem-solving assumptions that hold knowledge to be a property of individuals. Pedagogy still concentrates on the individual and individual performance, even though most work is ultimately collaborative and highly social. This apparent incongruence leads to our third pair, individual and social.

Attempts to build computer networks at least acknowledge the need to support communal work. Bannon (1986) notes that many of the difficulties computer networking encounters arise in part because the individual links in the chain are originally conceived in wholly individual and unrelated terms. By focusing attention primarily on the individual, user-interface design has lost sight of the mutually constitutive relationship of the individual and the social.

Once again, it is important to stress the interrelationship of the two members of this pair. We are not presenting individual and social as alternative approaches to design. Although historically there has been a gradual movement separating one from the other, they are inextricable in concept, as Williams notes:

> "Individual" meant "inseparable," in medieval thinking ... [and] became a term used to indicate a member of some group, kind or species. The complexity of the term is at once apparent in this history, for it is the unit that is being defined, yet defined in terms of its membership of a class. The separable identity is being defined by a word that has meant "inseparable." (Williams, 1961, p. 73)

To reverse the current focus by accommodating the social to the exclusion of the individual will do equal violence to the nature of the interrelationship. Reversal will not resolve the problems previously created by concentrating on individuals to the exclusion of the social. People do act individually and design must respond accordingly. But what people do takes on its meaning and can only be recognized within a social context. Concentrating on individuals has led pedagogy and design to overlook the way in which the implicit understanding of individuals—what Winograd and Flores (1987) call their "background" to interpretations—is constructed socially. By losing sight of this, design loses one of its most significant resources—the social construction of understanding.

Design also needs to be conscious of the way in which this understanding is not only socially constructed but also socially distributed. The social distribution of knowledge resembles the way in which the words of a play are distributed among the cast. If each actor were asked to perform on a separate platform, the resulting performances would make no sense. Nor, indeed, could any one actor proceed very far, lacking the necessary cues from the rest of the cast. The sense of what each one knows is only evident in the ensemble. Hutchins (forthcoming) provides a good example of the social distribution of tasks in navigation. No one member of the teams he describes can be said to navigate the aircraft carrier—but together, it can be said, they navigate the ship.

With this larger sense of social ensemble, as opposed to the individual cranium, design begins to expand its horizons. Not only must designers concentrate on supporting communal work; they must act with awareness of their role in productively developing or destructively preventing the formation of communities. Tools that isolate people physically, socially, or conceptually either deliberately or inadvertently work against the formation of those essential components of practice.

Novices Becoming Experts and Experts Becoming Novices

Reflecting pedagogical separations between learning and working, much current design for learning rests on the extremely influential dichotomy between novices and experts—our fourth pair. Novices are learners; experts have learned. This overly simple distinction fails to appreciate the way in which expertise is a fluid, social construction that is constantly subject to redefinition, the more so in times of rapid change. Learning is continually demanded. But learners are subject to social pressures. The novitiate is typically cast as an "entry-level" condition. People who have been definitively nominated "experts" can be prevented from acknowledging their need to learn by the loss of status involved in becoming a novice, as these people are defined as having learned enough. Technology, to its own detriment, can reinforce this inhibition.

In fact, the conditions of being a novice recur in different forms and do not disappear with increasing competence. Indeed, it is possible for people to be simultaneously novice and expert. The novice–expert distinction, when it gets reified in technology as an act of graduation rather than as a process of gradation, fails to deal with the needs of experts to learn. Experts can thus be left on plateaus of expertise beyond which they are understandably reluctant to go. Designing technology to support learning as it is needed, not when it is prescribed, is an important challenge. But the challenge is as much a social as a technological one.

This dichotomy and the resulting tendency of information technology to isolate novices from experts creates problems for conventional novices as well as for already competent practitioners. Brown and Newman (1985, p. 374) describe an "excellent administrative assistant" whose physical and personal isolation from the rest of the community of practice allowed her to believe that the office system she could not fathom was absolutely transparent to everyone else. As a newcomer, she was reluctant to reveal her difficulties to others, but unable to overcome them alone. She became deeply frustrated and depressed by her inability to learn what she assumed everyone else knew. When she was moved to a location from which she could see "oldtimers" at work, she quickly discovered that everyone else also had trouble with the system, and that the entire work culture was highly responsive to confessions of failure and frustration.

The social milieu can thus be responsible both for creating and resolving novice-expert problems. The hierarchic structure of most organizations, which the administrative assistant understandably assumed to obtain, inhibits confessions of ignorance, whereas the work culture that she eventually found encouraged exploration. As Orr (1990a, 1990b) shows, this productive sort of work culture often is interstitially formed and remains unseen or opposed in the organization as a whole. Zuboff (1988) argues that the demands of information technology are, in fact, breaking down conventional distinctions between novices and experts simply because everyone needs to learn.

A more suitable model for a learning culture can be found in the enormously successful computer user groups that have sprung up around the country. In these there is a vast and incommensurable range of expertise in which the novice–expert distinction is neither rigid nor important. Given the rapidly changing technology, the user groups implicitly understand that, at some time and in some way, anyone can be both a novice and an expert.

A group structure similar to that of user groups was developed around SHERLOCK, a training system for apprentice technicians in the United States Air Force (Gott, 1989; Lesgold et al., 1988). One of the most interesting and perhaps most salient features of SHERLOCK is the social framework in which this training takes place. The system is designed to model all levels of expertise; so all levels train together. One of the benefits of the system seems to be that every participant has the opportunity to see that everyone is a beginner in one or another aspect. And each has the opportunity to discuss the subject matter with or hear it discussed by people at different levels of competence. Similar conclusions as to the benefits of this sort of situated observation and discussion are reached by Orr (1990a) and Roshelle and Behrend (1991).

SHERLOCK's tutoring technology has been highly successful. Twenty hours of work with the system reportedly produce the equivalent of 11 months of on-the-job training. The success of SHERLOCK suggests that, among other things, design should ignore rigid learner–worker, novice–expert, user–tool distinctions, and design for continuous, participatory learning in a larger context. In particular, design should aim to foster just the sorts of multilevel social discussions that SHERLOCK supported, on the assumption that constructive knowledge is circulated along with the building of a multileveled community of interpretation.

DESIGN AND INNOVATION

Systems Narrowly Construed and Systems Broadly Construed

As we move from the individual into the community of practice of which the individual is a member, it becomes necessary to expand conventional notions of systems. This change in perspective gives rise to our fifth pair, the system narrowly construed and the system broadly construed.

A system is, in the end, a purely theoretical construct. Where boundaries are drawn is no more absolute for a system than it is for the dividing line between urban and suburban neighborhoods. As Nygaard argues:

> A *system* is part of the world, *which we choose to regard as a whole,* separated from the rest of the world during some period of consideration, *a whole which we choose to consider as containing a collection of components,* each characterized by a selected set of associated data items and patterns, and by actions which may involve itself and other components.   (Quoted in Ehn, 1988, p. 48)

Nevertheless, boundaries around systems tend to be drawn as tightly as possible. "Peripherals," "software," and even "users" tend to be defined by exclusion. If, however, the social world and peripheral features are essential to individual involvement with any system, however defined, then there are good reasons for trying to take the broadest, most connected view possible—to be inclusive rather than exclusive.

Again, we are not presenting a choice of either/or. Rather, we want to explore the advantages of looking at different levels of communities of practice and their internal and external relations, shifting the focus from the local work group to the organization as a whole and to the organization and its environment. Each can usefully be seen as a system in itself or as part of a larger system.

It is important to regard organizations (corporations, universities, bureaucracies) as systems in order to develop a sense of the interrelations of all their parts. Only from this perspective, as Barley (1988) argues, can complex concepts such as "deskilling" be understood. Systems, from this viewpoint, are not individual tools, but social organizations. The introduction of new processes and new products into an organizational subsystem must be expected to send shock waves throughout the organization and indeed, in many cases, beyond it. Only by understanding all the interconnections is it possible to predict where effects will be most strongly felt and what those effects might be. If the interrelations of the larger system are ignored, shock waves will not be noticed until they produce a breakdown, at which point, unfortunately, they may be dismissed as unconnected rather than just unexpected. Furthermore, we suggest that organizational innovation and its effects on the organization can only be understood in the context of a larger, less rigidly bounded system that includes the conventional organization and its environment. To grasp the sources of innovation, we need to move beyond the individual organization and explore its relationship to its environment.

Design for Reacting and Design for Enacting

The idea that boundaries are impositions upon the world and not natural features is an important distinction in Daft and Weick's (1984) powerful analysis of innovative organizations. Their analysis of what constitutes an inherently innovative organization leads us to propose that design has a critical role to play in making an organization capable of constant innovation.

Daft and Weick (1984) propose a matrix of four different kinds of organization, each characterized by its relationship to its environment. They name these relationships "undirected viewing," "conditioned viewing," "discovering," and "enacting." Only the last two concern us here; they form our sixth pair: reacting and enacting.

The *discovering organization* is the archetype of the conventional innovative organization. It reacts—often with great efficiency—to changes it detects in its environment. But, significantly, it presupposes an essentially prestructured environment and implicitly assumes that there is a correct response to any condition it discovers there.

By contrast, the *enacting organization* is proactive and highly interpretive. It not only constructs responses to its environment, but also creates the very conditions to which it must respond. Daft and Weick describe enacting organizations as follows:

> These organizations construct their own environments. They gather information by trying new behaviors and seeing what happens. They experiment, test, and stimulate, and they ignore precedent, rules, and traditional expectations. (Daft and Weick, 1984, p. 288)

Inherent in this analysis of organizations is a notion that the source of innovation lies in the interface between an organization and its environment. Innovation is produced neither in the environment nor in the organization, but in the interplay between the two. Reframing the environment is a key means to drive innovation. By reinterpreting its environment, by reregistering the world, and by both anticipating and responding to the effects these actions produce, an enacting organization can instigate change in both its world and itself. In sum, enacting organizations do not simply respond to a changing environment; they involve themselves in generating it.

The enacting process can be seen in the introduction of the IBM Mag-I memory typewriter, billed "as a new way of organizing office work" (Pava, cited in Barley, 1988). To make full use of the power of this typewriter, the conditions in which it was to be used had to be reconceived. In the old milieu of office work, the potential of the machine could not be realized. But in a newly conceived approach to office work, the machine could prove highly productive. Although the new conception could not be achieved without the new machine, the potential of the new machine could not be fully realized without the conception. The two changes went along together. Enacting organizations differ from discovering ones in that, instead of waiting for changed practices to emerge and then responding, they enable them to emerge and prepare for them.

In the process of implementation, design can play two different roles. Like the organizations themselves, one role is reactive, the other is proactive. In the latter case design lies between the changing organization and the changing environment. Its Janus-like position, looking both within and without and provoking changes in both, makes it an essential part of the enacting organization's ability to innovate. Not only does it provoke changes in the environment; it prepares the organization internally for those changes. The designers of the IBM Mag-I memory typewriter not only had to envision changed external office practices that would accept the product, but they first had to help their parent organization envision those changes and their significance in order to have the Mag-I manufactured and marketed at all.

Design, then, reconceived in enacting terms, has an important part to play in gaining acceptance for new ideas both internally and externally. The necessary reconception, we argue in the next two sections, requires an awareness of two different aspects of design.

Internal and External

Unfortunately, industrial design is too often thought of as choosing product packaging or colors. It is rarely thought of—as it should be—as an integral part of innovation. Most attention is paid to how design can help new devices flourish in the marketplace. Too little is paid to its ability to induce the reconceptualization within organizations necessary to permit development of new concepts in the first place. Designers therefore have internal and external missions—our seventh pair. For purposes of enacting, we argue, designers must be involved at a very early stage in the process of development.

The field is full of well-known war stories—the "Post-it" sticker, the Macintosh computer, Chester Carlson's xerographic process—that tell how a particular concept was rejected or overlooked by a parent organization unable to take the conceptual leap necessary to understand a new idea. Yet there are few adequate explanations of how reconceptualization can be supported in this, the first stage of the process of implementation.

Carlson's attempts to interest people in the idea of dry photocopying—xerography—provide an example of organizations' tendency to resist enacting innovation. Carlson and the Batelle Institute, which backed his research, approached most of the major innovative corporations of the time—RCA, IBM, A. B. Dick, Kodak. All turned down the idea of a dry copier. And it was the *idea* they turned down. They did not reject a flawed machine; indeed, they all seemed to have agreed that it worked. They rejected the concept of an office copier because they could see no use for one. Even when Haloid bought the patent, marketing firms consistently reported that the new device had no role in office practice (Dessauer, 1971).

What their evaluations concluded was that a machine was not needed to make a record copy of documents. Carbon paper already did that admirably and cheaply. What they failed to see was that a copier allowed a proliferation of copies and copies of copies. The quantitative leap in copies then produced a qualitative change in the way they were used. Copies no longer served merely as records of an original. Copies of copies, increasing exponentially and circulating widely, could participate in the productive interactions of organizations' members in a fundamentally new and unprecedented way. Only in use in the office, enabling and enhancing new forms of collaborative work, did the copier forge the conceptual lenses through which its value became visible and undeniable.

It is, then, at the start of innovation and not at the finish that the designer's role should begin. Designers can help an organization, through paradigm shifts, to develop a new understanding of itself and its environment. Only after the internal market has been satisfied does the next stage begin—the more recognizable process of preparing a concept for the external marketplace. Enacting designers should embrace both these roles. To do so, however, they must be capable of conceiving of *enacting design* as involving both process and product.

Design as Product and Design as Process

By failing to distinguish the process of design and its role in innovation from the product of design and its separate role in innovation, designers can fail both to realize their potential inside an organization and to achieve their purpose outside it. They fail, in short, to become enacting designers. This understanding of design as product and process forms our eighth pair.

Repair. "Repair" is a crucial feature in distinguishing design as process from design as product. Conventional communication divides into two-way communication and one-way communication. In two-way communication—paradigmatically, conversation—understanding advances partly through the repair of misunderstanding. That is, misinterpretations, recognized and repaired, can be an important means of clarification for both speaker and respondent. The repair of conversational breakdown is often so easy and so natural that it remains invisible. Nevertheless, it is important. A satisfying construction of a conversation depends significantly on rectifying unsatisfying attempts (Clark and Schaeffer, 1989).

The internal process of design, the process of aiding reconceptualization described above, is predominantly a two-way form of communication. Ideas, priorities, and goals are debated and negotiated. Misinterpretations, "mindbugs," and the like manifest themselves and are cleared up.

When a product moves out into the world, however, design becomes less of a two-way process and more of a one-way product. Conditions change and repair is far less easy (Suchman, 1987). Interacting with the finished design resembles reading a book rather than having a conversation. And, as with a book, once a product is in the hands of the public, its creator is no longer there to negotiate misinterpretation or control the context in which it is "read."

Confusion between the two aspects of design and the damage such confusion can do is evident in accounts of Xerox's attempts to introduce the concept of "Design for Operability." Many in the corporation thought that the company's designs were self-evidently operable and no such concept was needed. Managers who tried found they could operate the new machine with ease. This conclusion may have led to the unfortunate advertisement suggesting that the company's machines were so simple to use that a monkey could operate them. On site, it turned out, the machine was not so simple to run. As a result of the advertisement, however, key operators were inundated with offensive complaints and bunches of bananas whenever they could not operate the apparently idiot-proof machine (Jacobson and Hillkirk, 1986). The advertisement was quickly withdrawn.

The chameleonlike character of a machine that was apparently idiot-proof within the organization and a great deal of trouble outside arose from a confusion between the process of design and the product of design and the near invisibility of communicative repair. The people who found operation of the machine self-evident were, significantly, senior managers. Their position almost ensured that they could not come to a prototype as first-time users. They are usually not allowed to be novices. Instead, they are given an introduction and explanation, and they get some tactfully invisible help by omnipresent invisible hands. Repair of misunderstanding in these conditions is provided not by the instructions, but by an anxious engineer or designer ever ready-to-hand. But because the repair is so tactful, it is often presumed that the help stack—the instructions—was doing all the work.

The belief in instant operability to which this sort of invisible help gave rise was eventually dispelled. One factor contributing to the new appraisal was a video made by a research group for quite different purposes, which circulated quickly through the corporation. This video showed several people quite unable to operate the machine. What was not shown, but was revealed whenever the video was shown, was that these "incompetent" users were otherwise highly competent: One was a senior researcher, and another held an endowed chair at a major university. The significant distinction between these people and the managers was not their competence, but that none of the former was given any help, however discreet. They became novices with respect to this machine, and the video revealed that the novice's relationship with this particular device was rough. In delivering this message to senior management, the video exemplified one of the ways in which designers can help to bring about significant internal reconceptualization in an organization.

It is this sort of internal organizational reconceptualization that design as process can bring about. Design as product must deal with external operability, but generally through a form of one-way communication. The mechanisms of repair for processes and products are quite different in the two forms of communication. This brings us back to our earlier suggestion that designs are in a significant way read like books.

Reading a design. Although interpreting a machine in the workplace is more like reading a book than having a conversation, it is important to remember that books are not self-sufficient. They are not immune to breakdown. Their mechanisms for repair, however, are more limited and very different from those for two-way communication. Many of these mechanisms are not intrinsic to a book itself. Certainly they are not intrinsic to its text or "message." Interpretation and repair call upon resources distributed throughout the book's physical situation and its community of interpretation (Fish, 1980) and developed in a long historical process (Williams, 1961; Watt, 1958).

Despite all the powers of text to communicate, books do rely on a great deal more than the text alone to be understood. Consider, for example, a reader for a publishing house. Manuscripts are sent around with a cover note to indicate what sort of work they are, what genre they belong to. This note is meant to stand in for extratextual features of books—the binding, the cover illustration, the blurb, the section in the bookshop or library, the sort of bookshop or library in which the book is found—all of which convey its genre: whether it is fact or fiction, a detective novel or an autobiography. Text alone can be virtually uninterpretable.

These questions are answered, we suggest, by an implicit sense of genre and the interpretive mechanism that genre affords. It is to establish genre and begin interpretation that people ask such questions as "What sort of book is this?" "What audience is it for?" And it is in part from this implicit sense of genre and its social embedding that repair can come.

Like books, new artifacts are read as part of an entire situation. Like books, they are not self-sufficient. The materials of which a device is made and the shell designed for it, even the room in which it is put and the people authorized to work with it, can frame its status in a way more powerful than and quite contrary to any explicit claim. People must rely for help with interpretation and repair, in part, on the social and physical embedding of a device and the generic expectations to which it gives rise.

Thus, designers need to look for ways to foster interpretive communities and build within them a sense of genre in order to circumscribe interpretation and provide some of the mechanisms to repair misinterpretation. By contrast, we believe, many new artifacts are designed to be isolated from their environment and, misguidedly, to try to provide individuals with what are believed to be "idiot-proof" instructions.

DESIGN AND TOOLS

Idiot-Proof Design and Design for the Management of Trouble

Because communicative repair is more complex in designs as products, one tendency in design has been to overconstrain interpretation—to try to design idiot-proof machines, thus obviating the need for communication repair (Bannon, 1986; Brown and Newman, 1985; Suchman, 1987). The designer can choose to design to prevent all problems or to manage trouble when it occurs. Idiot-proof design and trouble management comprise our ninth pair.

Conceptually, idiot-proof design presents at least two significant sorts of problems. First, such designs are based on the mistaken premise that all problems can be anticipated. As Suchman's *Plans and Situated Actions* (1987) makes clear, "situated actions" can always circumvent the best-laid plans. Second, in trying to constrain the mistaken use of tools, idiot-proof design may also constrain creative use at the worksite, thus deterring a powerful, although usually unacknowledged, source of innovation (Brown and Duguid, 1991).

Action and Anticipation. A nice example of the impossibility of total anticipation is provided in the work on "How the West was Won," a user-modeling instructional game (Burton and Brown, 1976, 1979). Burton and Brown designed "West" with an AI coach to model the player's goals and provide assistance. The coach was designed not to intervene unless absolutely necessary lest it undermine the confidence of the player. Because the game needed only a limited number of player strategies, the coach could be built to contain an apparently exhaustive list to anticipate all strategies. Yet the record of one encounter with a player was completely unfathomable to the designers. This player's strategy could not be understood until it was realized that he had abandoned the conventional goals of the game entirely and instead set himself the goal of provoking the reluctant coach into intervening.

Attempts to constrain misinterpretation do not only run up against capricious responses such as this one. Plans, instructions, and explanations are inevitably set against a background of interpretation (Winograd and Flores, 1987), and if the background were to change, the plans and instructions would most likely fall apart, often with serious consequences. Akrich (1987) describes the plans of a group of designers who built a photoelectrically driven lighting system intended for use in less developed countries (LDCs). Their idiot-proof, maintenance-free DC battery system proved absolutely useless from the moment it confronted the electricians in the LDCs who had to install the lights. Although the designers had attempted to design a system to work in all conditions and with wholly inexperienced users, they had left out of their predictive equation the electricians who install the lighting system. The electricians in these countries only knew AC systems, and they reasonably assumed that the DC system worked in the same way.

Akrich notes:

> The technical object defines the actors it deals with: as it turns out, the lighting kit (and behind it the designer) proceeds by elimination and only tolerates a docile user to the exclusion of any other actors who might normally contribute to the constitution of technico-economic networks, like technicians or business people. . . . The designer's blueprint is merely a blueprint for action; the realization of the technical object follows a long process of the simultaneous fabrication of technical and social elements, a process which goes far beyond the frontiers of the laboratory or the workshop.   (Akrich, 1987, pp. 5–6)

Jordan's (1989) work on the grossly inappropriate retraining of experienced rural midwives by urban pedagogists similarly describes the unpredicted and unfortunate consequences that can follow when explicit instruction is assumed to be suited to all audiences. In Jordan's and Akrich's cases, predictions were made at an immense physical and conceptual distance from the conditions of use; but the same argument holds for all attempts to anticipate or model users. Orr's work (1990a,b) reveals similar consequences for the training of technicians, even though the distance between trainers and trained was circumscribed by a single corporation.

Instead of designing universal instructions for eliminating trouble, it seems wiser, as Suchman (1987) suggests, to design for repair, for the unexpected "always happens." Similarly, Brown and Newman argue:

> What is increasingly clear is that the classic goal of designing idiot-proof systems is profoundly wrong. Although such design goals as clarity in the user interface or consistency in the organization of system functionality are desirable, one can never anticipate and "design away" all of the exigencies, misunderstandings, and problems that will arise in people's use of complex systems. Instead, we need to recognize and develop system resources for dealing with the fact that the unexpected always happens. In other words, we must widen our focus from designing for the avoidance of trouble to designing for the *management of trouble*—of both a communicative and an operative nature. From this perspective the notion of repair becomes a crucial construct for interface design.   (Brown and Newman, 1985, pp. 367–68)

This, as we have suggested, requires designers to go beyond trying to make new devices internally self-sufficient and idiot-proof. They should try instead to gain leverage from the ambient circumstances, in particular the community of practice in which the devices will be used. Instead of being closed systems, devices should be open to the community's interpretation and development.

Design and Worksite Innovation. This brings us to our second argument against closed design: that it may constrain creative use. Repair, it should be remembered, is not simply a matter of "damage control." It is part of a highly constructive process.

Two hundred years ago, the economist Adam Smith encountered improvisation in daily work:

> It is naturally to be expected ... that some one or other of those who are employed in each particular branch of labour should soon find out easier and readier methods of performing their own particular work, wherever the nature of it admits of such improvement. A great part of the machines made use of in those manufactures in which labour is most subdivided, were originally the inventions of common workmen.   (Smith, 1937/1784, p. 9)

One premise for this sort of innovative behavior is that people are able to go beyond the explicitly described "functionality" of any device, to use it in new ways, to see its potential for new processes. Restrictively constrained devices, of course, inhibit such activity. Design that is itself potentially innovative must be sympathetic to this sort of improvisation and try to foster it. Design should be capable of helping to generate, circulate, mutate, and preserve emergent practices.

The work on "Buttons" (MacLean et al., 1990) is a significant example of such successful design. It provides a tailorable means for people using office workstations to embed unfamiliar technological innovations in a familiar and transferrable form: screen icons. Screen icons can be placed on electronic bulletin boards from where they can easily be taken and installed on personal systems. Once installed, they can be modified quickly to suit individual uses. "Buttons" thus helps both to circulate and to promote innovation. With this sort of technology, tools have progressed back to the point described by Smith 200 years ago, where they can again be designed by working people.

But as MacLean et al. point out, "Buttons" is not simply a technological fix. Its use depends on the community of practice involved. At a simple level, of course, the community must have a concept of icons and the ways to explore and use them. But at a more complex level, the work culture must also implicitly allow workers to feel able to explore and experiment.

Technology alone does not determine this cultural quality, although technological design can tend to support or inhibit exploration. Technological adventurousness also relies on the social work practices that obtain in a particular workplace.

Opacity and Transparency

A great deal of information technology is thoroughly opaque and frustrating. Transparency seems to be the desirable conceptual alternative. Opacity and transparency form our tenth pair of concepts for exploring design.

Glass Box Tools.   The benefits of transparency lead to the idea of "Glass Box" tools. (For an extended discussion of Glass Box tools, see Wenger, 1988.) The idea seems simple, but its ramifications are complex.

It can be important for some tools that might be invisible to be made visible, so that their role in activity is evident and can be examined. But tool transparency is not an unquestionably desirable end. In relation to visibility and invisibility, Lave and Wenger argue:

> Mirroring the intricate relation between using and understanding artifacts, there is an interesting duality inherent in the concept of transparency. It combines the two characteristics of *invisibility* and *visibility*: invisibility in the form of unproblematic interpretation and integration into activity; and visibility in the form of extended access to information. This is not a simple dichotomous distinction, since these two crucial characteristics are in a complex interplay, their relation being one of both conflict and synergy. It might be useful to give a sense of this interplay by analogy to a window. A window's invisibility is what makes it a window, that is, an object through which the world outside becomes visible. The very fact, however, that so many things can be seen through it makes the window itself highly visible, that is, very salient in a room, when compared to,

> say, a solid wall. Invisibility of mediating technologies is necessary for allowing focus on, and thus supporting visibility of, the subject matter. Conversely, visibility of the significance of the technology is necessary for allowing its unproblematic—invisible—use. This interplay of conflict and synergy is central to learning: it makes the design of supportive artifacts a matter of providing a good balance between these two interacting requirements. (Lave and Wenger, 1990, p. 27)

Nevertheless, some circumscribed notion of transparency is useful; it can be helpful to think of designing tools as designing glass boxes. But even then, there are several different forms of transparency:

> Transparency in its simplest form may just imply that the inner workings of an artifact are available for the learner's inspection: the black box can be opened, it can become a "glass box." But there is more to understanding the use and significance of an artifact since knowledge as accumulated by a community-of-practice and ways of perceiving and manipulating objects characteristic of the practice are encoded in artifacts in ways that can be more or less revealing. Moreover, the activity system and the social world of which an artifact is part are reflected in multiple ways in its design and use and can become further "fields of transparency," just as they can remain opaque. (Lave and Wenger, 1990, p. 26)

Furthermore, because opacity is partly a function of "the activity system and social world of which an artifact is a part," transparency is not simply a technological attribute. Transparency, like genre (to which it is related), extends across the system narrowly construed to the broader system of which the tool is only a part. Lave and Wenger continue:

> Obviously, the transparency of any technology always exists with respect to some purpose and is intricately tied to the cultural practice and social organization within which the technology is meant to function: *it cannot be viewed as a feature of an artifact in itself but as something that is achieved through specific forms of participation, in which the technology fulfills a mediating function. . . .* In focusing on the epistemological role of artifacts in the context of the social organization of knowledge, this notion of transparency constitutes, as it were, the cultural organization of access. As such, it does not apply to technology only, but to all forms of access to practice. (Lave and Wenger, 1990, p. 26; emphasis added.)

This leads us to propose (based on Wenger's 1988 analysis) three central kinds of transparency: domain transparency, internal transparency, and organizational transparency.

Domain Transparency. The aim in domain transparency is to make apparent to users the causal reasoning involved in the interaction of various mechanisms in a particular practice. Highly complex systems, particularly highly complex information systems, tend to "hide" causality and connections from people. In mechanical systems, connecting rods, drive belts, gears, bearings, and the like provide access to the causal functioning of a machine and reveal how it engages its environment. Even simple electronic circuits manifest a topological relationship among parts from which it is sometimes possible to infer causality.

To achieve similar insight into information systems, however, it is not sufficient to lay bare the circuitry of its boards, whose configuration has no easily perceptible relation to function. It is possible in certain circumstances to build a representative model of the relevant causality that allows users to develop a helpful sense of their own role and their tool's role in ongoing activity. The Xerox/Macintosh "desktop" is a simple but extremely potent example of such an explanatory model. STEAMER (Williams, Hollan, and Stevens, 1981), a system that provides a top-level, causal model of a propulsion plant—animated, interactive, and inspectable—provides another. Use of the term *relevant causality* indicates the relative nature of transparency: Explanations, as Winograd and Flores (1987) argue, must be seen against a background. Different backgrounds require different explanations. There are inevitably certain positions from which any Glass Box, like any glass pane, will simply throw light back at the viewer, blinding rather than enlightening.

Internal Transparency. Internal transparency is especially relevant to expert systems, which deal with the explicit reasoning of particular and highly circumscribed fields. Here, the aim of internal transparency is to reveal the hidden reasoning in such systems and to allow people working with the system to concur or override its conclusions. This option would provide people working with diagnostic systems, for instance, with the means to discover more than that x is a case of shattered piston rings and y is a case of meningitis. It would allow the car mechanic or the medical intern to follow the reasoning that led to those conclusions.

While many authors discuss the inadequacy of such representations of full-blooded practice, the formal reasoning involved can provide extremely valuable information to the people working with the system (Clancey, 1990). Denying access to that reasoning, in contrast, can be fundamentally alienating and deskilling (Garson, 1988).

Organizational Transparency. In our earlier discussion of systems, we argued that it is important to be able to construe the system as widely as possible, to search beyond an individual tool to the social as well as the technical milieu in which the tool is embedded. Unfortunately, the narrow construal of systems has isolated people from the overall organization rather than situated them within it. People can come to feel a little too like the human subjects in Searle's Chinese room, receiving instructions through one slot and responding through another, not knowing where these instructions come from or where the responses go. Organizational transparency is aimed at relating, through the processes of work, the individual worksite and the work done there to the workings of the organization as a whole.

User-Oriented Design and User-Orienting Design

For a transparency to be useful within a particular practice, a design needs to have the perspective of that practice. Cooley (1988) points out, however, that dominant design approaches today enforce a separation between designing and doing rather like the separation between learning and working which we have already noted. This separation gives rise to our eleventh pair—user-oriented and user-orienting design. The division has a long history:

> Around the sixteenth century, there emerged in most of the European languages the term "design" or its equivalent. The emergence of the word coincided with the need to describe the occupation of designing. That is not to suggest that designing was a new activity, rather that it was being separated out from wider productive activity and recognized as a function in its own right. This recognition can be said to constitute a separation of hand and brain, of manual and intellectual work; and the separation of the conceptual part of work from the labour process. Above all, the term indicated that *designing* was to be separated from doing.   (Cooley, 1988, p. 197)

It has resulted in systems design that is centered on abstracted models of espoused practice—a position that has increasingly been challenged in recent years.

Suchman (1987) reveals the distance between abstract, programmatic descriptions of work and the way work is actually conducted. George Eliot provides a splendid analogy of the difference between the two:

> Fancy what a game at chess would be if all the chessmen had passions and intellects, more or less small and cunning: if you were not only uncertain about your adversary's men, but a little uncertain about your own; if your knight could shuffle himself on to a new square by the sly; if your bishop, in disgust at your castling, could wheedle your pawns out of their places; and if your pawns, hating you because they are pawns, could make away from their appointed posts that you might get checkmate on a sudden. You might be the longest-headed of deductive reasoners, and yet you might be beaten by your own pawns. You would be especially likely to be beaten, if you depended arrogantly on your

mathematical imagination and regarded your passionate pieces with contempt. (Eliot, *Felix Holt*, II, xxix)

Orr (1990a, 1990b) more soberly maps the distance between documentation and training syllabuses on the one hand and actual practice on the other, and revealed how disturbingly great the disparity could be.

Schön (1987) directs attention in particular to the importance for designers of being able to "converse" with situations, not with abstractions of situations. He argues that "human beings, in their interactions with one another, *design* their behavior" (1987, p. 255). These interactions are therefore crucial to design. Schön posits a sort of hermeneutic circle, moving back and forth between engaged practice and partially disengaged reflection on practice. In this vein, Winograd and Flores (1987), Ehn (1988), and many of the authors in Norman and Draper (1986) argue for some sort of user-oriented or user-centered design. Ehn's TOPOS and UTOPIA projects were built in a densely collaborative process involving the people who would ultimately use the tools that were being designed (Ehn, 1988).

When a designer takes this approach, the catchment for design moves beyond a particular tool or a particular task. Ehn insists that "artifacts not only reflect social relations, but are social relations" (1988, p. 162), and he points to the significance of social and labor relations in Scandinavia for the designs produced on the TOPOS and UTOPIA projects. It is therefore understandable, as Zuboff (1988) argues, that the introduction of profoundly new systems into the conventional workplace will start to break down the conventional divisions of labor and Tayloristic hierarchical structures. This argument does not rely on any sort of technological determinism. It simply holds that technological systems are part of social systems and the two necessarily move together, but not necessarily as cause and effect.

Ehn himself recognizes that one of the problems for this sort of design is that it can too easily be replaced by situations in which designers merely respond to wish lists created by practitioners. A second and more worrisome problem arises from the first: User-oriented design can too readily cast existing fluid work practices in a concrete form that makes them harder to change. Both individuals and organizations have an inherent tendency to resist change (Schön, 1971), and this resistance is likely to increase when they have invested their resources in a purpose-built system.

These apparently paradoxical aspects of user-oriented design—that on the one hand it is a force for change, while on the other it is a force for conservatism—may be resolved with a better understanding of one particular way in which change affects organizations.

How Organizations Afford Knowledge. Anderson and Sharrock's provocatively titled paper, "Can Organizations Afford Knowledge?" (1990), argues convincingly in Gibsonian terms that organizations, by their very organization (that is, their structure or "organizational architecture"), afford knowledge:

> We do not have to ask whether organizations can afford to afford knowledge. Simply by being organizations they do. The questions are (a) how is any local organizational environment organized so that the participants to that setting can find their way around in it and do what they do in it, in the routine, unproblematic ways that they do; and (b) in what ways can this process of sharing, training, or "enculturation" be made easier, more flexible, and more broadly based. (Anderson and Sharrock, 1990, p. 18)

This analysis suggests why change can be so threatening. If working knowledge were dependent on an "organization's organization"—physical, social, technological—any change in the organizational structure would disorient members and deny the affordances on which they rely to get their work done. Every structural change would require rebuilding, to a greater or less extent, the background to each member's working knowledge.

To avoid resistance, then, designs that bring about this sort of structural change need to be not only user-oriented, but also user-orienting. That is, they need to be capable of re-establishing the relationship between the members of the organization and the reformed organizational structure in such a way that the working knowledge this relationship affords can be redeployed.

Architectural concepts provide both an important means and an important image for this sort of reorienting. They provide the means because the architecture of actual buildings, such as plants and offices, must change to accommodate new work practices. They also provide the image because organizational architecture and systems architecture must also change, and structural architecture provides analogical insight into how this might be done.

The architecture of buildings has developed and continues to develop a powerful language that people read quite unconsciously as they find their way around designed spaces. This is most evident in urban design (Frampton, 1988; Coates, 1988; Rasmussen, 1982; Alexander, 1988), but is equally true of individual buildings (Rasmussen, 1962; Perin, 1970; Sommer, 1969; Alexander et al., 1977). The irritation that badly designed buildings bring out in Norman (1988) and in most people reflects the extent to which we rely on good design to guide us.

Good architecture allows people to organize and direct themselves. It is not coercive; it does not force people in one direction. It is supportive; it helps people to navigate, to read structure into juxtapositions and oppositions and to perceive relations between the built and its environment. The static and the dynamic interact in compelling ways, as Alexander (1988) argues with his simple examples of flow around a traffic light, a drugstore entrance, and a newspaper rack.

Many of the most salient arguments against badly designed buildings point out simply that they disorient people. Such buildings lack reliable cues to guide people. This is particularly true of buildings that, however exquisitely or practically the parts are designed, fail to relate those parts to one another and to the whole and fail to connect the invariant and the dynamic—to coordinate the building and its users.

Orienting people is not simply a matter of producing better maps. As Coates (1988) argues, the *"experiences* of cities do not mix with maps or plans" (p. 97). Architecture, he claims, needs to learn how to "build on the nature of experience" (p. 99). And this, we maintain, extends to the architecture of organizations and systems, which must not only build on the nature of experience but also be capable of resurrecting experience after a reorganization.

Center and Periphery

> What constitutes a problem is not the thing, or the environment where we find the thing, but the conjunction of the two.
> Jeanette Winterson, *Oranges Are not the Only Fruit*

As architectural systems, organizational systems, and information systems become more interrelated, design must consider the means available for user-orienting coordination. The concept of a boundary, for instance, can change its prescriptive, limiting ontology to become, as Heidegger describes it, "not that at which something stops, but . . . that from which something begins its presencing" (1971, p. 154). Some of the most important relationships in architecture are those that do not stop at boundaries, but relate a building to its surroundings. By deliberately including surroundings as part of the conceptual system, design establishes an important orienting relationship between "center" and "periphery," which form our twelfth pair.

Again, as with many of our other pairs, the two are mutually constitutive. The relationship of any periphery to any center is quite capable of change. Two features that, from one aspect, are related as center to periphery may, from another aspect, form part of the periphery of a third object, or both might form the center for a fourth. What is most important is that center and periphery, or even two parts of any periphery, enter into a constructive relationship—for the purposes of both orientation and interpretation.

In expanding the notion of a system and in moving beyond a well-defined artifact to include its setting and surroundings, we are espousing Thackera's (1988b) suggestion of going "beyond the object in design." Appreciation of the part played by what are usually regarded as peripheral or even epiphenomenal features is, we maintain, necessary for recognizing the canonical center in both physical and social systems. This orienting process is analogous to the art of composition in painting, wherein painters construct the outer margins of their paintings (sometimes including the frames) in order to guide the viewers' attention to the aesthetic center of activity. Murals, and particularly *trompe l'oeil* murals, of course, extend indefinitely into their peripheries.

Peripheral features do not simply guide a viewer to the center. In the process of guiding, they set up certain expectations about what will be found there. Just as people interpret paintings or books against an implicit background of interpretation, so they "read" right across designs into and out of the periphery, placing features in the foreground and background according to available cues. Many of the broad arrays of cues that people use to interpret signs are not situated in the canonical message. (Expressions on a face are often more important than the words being spoken. The person standing behind the speaker might be more important yet.) Among other things, focusing cues allow people to identify a genre with which, as we suggested, interpretation begins. Just as book covers help distinguish between fiction and nonfiction, so too does the material substrate of artifacts help distinguish, for example, office from domestic appliances. That distinction made, certain conventions can be expected to follow. In contrast, a formalist predilection to make center–periphery disjunctions like those between "medium" and "message" or "form" and "content" can and does disguise the fluid interdependence of foreground and background.

Moreover, the periphery that is not consciously used by the designer does not remain obligingly inert. People will use it, designed or not, to interpret the center. The designer's negligence can therefore easily set up sources of conflict and contradiction. This result is similar to that when the implicit is overlooked in learning.

Many successful designs do use the periphery to which they have access in skillful ways. By beginning outside the narrowly construed system itself, such designs deal with the problem of focusing the user at a very early stage. For instance, packaging sometimes starts to paint a picture of how the device inside works. As boxes are opened layer by layer, they can provide a conceptual sequence, just as the path to the main entrance may afford an informative overview of a building.

Many people remember their early experiences with a Macintosh computer. Opening the package began a carefully structured exploration. The outside foreshadowed the inside, with boxes leading to boxes and icons leading to icons. The first layer revealed the instructions on a palette of color, which sat like a greeting card atop a gift. With admirable simplicity, these instructions (whose indexed relationship to their surroundings was so well established as to furnish almost instant communicative repair mechanisms) led to another box, the "Mac" itself, whose handle simply presented itself to the hand. Out of the box, hook-up was carefully prescribed by a series of what Norman (1988) calls "forcing functions." And at the bottom of the box lay a floppy disc that opened up the computer box with its "Tour of the Macintosh." It was all a brilliantly constructed tour, from the periphery to the center.

Constraints and Resources

The disjunction between center and periphery rests, we believe, on presuppositions about what are resources and what are constraints (for a similar argument, see Norman, 1988). Resources and constraints form the thirteenth and last pair.

The simple design goal of adding resources and the reciprocal one of removing constraints is deeply misleading. In simple terms, it might have been possible to design a way to ship a Macintosh without a box, for example, but it was far wiser to turn the constraint of the box into a powerful resource for understanding. So here again we have a dichotomy that should be dismissed. The distinction between constraints and resources (like that between "bugs" and "features") is impossible to pin down. Constraints can be turned into resources, and resources (such as added functionality or hideable controls) can turn out to be severe constraints.

Confusion between constraints and resources may, for example, lie behind the lack of enthusiasm for the on-line book and newspaper. These ideas have been talked about for several years, and the means to implement them have long been available, but they have not appeared in any very significant form. Over time, people have learned to use the constraining substrate of newspapers and books as an extremely useful resource. Viewing the substrate as a constraint to be replaced might lead to quite unanticipated difficulties.

With a book, for instance, the reader implicitly knows that he or she is approaching the end by the proximity of the finger to the thumb on the right hand. The author also knows this and can use it as a resource for accepting or resisting closure. (The final chapter of David Lodge's novel, *Changing Places*, 1978, provides an amusing account of the physical and imaginative closure of a book.) From the spatial relationship of articles on a newspaper page, readers quickly pick up a sense of the relative importance a story has been given. The width allotted to columns, the weight given to headings, the space provided for illustrations, and so forth are resources that allow people to scan. Editors, of course, know how to take advantage of this. In both cases, the book and the newspaper, it is improvident to try to remove the constraints without understanding how they are also resources.

Furthermore, it is important to understand the way in which apparent constraints reflect the cultural role of an artifact. The modern newspaper, for instance, grew out of a long historical, social development (Williams, 1961; Habermas, 1989; Carey, 1989). A newspaper is not simply an aggregate of "information" that can be selected by readers and transmitted in any form. The newspaper is a cultural artifact in a political and cultural tradition that goes back at least to the eighteenth century. It draws a great deal of its political and social effect from the fact that many thousands and even millions of people are reading roughly the same copy at the same time. Journalism presupposes a reading public engaged in reading a common text. To destroy the uniformity of a newspaper will be to destroy its particular cultural role. What remains will not be just a paperless newspaper; it will not be a newspaper in the conventional sense at all.

In general, the particular resources lost in changing substrate in any particular case may seem relatively unimportant. From the perspective of design, however, the embedding circumstances or the periphery of a device—whether it be the metal that supports a typeface, the covers that bind the sheets of a book, the frame that surrounds a picture, the social milieu in which work takes place, or the box in which a new device is sold—play a crucial role in its acceptance and use. By regarding them as constraints to be removed or disguised, designers may be trying to advance at the direct expense of their most useful allies. In particular, as we suggest in the case of the paperless newspaper, designers may overlook the way in which technical constraints are in fact extremely powerful cultural resources.

Learning to involve apparently peripheral phenomena—in particular, necessary social and technical constraints—in the construction of interpretation and orientation may be much more helpful than trying to designate constraints for removal or resources to add. Using form to further function has a long and successful history. In times of rapid change, when learning and interpretation are so important and disorientation such a challenge, understanding how far form extends into the periphery and its technical and social manifestations and potential may become one of design's most important tasks.

CONCLUSION

In the course of our thirteen sections, we have attempted to unravel the concept of design for work to reveal the broad array of mutually interdependent strands of successful implementation that design must unite. A design must be capable of interweaving what have often been regarded as incompatible opposites into a rich pattern that corresponds to and embodies the circumstances of its production. Design thus needs to be a situated process aimed at reconciling conflicting but integral contributions, and responding to human needs.

In the process of looking at design in this way, we have also addressed the important role design can play in making organizations innovative. Thackera (1988b) argues that "design has emerged in the past five years as a principal element in innovation strategy," but at the moment this discovery is neither widely recognized nor well understood. We believe that the innovative capacity of what we have called *enacting design* can only be understood within a context larger than any particular designed artifact. Only in this larger context can designs be deemed "usable," "functional," "learnable," "transparent," or even "innovative."

Acknowledgments

In developing the ideas in this chapter, we have drawn upon a broad array of resources and resourceful colleagues at the Institute for Research on Learning and Xerox Palo Alto Research Center. Canonical texts for us include Pelle Ehn's *Work-Oriented Design* (1988), Jean Lave and Etienne Wenger's *Situated Learning: Legitimate Peripheral Participation* (1990), Julian Orr's "Talking about Machines" (1987), and Lucy Suchman's *Plans and Situated Actions* (1987). We have also benefitted greatly from conversations with the authors of these works and with Bill Hartman, David Nadler, Geoff Nunberg, John Rheinfrank, and Terry Winograd. And invaluable insights, both explicit and implicit, into the work and world of design and architecture have been provided by Laura Hartman and Susan Haviland.

We also thank Paul Adler for the help, energy, and foresight he provided in arranging the conference on "Technology and the Future of Work," for which this chapter was prepared.

REFERENCES

Akrich, M. (1987). How can technical objects be described. Working paper, Center for the Sociology of Innovation, Paris. Published as Comment décrire les objets techniques. *Technique et Culture* **5**, 49–63.

Alexander, C. (1964). *Notes on the Synthesis of Form.* Cambridge, Mass.: Harvard University Press.

Alexander, C. (1988). The city is not a tree, in John Thackera (ed.). *Design after Modernism.* London: Thames & Hudson.

Alexander, C., S. Ishikawa, and M. Silverstein (1977). *A Pattern Language: Towns, Buildings, and Construction.* New York: Oxford University Press.

Anderson, R., and W. Sharrock (1990). Can Organizations Afford Knowledge? Rank Xerox, Europarc.

Austin, J. L. (1962). *How to Do Things with Words.* Oxford: Clarendon Press.

Bannon, L. J. (1986). Helping users help each other, in D. A. Norman and S.W. Draper, (eds.). *User Centered System Design.* Hillsdale, N.J.: Lawrence Erlbaum.

Barley, S. R. (1988). Technology, power, and the social organization of work: Towards a pragmatic theory of skilling and deskilling. *Research in the Sociology of Organizations* **6**, 33–80.

Bourdieu, P. (1989). Scientific field and scientific thought, in S. Ortner (ed.). *Author Meets Critics: Reactions to "Theory in Anthropology Since the Sixties."* CSST Working Paper no. 32, Ann Arbor, Mich.: University of Michigan.

Brown, J. S. (1986). From cognitive to social economics, in D.A. Norman and S.W. Draper, (eds.). *User Centered System Design.* Hillsdale, N.J.: Lawrence Erlbaum.

Brown, J. S., A. Collins, and P. Duguid. Situated cognition and the culture of learning. *Education Researcher* **18**(4): 1–12.

Brown, J.S., and P. Duguid (1991). Organizational learning and communities-of-practice, *Organization Science* 2, 1, Feb., 40–57.

Brown, J. S., P. Duguid, and G. Nunberg (1991). Design as Communication. Palo Alto, Calif.: Xerox PARC.

Brown, J. S., and S. Newman (1985). Issues in cognitive and social ergonomics: From our house to Bauhaus. *Human Computer Interaction* **1**, 359–91.

Burton, R. R., and J. S. Brown (1976). A tutoring and student modeling paradigm for gaming environments, in R. Colman and P. Lorton (eds.). *Computer Science and Education. ACM SIGCSE Bulletin* **8**(1,) 236–46.

Burton, R. R., and J. S. Brown (1979). An investigation of computer coaching for informal learning activities, in D. H. Sleeman and J. S. Brown (eds.). *Intelligent Tutoring Systems.* London: Academic Press.

Burton, R. R., J. S. Brown, and G. Fischer (1984). Skiing as a model of instruction, in B. Rogoff and J. Lave (eds.). *Everyday Cognition.* Cambridge, Mass.: Harvard University Press.

Carey, J. (1989). *Communication as Culture: Essays on Media and Society.* Boston: Unwin Hyman.

Carr, E. H. (1964). *What Is History.* Harmondsworth, Middlesex: Penguin Books.

Clancey, W. C. (1990). The Frame of Reference Problem in the Design of Intelligent Machines. IRL report 90-0016. Palo Alto, Calif.: Institute for Research on Learning.

Clark, H. H., and E. F. Schaefer (1989). Contributing to discourse. *Cognitive Science* **13**, 259–94.

Coates, N. (1988). Street signs, in John Thackera (ed.). *Design after Modernism.* London: Thames & Hudson.

Cooley, M. (1988). The product of illusion, in John Thackera (ed.). *Design after Modernism.* London: Thames & Hudson.

Daft, R. L., and K. E. Weick (1984). Toward a model of organizations as interpretation systems. *Academy of Management Review* **9**(2), 284–95.

Derrida, J. (1987). The law of genre. *Glyph* **7**, 55–81.

Dessauer, J. H. (1971). *My Years with Xerox: The Billions Nobody Wanted.* Garden City, N.Y.: Doubleday.

Dreyfus, H. (1979). *What Computers Can't Do: A Critique of Artificial Reason* (second edition). New York: Harper & Row.

Eckert, P. (1989). *Jocks and Burnouts.* New York: Teachers College Press.

Ehn, P. (1988). *Work-Oriented Design of Computer Artifacts.* Stockholm: Arbetslivscentrum.

Eliot, G. (1980). *Felix Holt, The Radical,* Oxford: Clarendon Press.

Fish, S. E. (1971). *Surprised by Sin.* Berkeley, Calif.: University of California Press.

Fish, S. E. (1980). *Is There a Text in This Class? The Authority of Interpretive Communities.* Cambridge, Mass.: Harvard University Press.

Foucault, M. (1971). *The Archaeology of Knowledge and the Discourse on Language.* New York: Pantheon.

Frampton, K. (1988). Place-form and cultural identity, in John Thackera (ed.). *Design after Modernism.* London: Thames & Hudson.

Garson, G. (1988). *The Electronic Sweatshop.* New York: Simon & Schuster.

Gibson, J. J. (1979). *The Ecological Approach to Visual Perception.* Boston: Houghton Mifflin.

Gott, S. P. (1989). Apprenticeship for real world tasks. *Review of Research in Education* **15,** 97–169.

Habermas, J. (1979). *Communication and the Evolution of Society.* Boston: Beacon Press.

Habermas, J. (1989). *The Structural Transformation of the Public Sphere.* Cambridge, Mass.: MIT Press.

Heidegger, H. (1962). *Being and Time.* J. Macquarrie and E. Robinson (trans.). New York: Harper & Row.

Heidegger, H. (1971). *Poetry, Language, Thought.* New York: Harper & Row.

Hutchins, E. (forthcoming). Learning to navigate, in S. Chalkin and J. Lave (eds.). *Understanding Practice* New York: Cambridge University Press.

Iser, W. (1974). *The Implied Reader.* Baltimore: Johns Hopkins University Press.

Jacobson, G., and J. Hillkirk (1986). *Xerox: American Samurai.* New York: Macmillan.

Jordan, B. (1989). Cosmopolitical obstetrics: Some insights from the training of traditional midwives. *Social Science and Medicine* **28**(9), 925–44.

Kant, I. (1934). *The Critique of Pure Reason* (second edition). London: J.M. Dent and Sons (first published, in German, 1787).

Latour, B., and S. Woolgar (1986). *Laboratory Life: The Construction of Scientific Facts.* Princeton: Princeton University Press.

Lave, J. (1988). *Cognition in Practice.* Cambridge: Cambridge University Press.

Lave, J., and E. Wenger, (1990). Situated Learning: Legitimate Peripheral Participation. IRL report 90-0013. Palo Alto, Calif.: Institute for Research on Learning.

Lesgold, A., S. Lajoie, M. Bunzo, and G. Eggan (1988). *SHERLOCK: A Coached Practice Environment for an Electronics Troubleshooting Job.* Pittsburgh, Penn.: Learning Research and Development Center.

Levi-Strauss, C. (1966). *The Savage Mind.* Chicago: Chicago University Press.

Lodge, D. (1978). *Changing Places.* Harmondsworth, Middlesex: Penguin Books.

Lukács, G. (1966). Technology and social relations. *New Left Review* **39,** 49–60 (first published, in German, 1925).

MacLean, A, K. Carter, L. Lövstrand, and T. Moran (1991). User-tailorable systems: Pressing the issue with Buttons. *Proceedings of CHI'90.* New York: ACM.

Martin, J. (1982). Stories and scripts in organizational settings, in A.H. Hastorf and A.M. Isen, (eds.). *Cognitive and social psychology.* Amsterdam: Elsevier.

Norman, D. A. (1988). *The Psychology of Everyday Things.* New York: Basic Books.

Norman, D. A., and S. W. Draper (eds.) (1986). *User Centered System Design.* Hillsdale, N.J.: Lawrence Erlbaum.

Nunberg, G. N., and P. Duguid (1991). Genre and technological base. Palo Alto, Calif.: Xerox PARC.

Orr, J. (1987a). Narratives at work: Story telling as cooperative diagnostic activity. *Field Service Manager: The Journal of the Association of Field Service Managers,* **11**(6), 47–60.

Orr, J. (1987b). Talking about machines: Social aspects of expertise. Report for the Intelligent Systems Laboratory, Xerox Palo Alto Research Center, Palo Alto, Calif.

Orr, J. (1988). Transparency, representation, and embodied knowledge: Some examples from the diagnosis of machines. Paper presented at the 87th Annual Meeting of the American Anthropological Association, Arizona, November, 1988.

Orr, J. (1990a). Talking about machines: An ethnography of a modern job. Ph.D. Thesis, Cornell University.

Orr, J. (1990b). Sharing knowledge, celebrating identity: War stories and community memory in a service culture, in D. S. Middleton and D. Edwards (eds.). *Collective Remembering: Memory in Society*. Beverly Hills, Calif.: Sage Publications.

Perin, C. (1970). *With Man in Mind: An Interdisciplinary Prospectus for Environmental Design*. Cambridge, Mass.: MIT Press.

Rasmussen, E. S. (1962). *Experiencing Architecture*. Cambridge, Mass.: MIT Press.

Rasmussen, E. S. (1982). *London: The Unique City*. (Revised edition.) Cambridge, Mass.: MIT Press.

Reddy, M. J. (1979). The conduit metaphor: A case of frame conflict in our language about language, in A. Ortony (ed.). *Metaphor and thought*. New York: Cambridge University Press.

Roshelle, J., and S. Behrend (1991). The construction of shared knowledge in collaborative problem solving. IRL Report no. 91-0026. Palo Alto, Calif.: Institute for Research on Learning.

Sacks, H., E. A. Schegloff, and G. A. Jefferson (1974). A simplest systematics for the organization of turn-taking in conversation. *Language* **50,** 696–735.

Sartre, J-P. (1978). *What Is Literature*. London: Verso.

Schön, D.A. (1987). *Educating the Reflective Practitioner*. San Francisco: Jossey–Bass.

Schön, D.A. (1984). *The Reflective Practitioner*. New York: Basic Books.

Schön, D.A. (1971). *Beyond the Stable State*. New York: Norton.

Scribner, S. (1984). Studying working intelligence, in B. Rogoff and J. Lave (eds.). *Everyday Cognition: Its Development in Social Context*. Cambridge, Mass.: Harvard University Press.

Sommer, R. (1969). *Personal Space: The Behavioral Basis of Design*. Englewood Cliffs, N.J.: Prentice-Hall.

Smith, A. (1937). *Investigations into the Wealth of Nations*. (fifth edition). New York: Random House (first published 1784).

Stevens, A.L. (1982). Quantitative and qualitative simulation in portable training devices. Report to the National Academy of Sciences. Cambridge, Mass.: Bolt, Beranek and Newman.

Suchman, L. (1987). *Plans and Situated Actions: The Problem of Human–Machine Communication*. New York: Cambridge University Press.

Thackera, J. (ed.) (1988a). *Design after Modernism*. London: Thames & Hudson.

Thackera, J. (1988b). Beyond the object in design, in John Thackera (ed.). *Design after Modernism*. London: Thames & Hudson.

Watt, I. (1958). *The Rise of the Novel*. Berkeley, Calif.: University of California Press.

Wenger, E. (1988). Glass-box technology and integrated learning: Information, communication, and knowledge in computerized environments. Thesis proposal submitted to the Department of Computer Science, University of California at Irvine.

Williams, M. D., J. D. Hollan, and A. L. Stevens (1981). An overview of STEAMER: An advanced computer-assisted instruction system for propulsion engineering. *Behavior Research Methods and Instrumentation* **13**(2), 85–90.

Williams, R. (1961). *The Long Revolution: An Analysis of the Democratic, Industrial, and Cultural Changes Transforming Our Society*. New York: Columbia University Press.

Williams, R. (1975). *Television: Technology as Cultural Form*. New York: Shocken Books.

Williams, R. (1976a). *Communication*. Harmondsworth, Middlesex: Penguin Books.

Williams, R. (1976b). *Keywords: A Vocabulary of Culture and Society*. New York: Oxford University Press.

Winograd, T., and F. Flores (1987). *Understanding Computers and Cognition: A New Foundation for Design*. Menlo Park, Calif.: Addison Wesley.

Winterson, J. *Oranges Are not the Only Fruit*. London: Pandora/RKP.

Zuboff, S. (1988). *In the Age of the Smart Machine: The Future of Work and Power*. New York: Basic Books.

Name Index

Subject Index